# Fearful in Gaza

## Abdalhadi Alijla

# Praise for Fearful in Gaza

*Fearful in Gaza* is a finely tuned and powerful autoethnographic account that documents Gaza's modern history and the lives of its people across changing social and political contexts. Alijla's vivid narrative style establishes the strong connection of Palestinians in Gaza with the place, the time, and each other. The choice of a dual-voice narrative style shifting between "The Son" and "The Mother" intensely reflects the paradoxical relationship and interconnection of sorrow and love, home and exile, longing and aspirations that are central to Palestinian lives. Written at the time of the genocide and the devastating erasure of Gaza's history and life, this book represents an affirmation of Palestinian life, struggle, and identity. *Fearful in Gaza* is a splendid, yet heart-wrenching account written by Abdalhadi Alijla at the time of the genocide—an affirmation of Palestinian life, love, and struggle in the face of ongoing erasure and exile.

— Dr. Nidal Al Haj Sleiman, Middle East Centre, London School of Economics and Political Science

This shimmering text is a melancholy memoir of Palestinian childhood under colonial occupation, before the genocidal violence of the last two years laid waste to Gaza. The voices, stories, and memories recalled here beautifully bind together the people, the trees, the stones, and the sea.

— Laleh Khalili, author of *Heroes and Martyrs of Palestine: The Politics of National Commemoration*

Abdalhadi Alijja's portrait of family life in '90s Gaza is as vital and vivid as his stunning prose in this heartbreaking, haunting memoir. At once unflinching and compassionate, this is a story of survival, community, and the unbreakable bonds of love. Truly unforgettable.

— Aamina Ahmed, author of *The Return of Faraz Ali*

A birth announced with "a smile longer than the sea" breaches the spatial and temporal ordering of occupation in Abdalhadi Ajila's haunting countermap tracing life, death, and exile from Gaza. The stubborn insolvency of kinship ties is enfleshed through Ajila's decision to alternate narration from Mother to Son and back again, and as the site of inquiry where both seek to make sense of their circumstances. But delight in our precocious child narrator dances with terror as they (and we) are forced to confront the impossibility of childhood under genocidal occupation.

— Khadijah Abdurahman, Editor-In-Chief, Logic(s) Magazine

A haunting, lyrical evocation of life in Gaza, and the burdens of leaving it. A deeply eloquent answer to those who dehumanize Gaza's people and rationalize the crimes against them.

— Peter Beinart, author of *Being Jewish After the Destruction of Gaza*

In an extraordinarily successful blurring of the genres of memoir and novel, Abdulhadi Alijla, a social scientist by training, tells his Palestinian family's story through the voices of its members, including his own first-person recounting of his experiences, as well as those of his mother and sister. The power of the work lies in Alijla's ability to center the human emotions of love and longing, of awkwardness, of sorrow, and joy while telling a story of extraordinary political weight.

*Fearful in Gaza* is about what it means to be Palestinian —a people caught between exile, occupation, and genocide, implicated in the most harrowing political issue of our time. But it is also a story of what it means to be human, what it means to be "Free" and "unfree," what it means to be home. Fearful in Gaza, in its creativity, in its refusal to conform to the expectations the world lays out for Palestinians, to be either victims or survivors, in its refusal to fit neatly into any literary genre, is a must-read.

— Heba Gowayed is an associate professor of sociology at CUNY Hunter College and Graduate Center. She is the author of *How the State Shapes Human Potential*

**Fearful in Gaza**

Copyright © 2025 by Abdalhadi Alijla

All rights reserved.

No part of this book may be reproduced, stored in a retrieval system, or transmitted in any form or by any means—electronic, mechanical, photocopying, recording, or otherwise—without prior written permission from the author, except for brief quotations used in reviews or critical articles.

For permissions or inquiries, contact: permissions@casacarlini.com

ISBN: 978-1-943657-22-3 (Paperback)

ISBN: 978-1-943657-22-3 (Hardback)

First Edition: 2025

Printed in the United States of America

*Visit us online!*

*I long for my mother's bread,
My mother's coffee,
Her touch.
Childhood grows inside me,
Day after day
I cherish my life because
If I die,
I would be ashamed of my mother's tears.*

*A greeting... and a kiss,
And I have nothing more to say.
Where do I begin?
And where do I end?*

— MAHMOUD DARWISH

*To my beloved mother, taken from the land she loved, by the cruel hands of colonial oppression—your absence is a wound that time cannot heal.*
*Your love was my first home.*
*Though you were silenced before you see this book, your spirit roars within me, with every thought, and every breath of this work.*
*This book is for you. A promise that your story will never be forgotten, and a commitment to justice.*

# Author's Note

The characters in this book are real, and the stories are rooted in true events and lived experiences. While every effort has been made to present them faithfully, some accounts may not fully capture the perspectives or versions of others who were also part of the events.

# How to Read this Work

This piece employs a dual narrative structure. The primary storyline is narrated by Ayk, the main character and narrator, while additional perspectives are conveyed through conversations with Ayk's mother, offering their views on the same events. Sections narrated by the mother are indicated at the beginning with "(The Mother)," while those narrated by Ayk are marked as "(The Son)." Different sections contain the same timelines.

# Part One
# The Cruel Passage of Time

*"But that life, that time,
seems like a dream now,
Even to me,
Like some long-dissolved rumors"*

— Khalid Hosseini, Sea Prayer

# Sweden, Winter 2014
## The Son

I grew up suddenly like a tree. I once had a dream when I was five years old. This dream revisited me one night in Sweden years later. I slept for only ten minutes that night. The medicine that the psychiatrist prescribed to me did not work. Tranquilizers had not worked for me in the past and would not work for me this time. I did not take them the night before. I had taken them in the past to take the edge off my fear. The previous night, something paddled through my mind, convincing me that tranquilizers were not for me; my mind was like a pot-holed, narrow way in an ancient town. I had a nightmare that I was a child in Gaza, on top of one of the city's highest towers. I was riding a camel over another smaller camel, and a storm was coming from the seaside. Suddenly, I fell, and the sea swallowed me. I woke up shuddering. I've feared the sea since I almost drowned in Gaza at the age of nine. I woke up wondering, *Why is the sea chasing me?*

My small Swedish studio was more cell than home; a bed, a desk, and a narrow kitchenette.

I opened my eyes and suddenly clenched them shut again. They were swollen after a night of nightmares, preceded by four hours of reading and writing. It is difficult for the eyes to open immediately after a terrifying nightmare or a beautiful late night.

*Shall I go to work?* I thought while my eyes were still shut. I could not decide if I would go or not. The cranks and dials in my head were still working. *I will stay here in this four-walled flat,* I said to myself. I opened my eyes again. This time, I did not look at the white ceiling but back toward the window. I wanted to see the sky.

"Is there sun today? Will it visit us today?" I asked, letting myself hear my voice.

We had not seen the sun for two weeks. In this northern city, the sun rarely shines after August. It rises and sheds light, bringing a cold breeze and chilling weather to remind people of its existence. My eyes widened.

"There is sun." This time, my voice was louder.

Today could be a beautiful day. I pulled my leg, put it down, and stood on my bed. I looked at the desk and found a few books that I needed to return to the library. I had a bad habit of borrowing many books at once, but after I bought a new collection, I ended up reading half of what I bought and half of what I borrowed. I cherished my relationship with books. Books were my family, friends, and soulmates. When people lose the meaning of family, they turn to new things, sometimes drugs and crimes, or occasionally noble things such as charity and volunteering. I turned to books. I could speak to them and learn from them. They never complained, and neither did I. Luis Borgese once said that all human inventions are extensions of his senses. The microscope is an extension of sight; the telephone is an extension of hearing, and a plow is an extension of arms and movement. However, the book is an extension of something invisible, inaudible, and intangible. It is an extension of memory and imagination.

I had to return those books. I made myself get up, looking at the pack of cigarettes. I had not smoked for two days, but today could be the day for resuming the habit of smoking once or twice a day. I prepared the Swedish coffee machine, turned it on, and went toward the shower. I walked oddly, almost a sidle, pushing my right leg in front of me as if I were testing a loose wooden floorboard. I wanted to shower, to have energy despite knowing that a hot shower would make drowsiness my friend again. I looked in the mirror. My reflection was blurred, a bearded face with shapeless, swollen eyes.

"There are more grey hairs," I mumbled.

"God morgon," I said to my own reflection in the mirror. Good morning in Swedish.

I imagined my reflection answered, "God morgon."

After I got dressed, I left and took the stairs down. The postman had started to distribute the post in the twenty-four mailboxes in my building. I was not expecting anything, but he suddenly took out a confidential post and put it in my box. I stopped and threw one leg back, standing behind him with a smile. Once he was away, I opened my box and took out the paper. It was a notice informing me that I had an important post that I must pick up from the post office. They stressed that I had to bring a valid ID. This was strange as I was not expecting anything. The post office was close to my home, just a 10-minute walk, so I decided to pick it up on my way to the library.

I put my bag on my back, filled with books and my laptop, but before locking the door, I changed my mind. I decided to leave the bag, collect the post, buy some groceries, come back home, and then go to the library. On my way to the post office, I was unnerved. *Who sent me the post? What is it? A gift?* Many questions such as these continued to muddle my mind.

The sun started to take on the weather, the temperature hitched another notch, and the smell of last night's rain filled my nose. A few crows were around, following me, causing my temples to pound with steady pulses. I grew up believing that crows are a bad sign; they mean bad luck. A small wet leaf fell on the post paper I held. Everything was silent around me, and the leaf was sticking to the paper, spiraling as if in a dance. I smiled.

"Hej," I said to the service man. Hello, in Swedish. I handed the paper to him, along with my driver's license. The sounds of the machines were loud.

He scanned the barcode of a big envelope. "Sign here, please, and write your name."

I did, eager to get the envelope, the curiosity killing me.

"Here we go."

The envelope from Sweden's Migration Board trembled in my hands. Inside was my new reality: I had become a Swedish citizen.

Inside the envelope was my Palestinian travel document and other papers. I was mellowed, somehow now calm and quiet, yet I was sure the service man inside could hear my pulse and feel my hot, painful breath. Two meters away, I put the passport back inside my pocket and pulled the paper from inside the envelope to read, expecting a letter explaining what I needed to do next.

As I read, everything changed. My eyes and mouth were wide open, my mouth was wide open, and the hot breath fog in front of my face became more intense. I grinned.

It is here with the storm.

The journey of the ninth child, escaping death and life.

# Gaza 2014
## The Mother

The sun rose as usual, casting its warm rays into the room. I woke up at six like I always do. After saying my prayers, I prepared breakfast for your father, a routine I've followed for over half a century. However, I am not the same woman I was when I started. The years of battling for you and your siblings have taken their toll, depleting my strength. I struggle to walk for long minutes these days. I feel like a vessel searching for its final harbor in an endless sea.

This morning, I carefully arranged Za'atar, olive oil, cottage cheese, tomato, and labneh on a plate for your father. I also made him a cup of tea. The same pot that we had twenty years ago is still here with its over-used marks, darkened by the time as fires leave their marks on it, like memories leave their scars on humans. I would have prepared scrambled eggs, potatoes, or *shakshuka* in the past, but those dishes require me to stand in the kitchen for extended periods, and my legs no longer cooperate. I gave birth to 11, and it feels like making *shakshuka* at this age is more difficult than raising a child. No one here at home can lend me a hand. Your father is also unwell and barely able to make it to his prayers.

Last night, sleep eluded me as memories danced vividly before my eyes. I couldn't help but reminisce about the day you left. There are moments and days in life that one cannot let go of behind their eyes. These are the marks of life that our unconscious knew would have an impact on us. Your departure day was one of these scars. It was many years ago, during the autumn season. I recall how you carefully packed your bags, moving slowly as if each item held a part of your being. You bought your bag a month before you travelled, and I noticed the worry on your face even without you telling me. The weight of your decision to leave burdened me, and the memory continues to haunt me. I spent most of the night awake, lost in thoughts of you. Your brother told me that you haven't been feeling quite yourself lately.

In the depths of the night, I felt an uncommon ache, as if my cartilage was screaming with pain. Restlessness consumed me, preventing me from finding any respite on the bed or in stillness. My legs caused me unsettling pain. My cartilage has been my friend since the early 1990s and never stopped being my unwelcome guest. Since I married your father, I have spent all my life in this room; the door is the same, and I am reminded of the days and nights when I first arrived from Jaffa hospital after the first operation. It was midnight, and I saw you as a child waiting for me to wake up. Your face was mixed with the red lights of the ambulance that brought me to Gaza.

I walked through the spaces of home, a pilgrimage of heartache, pain, and sorrow. Each step echoed with the weight of memories as I clicked my fingers and tapped my feet against the guest room walls, serenaded by the melancholic chorus of crickets. And then, compelled by an invisible force, I found myself walking toward your room, which became your room not long ago. You had no room for yourself until you were 14, but I wanted you to be educated and grow to make us proud. In passing the other rooms, a surreal blend of days melded together as if time swayed beneath my weak feet.

I was wrestling with a question. Should I knock on the door, adhere to my old ways, and call out your name before entering the room? My tongue thickened, my voice was consumed, and silence seized me every time I was about to call your name. For a lasting second, a sickening sensation overwhelmed me as if I were trapped within the walls of the corridor. You were not there, and I was daydreaming from the pain.

A moment seized me as if I stood as a spectral guardian, gazing upon your countenance, much like those final hours we shared before you left. Now you have traversed three decades and more, walking your own uncharted path. You have become both a child, forever imprinted in my eyes—your eternal place in my heart—and a man who continues to kindle an everlasting pride within me.

Two days ago, I sought solace in your brother's words, longing to hear tidings of you. He shared that you had conversed with them, but you were feeling sick. I felt it resonating within me. Is it not said that a mother's heart serves as the most steadfast compass? They say that the mother's heart feels and knows everything.

I yearned to confess a long-held secret last night, wishing you had been present by my side. When I discovered my pregnancy with you, it was too late to alter the course. I harbored an overwhelming desire to unburden myself, to have an abortion. In desperation, I even contemplated hitting my belly, but the depths of my spirit forbade me.

---

Today, I braved going to the shop by myself, a victory following a fortnight shackled to my bed. The doctor's recommendation echoed in my mind, warning against strenuous movement. But truth be told, the necessity to move is a rare occurrence, a result not just of the pain that scales my legs and spine like an unwelcome climber but of the fact that there is no purpose in moving.

Returning home today, our age-weathered neighbor, Um Ahmad, paused her day to inquire about my health. It didn't require the keenest observation to understand that I was not feeling well. My legs were moving slowly, and I rested for five seconds after each step forward. I carried myself and the small, seemingly weighty plastic bag I clutched tightly, but a five-year-old boy could have carried it easily.

"*Salamtik*," she intoned, a well-meant wish for my wellness. "Where are the children to bear your burdens?" she continued with a loud voice, one of her arms moving around her right side in a movement signaling curiosity.

A cold sensation contrasted sharply with the sweltering heat around me as I thought of her question. A sad smile drew on my lips, a silent acknowledgement of the void her words had unintentionally ripped open. She was unaware of the silence that had invaded our home. In times gone by, it would indeed be the young ones making these market runs. Now, you're miles away and your brother is at his work and comes home late.

"There are no more youth in our home," I confessed. "It's just my husband and me."

Indeed, the children's laughter was replaced with the clock's ticking.

A wave of annoyance mingled with a whisper of anger sprouted within me, prompting me to cut the conversation short. I set my legs homeward, pushed open the door, and settled into the chair I had strategically positioned to sit on as soon as I opened the door. Every home in Gaza seems to have an elderly person who sits in a small chair at the entrance. I once thought that day would not come, but here it is. One never knows what the future holds.

I found myself reflecting on how the relentless nature of life has shaped me. My entire world revolved around watching you sprout like a tree for many years and thousands of days. I was nurturing you, laying brick by brick your foundation to be a man. That was my encounter with the ruthless journey of time and existence. My life was devoid of other priorities. Like most women my age in Gaza, we had limited experiences; our lives did not have many options, making it improbable to consider different hues. And now, at this age, I have to go shopping alone. I felt that life was unfair to me.

Since I left my father's home for your father's home, or now our home, this house has remained largely unchanged. I stayed in the same room until your father passed away. I never left it. The only times I slept elsewhere were during hospital stays and our sacred pilgrimage to Mecca and Medina. Your father's story paralleled mine. His early years were spent in the old house before he moved to what we called the eastern house, near *Al-Muntar*. The only occasions he left home were during hospital visits with me, the Hajj, and occasional training trips to other cities. Our life was simple and unadorned. Although we didn't live in many homes, our struggles were a far steeper climb than most, our journey through the harsh realities of time and existence a different one, yet in some ways more direct. We were two warriors fighting for our tribe of eleven sons and daughters.

I recall joking once with your father that our eleven children made an ideal football team, and we fit perfectly as the coaches. Our understanding of the situation was as unclear as a foggy dawn; all we knew was our desire to create a family. It still astonishes me—I reflect, filled with wonder and disbelief—that I survived the numerous surgical challenges. It feels as if I have crossed the finish line of a catastrophe but remain haunted by its lingering echoes—the phantom pains and the longing for my scattered eleven stars across the vast universe.

After bringing eleven children into the world, I've come to realize that the hardest rite of passage isn't childbirth, but rather the deep sense of yearning when children grow up. The ache for those intangible connections, for the dear ones who have set forth on their own paths—unaware of when we might cross paths again—remains the most challenging trial of all. Just last week, I quietly expressed my gratitude, thanking God that you have been spared from these current hardships.

Yesterday evening, the darkness was more profound than ever, with the power cut off for over two days. The hot July air stifled our house. Yet, a cool gust from the trees outside our home made it tolerable to sit in the main hall. As I sat there, lit by the soft glow of two candles, a sudden gust of wind snuffed out their flickering flames like a playful sprite in the moonlit darkness. A sharp jolt of surprise made me grip the chair's armrest tighter, stirring thoughts that echoed like bells in the still night. What are the two most significant life events? Could they be as profound, inevitable, and contrasting as birth and death?

These moments awaken the longing that has simmered within me over the years, as I try to extract its ache from my soul. It is in these instances that I see your peers and friends grappling with life's harshest challenges, and my heart throbs most intensely.

# Gaza, Winter 1994
## The Son

"Where did I come from, Yabba?" I asked, my curiosity like a young bird fluttering its wings. In my community, we say "Yabba" instead of "Papa." The term "Papa" is typically used by those viewed as more educated and "civilized," often having traveled abroad and not stemming from farming backgrounds. Additionally, when spoken by a man, "Papa" can carry a feminine connotation.

Caught by surprise, my father paused. When my question echoed again, breaking the silence, he found words.

"We all come from mud," he shared, his words dropping like a pebble into the still pond of my understanding.

Eyes wide as the full moon, mouth agape, I echoed, "Mud!"

Without hesitation, I rushed to the backyard, my tiny hands collecting a small amount of sand. "I was born like this?"

Father was unable to give more explanation, leaving me confused. Later, a teacher clarified that our ancestry goes back to Adam, who was created from mud.

The day after, my mother saw me barefoot. Her voice, sharp as a hawk's cry, halted me. "Come here! Go inside."

That day, her insights on life resembled a jigsaw puzzle with missing pieces. I questioned her directive to remain indoors, to which she replied, "You are my hero. Without you, I would likely be a divorced woman today."

Her mysterious words hinted at untold stories beneath the surface. In an instant, a commanding voice disrupted the tranquility.

"Zeinab... Zeinab... Get over here. Where's the coffee? I asked you to prepare it!" My mother's sobs revealed that it was my paternal grandmother calling for her.

I later realized that my arrival as a male was the lifebuoy sustaining my mother's marriage. My paternal grandmother had threatened to introduce another woman into my father's life, a threat intensified by the rumor of my mother expecting another girl. Having already given birth to two boys and six girls, the period leading up to my birth was a turbulent time marked by bleak moments.

At times, I playfully teased her, proclaiming myself the knight rescuing her from the dragon of a second wife, or as we call it in Arabic, *"Dorra"*. She often replied with a faint smile and an enigmatic comeback.

"You could have been her son instead of mine. Perhaps the one with the prominent nose."

We laugh together, but she still faces the past without hesitation.

"I considered aborting you several times, just like I tried with your sister. If I bore another girl, your grandmother would have pushed for your father to marry a second wife." My mother would tell me.

Indeed, my older sister's struggles with walking painfully reminded me of my mother's frantic efforts to abort her. I sat with my knees drawn to my chest; my furrowed brows mirrored my mother's expression of distress.

Whenever my mother recounted these stories, she did so with acceptance.

"When I finally realized that I was pregnant, it was too late to alter my path. I held my secret like a silent anthem until I reached seven months."

In many Arab societies, there is a preference for males over females, but not because females are viewed as weak. When I was eight, my family gathered on a Ramadan evening before breaking the fast, and we were listening to the radio. A preacher was discussing women, and I paid close attention until he mentioned "*Wa'd Al Banat*" and the practice of burying them alive in pre-Islamic times.

While sitting next to my father, I stood up and said to him, "Why do you want to make her die?"

He said, "Who?"

I replied, looking at my older sister, "Zahra."

My father's head went back suddenly, and his wide eyes matched mine. "Who said that? What?"

"The radio said that!" I replied.

He smiled and took me in his lap, saying, "Before Prophet Muhammad's time, society was characterized by *Jahiliya* [ignorance], during which people acted cruelly, committing acts of murder and theft. In that era, men often did not desire daughters due to their unkindness."

My father made every effort to explain, but he ultimately instilled the belief that those men were bad while portraying himself as a good man who would never harm my sister.

He continued to try to turn it into a narrative. This marked the first time my father genuinely attempted to explain something to me, investing time in the process. He scratched his head several times, striving to be both creative and clear.

"In the past, men owned vast tracts of land and farms populated with cows, donkeys, and horses. They sought more workers for their farms, under the false assumption that women were significant consumers. Consider your mother; she consumes the least yet cooks and labors tirelessly throughout the day. Their perception was flawed."

One day, I happened to hear my father voicing his frustration about some men in the extended family.

He said, "One woman today can outdo a hundred men and overcome thousands."

That sentence stayed with me for years. I questioned, *if my father is truly that way, why did he allow his mother to interfere in my mother's life?*

I found the answer on my own years later. Humans are shaped by their environments, continuously evolving, often without awareness. The greater their exposure to new experiences, the more receptive they become to change and new ideas. It also showed me that generational differences can turn a morgue into a garden, or vice versa.

# Gaza 1989
## The Mother

One day, when you were just five years old, you had a question for me that is vividly etched in my memory. You opened the creaking front door and dashed inside, quickly kicking off your shoes in a motion like a skilled footballer. With urgency glimmering in your eyes, you approached me and asked.

"What is your birthdate?"

I returned your query with a gentle, "Why?"

"Since today is Mother's Day," you responded, echoing the discussions of the neighborhood kids. "Were you born on this day, similar to Mother's Day?"

"No, dear. Today is Mother's Day, but it isn't my special day," I responded, while my hands busily shaped falafel for the little shop we opened a few years ago to help your father support you.

Today wasn't my day, nor a day to celebrate my mother. I've dedicated my life to your well-being. From the moment my first child was born to the arrival of my youngest, my days have centered around nurturing my kids, leaving scant time for personal celebrations. Amid this relentless cycle, my own birthday has faded into obscurity.

"When were you born?" you inquired once more, your innocent

eyes gazing at me as you clutched a slice of bread topped with vibrant red chili and a fresh burst of tomato.

I paused, gazing at you with affection. I replied, "*Sanat Al-Nakba*," referring to the year of the Nakba, the Palestinian catastrophe. Instantly, your munching ceased, and your eyes widened with curiosity and confusion.

"What? Nakba? What is that?" you stammered, as if witnessing a meteor hurtling toward us. The word lingered heavily in the air—a term alien to your young mind but rich with emotion in my voice. Just like that, one answer triggered a flood of questions, and your single inquiry opened the door to countless explanations.

"The Nakba," I explained, "was when people from afar, who carried guns and spoke not a word of Arabic, descended upon our villages. They brought death and terror, expelling people from their homes to live among us."

You fell silent, processing the words that just washed over you. You stared at me for a seemingly endless minute, mouth slightly agape. Then, as if jolted by a bolt of lightning, you stood upright, and in a tremulous voice, you asked, "Did they kill my grandfather?"

I was taken aback by your question, not knowing where you had formed the idea that your grandfather was killed.

"Why do you ask about your grandfather?" I inquired.

"Because Dad told me he's dead. He died," you said.

I understood then that from your childlike perspective, death equated to murder, leading you to presume that anyone who had died must have been killed. After setting aside the falafel dough, I led you to a nearby mattress.

"Listen, sweetheart. While many people were indeed killed, your grandfather was not among them. People can pass away naturally," I reassured you. Your expression remained one of surprise, your body frozen as if on the verge of tears. Just as I prepared to head back to the shop, your curiosity resurfaced.

"And what about the Nakba? Where are the people?" you asked.

"The Nakba," I began, "was a time when some families, like

those now living on the *Muntar* and the family next to your uncle's house, were forced from their homes and lands, arriving here with nothing but the clothes on their backs. Their homes and their lands were stolen, and many of their men were mercilessly killed."

You were so captivated by my words that you didn't notice you had dropped your bread. I went on, "When they arrived, we welcomed them into our homes and shared everything we had. We offered food, clothing, and support until they were able to find their own homes."

"Why didn't my father help them return?" you questioned.

"Your father was just a child, much like you are now. And your grandfathers were helpless against the invaders, for they had no weapons," I replied.

"Can they go back now?" you pressed.

"Enough with the questions, for now, little one. Ask your dad when he returns from work," I instructed.

I felt fatigue testing my patience. It wasn't that I couldn't respond to your questions; I simply struggled to articulate the right words for your curious mind. Kids often ask the most insightful questions that can perplex even the wisest scholars, not because of their depth of knowledge, but because they see the world without filters, looking for straightforward, honest, and clear answers.

# Paths of Gaza 1950s
## The Mother

Cities, much like humans, experience growth, decline, emotional highs and lows, and bursts of energy alongside tedious frustrations. Gaza, a city entangled in historical upheaval, has seen empires rise and fall, altered its environment, overcome enemies, and forged alliances. It has served as a sanctuary for both fighters and peacekeepers. Nonetheless, this city has persistently remained strong, poised for the unpredictable.

Prior to the Nakba, Gaza City's roads featured distinct names and winding paths. The houses were identifiable structures, and the vibrant atmosphere, including its cuisine, had a unique essence. The Nakba, a devastating event committed by immigrant Jews, profoundly altered the lives of everyone living in Gaza.

Amid the rich landscape of Gaza, the Turkman district represented the core of the *Sheja'iyya* neighborhood, while the nearby *Al-Jadida* emerged as the "new" district. My father often noted that *Al-Jadida* featured only a small number of homes compared to Turkman. Before 1930, no houses extended beyond the cemetery's limits. Traditionally, cemeteries were located on the city's edges, symbolizing the boundary of the urban area; this cemetery delineated the end of Gaza and the adjoining neighborhoods, *Turkman* and *Al-Jadida*.

One memorable stroll with my father takes me back to our home as we made our way to the central market. As we walked, I noticed narrow paths extending eastward, bordered by cactus trees, whose prickly arms seemed to embrace our route.

During this walk, my father met a man named Hassan. He carried a pitchfork resting on his shoulders, a sickle firmly held in his hand, and a large bag hanging by his side. Hassan greeted my father with warmth and familiarity.

"May God bless you with a good morning, Abu Salman. Where are you going?" Hassan asked sincerely.

"I'm going to buy some meat, then I'll head east," my father responded.

The man nodded, his eyes reflecting a spirit of friendship. "I will wait for you in the *Diwan*; we will go east together."

Taking the eastern road meant entering the fields where wheat, vegetables, and fruits were planted. The air was rich with the aroma of the harvest, and my family, like many in *Sheja'iyya*, were part of the farming society. As our chat with Hassan wrapped up, he bid farewell to my father, his slow steps mirroring the swinging of his sickle and pitchfork. I observed the man from afar, wearing his *"Gombaz"*, baggy trousers, tied at the waist with a cord.

Curiosity tinged my voice as I queried my father, "Where is he off to?"

"He's on his way to *Darb Al-Tabana*, the Milky Way Road," my father said.

"What is out there?" I asked.

Father paused, casting his eyes westward as the man faded from view. "See, he's going down that road. They refer to it as *Darb Al-Tabana*—the Milky Way."

My naive mind fluttered with worry. "Isn't he scared of *Alwawi*, the golden Jackal?" I clung to my father's legs, searching for comfort.

A hearty laugh erupted from him as he squeezed my hands

tenderly. "No, my child. He is a man of strength, equipped with a lighter, and *Alwawi* only appears at night."

As we continued our trek, retracing our steps amid the towering and smaller trees, men exchanged friendly greetings, and my father responded to each one. It was then that I found the courage to ask him more questions.

"Why don't we live in *Darb Al-Tabana*?" I asked.

"We live in *Darb El-Muntar*," he responded.

As we walked towards the market, thoughts of *Darb El-Muntar* and *Darb Al-Tabana* stayed in my mind. These names encapsulated hundreds of years of Gaza's history. Today, however, they have faded into obscurity, becoming the past.

# GAZA 1950S
## THE MOTHER

In our history books, the narrative of Palestine or Gaza was absent. Meanwhile, Egypt's history was the one we studied, as Egypt controlled Gaza after the Nakba. A sense of curiosity compelled me to ask my history teacher, who had an Egyptian education, about our local history.

"*Ustaz*, why aren't we studying the history of Palestine?"

His unease reflected the silence that lingered after my inquiry, akin to the calm before a tempest. He looked around furtively, as if my question was something dangerous.

"I can't answer those questions," he stammered. "The curriculum is set by *Al-Hakem Al'askari* (the military governor of Gaza). That's the end of it."

My curiosity about history and Palestine left me feeling overwhelmed. I only understood Egypt through the soldiers in Gaza, tanks on the streets, distant radio broadcasts from Cairo, and a lone TV in the coffee shop where people watched Egyptian programs together.

One day, while waiting for my friend Laila outside our school, I suddenly had a realization: our school is a historical monument. It's an ancient palace, with its original mud colors still visible through the cement façade. In that moment, I understood something: one must step back to see the surroundings truly. Often, the tiniest details, which can only be seen up close, conceal the beauty of the whole. When Laila arrived, I eagerly shared my discovery.

"Look, Laila," I said, "it seems we study in a castle." I pointed out the principal's office and the storeroom with its arch, just like the ones in our history textbooks.

Later that day, my mind was teeming with questions. I was consumed by my newfound fascination with history and the enigma that was our school.

When my uncle returned home after studying in Egypt, I sought his advice. His smile reflected an interest. He requested that I prepare tea for him, my father, and myself. I thought he had just ignored my question.

As I returned with the tea, he began, "Your school was once the Pasha Palace, a legacy of the Redwan Family, constructed during the Mamluk period. It also served as Napoleon's fort during his campaign to Acre."

"But why is it called a palace when it's merely a small building?" I inquired.

His reply was cut short by my father, who was absorbed in the radio broadcasts, the antenna rising like a lighthouse amidst the news haze. Like many others, my father had a particular fondness for radios with large antennas, capable of picking up Arabic broadcasts alongside Monte Carlo and the BBC. He often carried the radio around the house like a compass, trying to capture the fleeting signal.

"They expect an attack from Egypt on *Al Yahud*," my father shared.

"Nasser will win this time," my brother declared, his tone underscoring his firm conviction. My brother enlisted in the Egyptian army as an officer and became a member of Mustafa Hafez's unit. Mustafa Hafez, a highly esteemed Egyptian military leader, had served in Gaza and was often called the "Father of the *Fedayeen*." He trained numerous individuals and led various operations against the Israeli army along the eastern Gaza armistice line. We used to call the Israeli army *Al Yahud*—the Jews.

The term *Al Yahud*, or Jew, was synonymous with soldiers, occupation, massacres, and war in our vocabulary. We couldn't distinguish between a Jew and a Zionist until we heard about Felicia Langer, a Jewish lawyer who defended Palestinians in Israeli prisons through international news broadcasts. Her name and noble cause were surprising revelations. Only when the BBC and Monte Carlo acknowledged her activism did we become aware of such a sympathetic Jew.

Once the conversation wrapped up, my uncle faced me, holding a copper teapot. The aged patina had deepened its base. He poured himself another cup of the strong tea.

"Ah, the castle was once much greater," he said. "The English dismantled a significant portion of it after using it as a prison."

"Why?" I asked, my curiosity rising.

"Because it stands as proof of our existence here in Gaza. By diminishing the palace, they believe they're erasing a piece of our history and existence," he explained.

His words were a puzzle whose meaning I would not unravel until much later. I came to understand that the locations of our first steps leave lasting marks on our hearts and become essential aspects of our identity. My school was a reflection of myself; it was the only school I attended until I turned eighteen.

# Gaza 1960s
## The Mother

The first time I met your father, I understood that life isn't an abstract notion; it is clear and tangible, much like the tasks and activities that fill our days. When my mother told us we were having a *Khutab*, I was overwhelmed by a sense of sadness. *Khutab* are a group of women who come first to visit homes who may have a potential bride for their male relative. I was nearing the end of my secondary school education and had aspirations of pursuing education. *Khutab* referred to your father's mother, who lived only three minutes away from my parents' home, separated by just a few hundred meters of trees and bushes. This term is also tied to a long-standing tradition, now less common, where a woman or a group of women (typically the mother and sisters of the man) visit a girl's home to propose an intermarriage.

Typically, they ask for a week to evaluate the girl, after which they either consent to the marriage or mention a cousin's interest in her. Nowadays, a frequent reply is, "The girl wishes to continue her education." Many say this playfully to sidestep a direct rejection.

This week-long timeframe is sometimes utilized to gather information about the prospective husband's family, character, conduct, and occupation. If he fits their social structure, they are likely to give a positive response. Conversely, if he does not meet their expectations, they may politely decline, often using the same phrases: "The girl wishes to continue her education" or "One of her cousins has proposed to her."

In today's world, societies have changed. Before the visit from the *Khutab*, the couple would have already set their direction, and the girl shared her story with her mother, who then would have informed the father. The ritual has simply become a performance of formalities.

---

There was a time when young girls could walk the street in short skirts without attracting any attention. At seventeen, we walked safely, with no one bothering us or saying a word. This was simply the fashion of the day, with men in *Gombaz* accompanying their daughters in short skirts. I can't pinpoint when I stopped wearing those skirts, but it must not have been long after I got married. In 1994, when I inquired about this shift with your father, he linked it to the aftermath of the 1967 war, known as Naksa.

The 1967 occupation of the Gaza Strip represented a significant turning point. Life, much like a river, altered its direction; individuals turned towards greater religiosity, while security disintegrated like a sandcastle under the tide. Additionally, the rise of new *Fedayeen* and freedom fighters loomed over lives, enforcing new orders, in life as much as in politics.

I noticed your father's daily journey west toward the Gaza center, which I believed was related to his work. He left at seven in the morning, coinciding with me and my friends' walk to Al-Zahra school. Our path took us along Baghdad Street, a daily reminder of history, which has remained unchanged since it was named in the early 1900s. Even after its expansion to the east, it has retained its original name, Baghdad. This street serves as a divider between the neighborhoods of *Turkman* and *Al-Jadida*.

Initially, many referred to the street as "*Fayysal*." However, as time passed, this name faded away, becoming akin to a leaf carried off by the winds of change. The street originated in the early 1920s to honor King *Faisal I* of the Hashemite dynasty. Yet, following rumors surrounding King Faisal's agreements with the Zionists and the eventual dissolution of the Kingdom of Arabia, prominent figures in Gaza gathered to deliberate on a new name for the street. A suggestion was made to rename it after the Iraqi president, Abdelkarim Amer. One individual proposed the name "Baghdad," stating, "Men come and go, but cities remain forever." Consequently, "Baghdad Street" became a part of our local history.

I was unaware of the meaning of *Sheja'iyya* until one day, after I married your father, I chose to ask him. "Mahmoud," I inquired, "what does *Sheja'iyya* mean?"

He thought for a moment before answering, "It doesn't have a specific meaning. It may come from 'Shuja,' which means 'courageous.'"

*Turkman* was one of the main districts of Gaza City, named after the Kurdish and Turkmani tribes that settled in the Gaza Strip during the ninth century. They arrived with Saladin, a Kurd, much like seeds carried by the winds of fate. Known for their valor and fortitude, they acted as ancient guardians of their land. Even now, Turkman's residents are celebrated for their resilience, stubbornness, and deep sense of dignity and protection, along with their unwavering connections and solidarity.

# GAZA 1984
## THE SON

My sister once described a vivid scene: "It was one of the first nights of *Al-Arba'aniya*." *Al-Arba'aniya* marked an annual retreat of forty days, stretching from the 22nd of December to the 31st of January. It represented a constant chill, rain, and the mourning of the wind.

Our grandmother's voice reverberated through the quiet: "Why are you still awake?"

"Just looking after the little one," my sister answered, her voice soft as a whisper in the quiet. My youngest sister at that time, barely fifteen months, appeared tranquil, her tiny face calm in the night's stillness. In contrast, our older sisters were enveloped in a world of dreams, sprawled on the floor, bundled in the *Lehaf*—a large duvet crafted from winter cotton. Its material recounted tales of harsh cold and the warmth it sheltered within.

Unfortunately, my mother was without her bride *Lehaf*, a treasured item from her dowry that my grandmother borrowed and never returned. This distinctive piece, customarily acquired by the bride herself, represented more than just a blanket. For newlyweds living together in shared family quarters, their room became their entire world, and the *Lehaf* emerged as a defining feature within it. The elegance of a bride's *Lehaf* was a source of pride; the more luxurious it appeared, the greater her sense of self-importance.

My siblings rested in the grand corridor, an open space with no doors or windows. When the southern wind blew, it swirled around them, whispering icy words as they slept beneath their *Lehafs*.

At the gentle whisper of dawn, just after the *Fajr* prayer, my mother experienced the unyielding waves of *Taliq*—the labor pains signaling that the time was near for the new arrival.

"I feel the baby descending," my mother told my father.

"Wait, let me get dressed first," he responded urgently.

In that moment, she paused, her expression reflecting deep concern, and asked, "What about the curfew?"

After a brief silence, my father checked his watch and announced, "It's 4:30. If we're caught, we'll say we're heading to the hospital. The curfew ends in thirty minutes. Let's hurry!"

Since 1967, the Gaza Strip had been under an Israeli-imposed curfew, a veil that descended every night at nine and lifted at dawn.

As she stepped out of the room, my mother's eyes landed on my sleeping siblings, strewn along the hallway like serene dreams. She told me that a wave of nausea washed over her at the thought of bringing another life into this uncertain world.

"Why should I bring one more into this life of struggles?" she told herself.

The sound of raindrops then captured her attention. "It's raining; how will we manage this?" she inquired, her voice tinged with both anxiety and determination.

"*Allah Bisahel* (May God help us), we will get a cart or car," my father comforted her.

Putting on her *Gataras* and *Dayer*—relics from a past time brought to Gaza after the 1967 war—she readied herself. The *Gataras*, a wide white headscarf, draped gracefully over her head, providing protection, while the *Dayer*, a dark cotton skirt, whispered stories of yesteryears.

She gathered a swaddle, several clothes, and a pair of towels she had collected weeks earlier. The baby's gender was still unknown, so she chose a white swaddle—a blank canvas for an unfolding story—representing the possibilities and mysteries of new life. Before long, this uncertainty would fade, as it had with her previous eight children, revealing a new chapter in their lives.

My grandmother was deep in her *Fajr* prayer when my parents walked in. Noticing their presence, she heightened her call, "*Allah Akbar*," her voice resonating brightly. However, her plea fell on deaf ears, as my parents were determined to follow their course ahead.

This story of my birth was not shared with me by my mother. Instead, it was a tale woven by our neighbor along with my two sisters, who were 14 and 17 at the time. They always laugh as they describe how I was whisked away from the hospital just two hours after I was born, as the sun began to extend its golden rays, the lingering morning chill faded into its warmth.

---

That morning began while my mother was not at home.

"It's a fascinating weather pattern," my grandmother noted. "It's hard to tell if the skies will weep or if the sun will shine." At the front door, she donned a brightly patterned scarf reminiscent of those traditionally worn by Chechen women. The captivating red and blue hues of her scarf drew everyone's gaze, overshadowing everything else nearby.

She was speaking to our neighbor as she passed by, her voice carried by the gentle breeze.

"Indeed. Nonetheless, sunshine is a genuine blessing, *Hamdellah*. It frees us from the need for extra clothing and covers," the neighbor replied.

Like many women her age, my grandmother often perched outside the house, comfortably seated on her favorite bamboo stool. Her small social spot featured a charming, large teapot and four transparent, empty glasses eagerly awaiting to be filled. Every passerby was warmly welcomed to enjoy a cup of tea, a lovely gesture of hospitality. Occasionally, an elderly lady would sit beside her, and their conversations became a delightful exchange of stories about old farms and unforgettable journeys to places like Jerusalem and Hebron, or imaginary tales about Istanbul. Sometimes an old man would join, sharing memories of his friendship with her husband (my grandfather), who had passed away decades earlier. Whether woman or man, rolling Arabic cigarettes became a treasured ritual among them. My grandmother's love for these cigarettes was well known, and their rich scent wafted through the air for meters around. Keeping the cigarettes lit required a steady flicker of fire, much like the vibrant stories that animated their gatherings.

While lighting her cigarette, my grandmother noticed another neighbor coming from a few hundred meters away, her face radiant like the morning sun.

"Why such a broad smile? *Khair*?" my grandmother asked.

"*Alf Mabrouk!*" the woman joyfully exclaimed as she approached my grandmother.

"What for?" my grandmother asked, her expression confused as she attempted to understand the woman's exuberance.

"Your daughter-in-law has just welcomed a baby boy!" the woman declared, her voice overflowing with happiness and her smile beaming even wider.

Upon hearing the news, my grandmother sprang up like a startled bird, her expression shifting swiftly. With a grin that gradually spread, she said to the woman, "Ah, that's why your smile stretched longer than the sea!"

"My sister was also giving birth. She was beside your daughter-in-law, and they both welcomed baby boys."

"Hold on," my grandmother interrupted before retreating into the house. She returned shortly, presenting a silky new headscarf. "This is for you, *Halwan* (gift), for sharing such wonderful news."

After the woman left, my grandmother collected her stool and teapot before heading inside. A few minutes later, she returned, wearing her *Dayer* and *Ghatars*. In her room, she gently opened a small purse concealed within her mattress and retrieved several notes of Jordanian Dinars. She returned the purse to its hidden spot and discreetly placed the notes between her breast and bra, a secret compartment known only to her.

In Gaza, currency embodies its complex history, political landscape, and societal dynamics. Jordanian dinars, Israeli shekels, American dollars, and even euros have all been in use since 2002. The dinar signifies value; it is utilized for assets, university fees, dowries, and savings. The shekel is primarily used for everyday transactions, wages, and salaries. Meanwhile, the dollar is for those employed by UNRWA. As a child, I once observed a neighbor discreetly tucking a purse into her bosom, which piqued my interest in this uncommon practice. I eventually discovered that women in Gaza have created an alternative to the traditional handbag.

As she left the house, her search for a donkey cart started—the rural equivalent of Uber these days. She made her way east along the narrow sandy streets. Unexpectedly, she noticed a UN vehicle parked near a location affectionately known as "Hunger" by the locals—the UNRWA food distribution center for Palestinian refugees.

Pausing her stride, she observed the morning bounty being unloaded from large pots until the driver appeared, met by her eager gaze.

"I need a ride," she said succinctly to the two men in the truck.

"And where might you be heading?"

"*To Al-Shifa*," she answered.

"But we're not going to that side of the city."

"Then take me to *Al-Sikka*, the railway."

In Gaza, *Al-Sikka* represents more than just a railway; it serves as a societal symbol. This name evokes memories from the pre-1967 period when a train connected the Gaza Strip to Egypt, with a station located on the western edge of the Turkman neighborhood. Although the railway has been destroyed and replaced by the vibrant

Souk *Al-Sheja'iyya* market, that area of Gaza continues to honor the name *Al-Sikka*, a tribute to its history. My childhood recollections of that railway station may be blurred and faint, yet they endure, offering a nostalgic view in sepia tones.

From *Al-Sikka*, my grandmother found it easier to reach *Al-Shifa* Hospital, located just four kilometers away. *Al-Shifa*, the sole hospital of healthcare in the Gaza Strip, lies close to the sea. It began as a treatment center for quarantined and febrile diseases during the British mandate era. After Egypt assumed control over Gaza, it was converted into a hospital in 1948.

As soon as she reached *Al-Sikka*, my grandmother waved goodbye to the driver of the UN vehicle. She stood at the roadside, her gaze pursuing the horizon for any taxi or cart. Her search was in vain; it was a curfew day for western and northern Gaza under Israeli occupation, leaving the streets devoid of cars or carts.

Across the road stood the Israeli military base. Clad in his authority uniform, a soldier approached my grandmother, issuing a curt command: "Go away, move from here, *Mamno'o Tajjawol*" (movement is forbidden, or curfew).

Instead of acquiescing, my grandmother paid him no heed, tilting her head to the east as if he were a ghostly apparition. Herein lies a peculiar form of resistance—to ignore one's oppressor is to deny them the satisfaction of their power, their very existence. This form of silence can be louder than any shout.

Furious over her indifference, the soldier snapped back, his flawed Arabic resonating like an amateur musician tackling a challenging piece: "*Roh Min Hun, Aw Batoukhik*" (Go away from here or I will shoot you).

"Be quiet. May a dark day come for you," my grandmother retorted, her words cutting like blades. With this, she started her walk westward, climbing the hill of old Gaza. Every step was a silent prayer for a car or cart to give her a ride.

"Where are you heading, *Hajja*?" a cart driver inquired as he came alongside her.

"To *Al-Shifa*, my son," she responded.

He nodded and assured her, "Come, I'm headed to a refugee camp. I can drop you off on the way."

She requested that he pull up close to the pavement side so she could use a large stone and the ground as makeshift steps. As she began her ascent, an aging blue Peugeot 404 roared past them. The car, clearly past its prime, groaned with every turn of its wheels.

*A stroke of misfortune,* my grandmother lamented silently. *If only I'd waited longer.*

Once settled on the cart, the donkey began to trot. She tried to engage the young driver in conversation, saying, "Your donkey is *Mashallah*, good and fast."

The young man, his sun-kissed skin, did not respond; his silence an unspoken plea for tranquility.

Undeterred, she asked, "Where are you from, *Ya Khalti*?"

This form of address—*Ya Kahlti or Ya Amti* (referring to a sister's son or a brother's son)—is typically used by older women when speaking to strangers, or by older individuals when addressing younger strangers.

He avoided her gaze, his voice barely above a whisper as he replied, "I'm from *Al-Sabra*, from the *Al-Hilali* family."

"Ah, I'm familiar with *Um Ahmed*, the midwife," she said, her eyes showing a hint of recognition.

"Yes, that's my grandmother. She's currently unwell and no longer works as a midwife," he responded, his tone carrying a trace of sadness.

"God! Please send her my regards. She was an incredible woman. Nearly half of Gaza owes its delivery to her," my grandmother remarked, her words reflecting a legacy of Um Ahmed.

"What is your occupation?" my grandmother inquired. Older women have a unique ability to engage in conversations with strangers, bombarding them with questions as if they were long-time friends. I recall my father mentioning that in the past, women frequently asked men if they were seeking a bride, particularly when those men were self-sufficient, esteemed, and came from reputable families.

"I work at the vegetable market. I ferry fruits and vegetables from the fields in the north from *Jabaliya* to *Feras* popular market every day," the young man answered.

"May Allah help you," she responded.

Despite his youthful energy, the young man appeared weary, his eyes intermittently closing before snapping back open. As they approached the hospital, an Israeli checkpoint obstructed their way.

Upon reaching the checkpoint, my grandmother promptly engaged with the soldiers. "*Beit Holium ya Khawja,*" she articulated distinctly, using the colloquial term *"Khawja"* for Israeli soldiers, a term with origins in the British Mandate period.

The soldiers requested the young man's ID, swiftly inspected it, and then handed it back with a terse command: "*Yalla, Roh albeit*" (go home).

"I wake up at four every day to begin my work. Those bullies frequently corner me, making me stand for hours with my hands against a wall. Just this week, they did it to me four times in various locations. Today, I feel fortunate to have you by my side, *Hajja*," he admitted.

Before getting off the cart at the hospital's main entrance, my grandmother turned to him and said, "We are guided and have no choice. When you crossed my path today, it was for a reason---to protect you from them. I felt a bit upset earlier when the car passed by, thinking I could have arrived faster. However, we saw it broke down just a few hundred meters from our starting point. Our paths are guided by Allah, not by humans."

# 22 December 1984, Gaza
## The Mother

Your grandmother rushed into the room, her voice shattering the sterile hospital silence with cries of *"Weno? Weno?"* (Where is he?). The moment I saw her, any remnants of strength or emotion in me seemed to vanish. She moved with desperate urgency, like a sprinter racing to catch the last bus of the day.

As I turned to my left, her gaze never met mine; it was focused entirely on you. Like a lighthouse guiding lost ships, I watched her every movement, my eyes widening as she drew closer. A knot formed in my throat, making it hard to breathe or swallow.

"This is my grandson. Mahmoud's son," she declared, erasing me from the scene with her words. In her story, I was reduced to a mere shadow, even as I lay there, the nurse who had just handed you to her still present in the room.

My heart quaked as she lifted you, swaddled in white, and turned to leave the room. My body yearned to rise, to intervene, but my sister-in-law and the nurse held me down like anchors in a raging storm. "Calm down, she's his grandmother. No need to make trouble," they consoled.

Moments later, a *Zagrouta* (a lively trill) resonated through the air, her voice soaring through the hospital halls—a vibrant herald of your arrival. And just as abruptly, she vanished. She departed the hospital, cradling my newborn son, and left me behind. Darkness enveloped me, rendering my world colorless. That's how I realized from the set of events.

I felt like a dam bursting, tears streaming down my cheeks, my face pressed into the hospital pillow. I cried, my sobs resonating with profound sorrow in my heart. My mind began to replay painful memories from my past and present, like a horror film on repeat. The grief of watching you being taken from me had settled deep within my heart, spilling over onto my face. My stomach twisted with a blend of disgust and rage, a poisonous brew that threatened to force out my pain.

Leaning against the wall for support, my sister-in-law helped me get dressed. Back then, women were expected to leave the hospital within just an hour or two after giving birth. I anxiously waited for your father to take me home and introduce me to his son. As I steadied myself, I glimpsed your grandmother through the window, where she cradled you in her *Dayyer*. You disappeared within its ample folds. Instead of gazing into your eyes, kissing your cheeks, and feeding you with my milk, I had missed those precious moments. Upon leaving the room, your father came in, his face brightened by a wide smile. Yet, when he saw my empty arms, his joy transformed, and his expression resembled the upside-down dish, Maqluba. He later shared that your older sister had called him at work to deliver the happy news.

"Where is the child?" he asked, his voice bouncing off the sterile walls.

"*Al-Hajja* took him home," my sister-in-law replied, her eyes glistening, forehead furrowed with worry, and lips pressed together tightly.

His audible sigh revealed his frustration; a deep breath punctuated with irritation. Cursing under his breath, we exited the hospital. He requested we wait while he searched for a taxi.

# The father, Gaza
## The Son

When my father came back, he exuded a noticeable unease, like an unexpected note in a familiar tune. It was midday, the sun high in the sky, as he passed through the ancient, metal-trimmed door, holding my mother's hand tightly. Each step they took was intentional, and he kindly cautioned her about the dangerous doorstep.

As they entered, my sisters, like birds flocking to a feeder, hurried over to help my mother with her careful walk. My father stood next to her, steadfast like a strong oak, maintaining their slow, shared pace. Wearing his faded beige jacket from the sixties, he led my mother into the comforting space of their room.

A weighty silence draped over everyone, broken only by the rhythm of their synchronized footsteps. Every gaze in the room followed their movements, instinctively sensing the tension that clung to him like a second skin. My sister later shared that his refusal to leave my mother's side was a nonverbal condemnation of my grandmother's actions.

Inside the room, words escaped him. Instead, he gently pulled me away from my eldest sister's embrace, asked for some soup and warm water for my mother, and requested that she be allowed to rest undisturbed.

At home, as he held me, his demeanor shifted like the sun breaking through a cloudy morning. His lips, hidden beneath a thick, dark mustache, formed a smile, lifting the hair along his jawline.

Cradling me securely, he whispered in my ear while my six sisters and older brother looked on, their curiosity visible as they lined the edges of the room: "'Allāhu 'akbaru, 'ašhadu 'an lā 'ilāha 'illā -llāhu, 'ašhadu 'anna Muḥammadan rasūlu -llāhi, ḥayya 'alā ṣ-ṣalāhti ḥayya 'alā l-falāḥi, 'Allāhu 'akbaru, lā 'ilāha 'illā -llāhu."

This was the Muslim *Adhan*, a traditional whisper into the ears of newborns, symbolizing their spiritual awakening, marking their first auditory invitation into the world of Islam.

There is a belief inherently interwoven into the cultural and religious fabric that the first sounds a baby hears should be these sacred verses, which are thought to influence their upbringing. Yet, as I matured and became capable of comprehending and performing the *Adhan*, I learned that this was possibly a folktale, lacking a basis in the Islamic traditions practiced by the Prophet and his successors.

"I'll head to the market to buy sweets before guests start to arrive," my father announced, breaking the serene silence in the room.

His leave was marked by his mother's voice echoing, "*Mabrouk! Mabrouk!*"

Instead of replying to her congratulations, he softly uttered, "God bless him, may he grow bathed in your honor." The strain in his voice revealed how difficult it was for him to reconcile his mother's actions against mine. Nevertheless, he stood with unwavering strength, a rock against the unending tide of community judgment.

During a quiet moment outside our home, he once shared with me, "A swell of pride washed over me, knowing that you were a boy, and I was blessed with a third son."

From the edge of our home, my father heard his mother declare that I would be named Abdallah, honoring my grandfather. It was a rainy December day, and the air was filled with the aroma of damp earth, as if nature had distilled its essence into one vivid scent. A brisk wind gusted, like an unwelcome visitor, shaking the long windows on the west side and urging everyone to seek warmth, either in the cozy room or around the fireplace, our beloved source of comfort known as the *Kanoon*.

The *Kanoon* consists of a solid metal base supported by four sturdy legs, holding the crackling wood at its center. Its promise of warmth drew everyone in like iron filings to a magnet, offering respite from the biting cold of the *Al-Arbiniya* winter.

"I shall name him Ayk," my father declared, the small *Kanoon* gently held in his arms, its belly filled with coal that radiated warmth, blending with the unique aromas of winter rain, rich earth, aged trees, and smoldering coal—the hallmark fragrance of winter.

My grandmother did not concur; instead, she emerged with a tempestuous disapproval. Confronting my father, her words pierced with conflict, she said, "Why not Abdallah, your father's name? Are you turning away from our heritage?"

"No, I feel no shame," my father insisted, "but my brother has already claimed the honor of naming a son after our father for his firstborn. You took that privilege from me, so I won't name any of my sons after him now."

My mother, the quiet martyr who carried me for nine long months, the one who would meticulously shape my future, was denied the chance to name her own son. My father looked at her as she nursed me, seemingly searching for her silent consent. Yet, she lowered her eyes, a quiet spectator in this drama. His eyes, reflecting his affection for his wife, yearned to convey a love that he struggled to articulate. A true man embodies a paradox—a blend of strength and vulnerability, love and determination, all tied together by his devotion to his partner.

Resolutely, my father declared, "I will name him after my ancestor, a rebel against the Ottomans."

That ancestor, a rare literate figure in early 1800s Gaza City, actively participated in the uprising against the oppressive Ottoman Empire and their local allies who exploited farmers. His resistance made him a marked man, leading the Ottomans to pursue him and ultimately forcing him to flee to Astana.

Weeks later, when the official records were finalized, I was named in honour of our revolutionary grandfather. I became the first grandchild to uphold his name, a living testament to his battle against injustice.

# PART TWO
# AGAINST THE TIDE

# WITHOUT A CHILDHOOD
## THE SON

In my early years, I felt as though I were not a child. I struggled with the loss of innocence, feeling confused and trapped in a dilemma. My home resembled an architectural puzzle, built decades before my birth, featuring a unique style that defied classification—four rooms, overlooking a shared space under the same roof. The kitchen, much like a lonely island, was separated from the rooms. Going to the bathroom outside the bedroom area on cold nights felt like an arduous journey into the frigid winter, forcing me to stifle my discomfort until dawn broke.

During my early years, I became familiar with the disquieting normalcy of life among those who used fear as their shield; these ominous figures occupied our land, spreading dread with the same ease as breathing. In my innocence, I mistook the flight of young men and boys from these soldiers for a whimsical game of hide and seek. Yet, as time passed, transforming days into weeks, months, and years, my naivety diminished. I started to see that these armed soldiers were not just foes but the very embodiment of oppression and brutality—relentless pursuers driven by an unquenchable thirst for death.

My first close encounter with the soldiers occurred when I was three years old. A loud, chaotic convoy of military vehicles disrupted my usual walk to the market with my mother. Soldiers stood on both sides of the road; their guns directed at homes and pedestrians. My mother tightened her grip on me, pulling me in closer as if to protect me from the imminent danger. As she held me, I could feel her heart racing against my small frame, becoming a silent anthem of fear. A wave of relief washed over me when she finally let go, only to be quickly replaced by confusion. Something felt wrong; my trips to the market with her were never to happen again.

The first game I played with my friends mirrored the war-torn surroundings we faced. We named it "Jew and Arab," a stark reflection of our grim reality. At first, I played the part of the Jew, representing the army, *Al Jaish*. Yet, when the roles were redistributed one day, I decided to object to it.

Rejecting the assigned role of *Jaish*, I asserted, "No. I want to be Arab."

"No, we are Arabs, you are a Jew; you're with them," one of the older kids shot back.

Distressed and furious, I insisted again, "I don't want to be the bad guy. I won't be a soldier."

I retreated to a nearby cement block, distancing myself from the game. As an observer, I watched the spectacle unfold, the "Arabs" hurling stones and verbal barbs at the "Jews," while the children embodying soldiers mimicked gunfire, their lips forming the shape of silent gunshots. Our games always ended with us constructing a makeshift checkpoint, cobbled together from rocks and tree branches, where we wielded our stick guns with false bravado.

Drivers reacted differently to our performance. Some participants joined in by joking and praising our courage, while others remained steadfast, hurling insults from a distance, signaling the early end of our play. These everyday experiences illustrated the mixture of discomfort and wonder that characterized our childhood in Gaza, a time of innocence abruptly snatched away before my eyes.

One day, I discovered a discarded newspaper that piqued my curiosity. The images fascinated me as I left dust prints with my bare feet. I sat on our doorstep, flipping through its pages, my small hands mimicking my father's gestures as he read his paper. I became absorbed in the vivid images—disturbing depictions of weeping women, lifeless bodies, blood-soaked landscapes, deceased children, and threatening soldiers.

While absorbed in the newspaper, haunting images of lifeless children struck me, leading me to wonder, *why didn't they shout?*

Years later, I learned that amid the slaughter, the innocent cries of children are drowned out by the overwhelming sound of gunfire. I scrutinized each photograph, and my youthful heart filled with anger.

Recognizing my increasing interest, my father started bringing home the *Al-Quds* Newspaper every day after work. This practice soon became a habit; each evening, I would rush to him, barefoot and enthusiastic, to help him carry the newspapers and whatever groceries he bought. It became my refuge, offering relief from the brutal truths reflected in our "Arabs and Jews" games.

# Gaza, Spring 1990
## The Son

In the early spring of 1990, warmth returned, and I started to walk barefoot through dusty sunlit streets. Sometimes I'd rinse off at home; other times, I'd forget, prompting my mother's frequent reminder: "Cover your feet when you go outside."

Years later, I still pondered why my mother would utter such remarks despite knowing I had just one worn-out shoe—a reliable friend throughout my school escapades. Its role ended with the school day; if I kept it on my foot afterwards, my mother would inquire, "Why are you still wearing that?"

One day, while I was home from school, I relished the freedom of being barefoot. I wandered into the kitchen, where my stomach growled with anticipation. Balancing pita bread in my small hands, I opened the fridge door. Inside the cool light, a bright, plump tomato caught my attention.

I reached for the chili jar on the high shelf, using a short wooden stool to grab it. After opening the jar, I scooped two spoonfuls of chili onto my pita bread.

As I finished up, a flash of worry hit me—was the lid tight

enough? The thought of chili spilling, especially into my eyes, made me cautious. I turned away as I put the jar back to avoid any accidents. I walked out of the house with a pita sandwich and tomato, unbothered by anyone.

The sheer ecstasy derived from the unhindered embrace of my bare feet and the earth was immeasurable. Each step was taken with purpose, as though responding to an important call or responsibility. I appreciated the warmth of the ground beneath my feet while enjoying a spicy sandwich, taking a moment to acknowledge the satisfaction it brought.

My aimless wandering brought me to the school's gate, which was unexpectedly secured from within. I stopped in my tracks, taking in the view around me. A donkey, burdened by a cart, ambled past. On the cart sat three women, their faces indistinct, alongside four colorful plastic baskets filled with vegetables.

A brief confusion struck me while I attempted to understand the ratio of baskets to women. Was one woman absent? Or did one woman have two baskets? This transient dilemma led to an unusual habit. In the months that followed, I examined every cart I came across for the basket-to-woman ratio. Although years have passed, I still vividly remember the three women and four baskets.

On the day I finally used my own plastic bag at the supermarket, each use brought back memories of the absent woman or the extra basket. Yet, a moment arrived when I had to carry two bags. After I paid, the thoughts of the missing woman and the additional basket surged in my mind. Yet, here I stood, carrying two bags, with no one missing.

People frequently struggle to comprehend others, seeing only their similarities or speculating about their motives. However, there are moments when the universe offers insights into the questions embedded in our early years. A particular moment occurred when my mother uncovered the identity of the enigmatic woman during a casual phone call while chatting about the neighborhood, well after I had departed Gaza. My siblings and mother consistently kept me informed.

"Ahmed, the son of the martyr, has a wedding," my mother shared.

"Who is he?" I asked, drawing a blank.

"Do you recall the woman who used to pass by weekly with her donkey cart and baskets?" she prodded, to which I responded affirmatively, thinking to myself, *I'm the one who knows that woman.*

"That's Ahmed's grandmother. Following his father's death by the Israeli soldiers, she took on the responsibility of two families alone. She is indeed a true warrior. May God reward her," my mother said. Then, like a fog lifting, I realized—the fourth basket was for the family of the martyr.

---

As I enjoyed the final bite of the juicy tomato, the school and its entrance slowly slipped from my mind. Moving past the tall gate, I glanced into the narrow gap between it and the concrete pillar. There, I saw a striking yet disturbing sight – my classmate Ali with a significantly older man. Emad, being in his twenties, presented a contrast to Ali and me, as we were only at the outset of our respective journeys.

*What could they be doing?* The thought emerged softly in my mind, filled with uncertainty. For a moment, I envisioned a lively football match starting, recalling how I had seen Emad engage in such games previously. However, the scene seemed out of place, like a puzzle piece that didn't fit. The schoolyard was deserted, and it was nowhere near the time when feet typically moved with soccer balls.

Emad's stern gaze and resolute presence pushed Ali, who seemed trapped and frightened. He looked like a caged bird longing to escape, visibly overtaken by fear. A wave of unease coursed through me, urging me to head home. Yet a surge of curiosity held me back, changing me from a carefree child into a quiet observer.

They headed toward the administrative building, which was typically locked and empty at this time. As they vanished from view, my inner six-year-old transformed into a detective, driven by an unquenchable curiosity to solve this mystery.

I moved quickly, keeping my hands moving in rhythm as I headed west. About 100 meters ahead was a tall wall belonging to another school, which had several holes that could be used for climbing. I reached the first hole, then the second, and soon was about two meters from the top. I glanced downward but was not afraid. Then, looking up, I tried to reach the next hole by extending my arm. After several attempts, I managed to get a grip. Once on top of the wall, I continued walking to observe what was happening behind the administrative building. Because the other school's wall was lower than the one I was climbing, I was able to position myself behind the separating wall between the two schools. I observed the area for any signs of movement but saw nothing, so I chose to climb the higher and thinner wall, which was one meter taller.

I moved slowly and carefully, concerned about the risk of falling. The wall loomed high above me, about five meters tall and only twelve centimeters wide, prompting me to lie on my stomach and crawl over it. Midway, I spotted Emad sitting on a small rock at the edge of the cafeteria, chatting and waving one hand as if beckoning someone. Moments later, he stood up, glanced around, and pulled Ali toward him. Ali appeared tiny next to Emad, which filled me with dread. I froze like a lizard clinging to the wall, watching as Emad gripped the fabric of Ali's shorts.

I sensed something was amiss, and Ali attempted to free himself but could not. Emad pulled Ali closer and forced him to sit on his legs. I could see Ali's face; he looked more fearful than his expression revealed. I noticed Emad unzipping his trousers and taking out his penis while pulling down Ali's blue shorts.

I struggled to concentrate and remained frozen until they eventually left. I stayed like that for a few more minutes after they were gone, which felt like ages or many days. Since that day, I have felt fear whenever I saw Emad or Ali. Fear of people calcifies in our veins and the chambers of our hearts without us understanding why we perceive it differently from the reality of those individuals who committed a wrong. Since that day, I ran away every time I spotted Emad, and if he was far off, I kept an eye on him.

Time felt like it was both dragging and racing at the same moment. I'll never forget the fear in Ali's eyes and Emad's grip on him. Each time I think of Emad pulling down Ali's shorts, I feel a jolt as if it were happening to me.

A few weeks later, in the late afternoon, as I waited for my father to come home from work, I saw Emad climbing over the school walls and jumping down inside. My previous curiosity battled against my fear of following him again.

Many years later, I understood that my curiosity and childlike innocence had shaped me into an adult who could burden myself and others. I had grown overly inquisitive and matured far too quickly. The rigidity within me made me believe that being flexible and kind was wrong. That day, my curiosity and stubbornness compelled me to enter the schoolyard. I feigned playfulness, yet my gaze was locked onto that madman, who filled me with dread. Several students were still in the school, and a few adults were playing football in the primary yard. When he vanished behind the school, I hurried around to keep him in view from a distance, making sure others could see both him and me. My eyes widened, and I sat beneath a large tree, hunched like an old man. There was Ali, playing with the other children.

Emad was coming for him again. Briefly, I thought his actions might help, but fear quickly took over. While playing with fallen leaves between my toes, questions flooded my mind, and I watched Emad closely. Earlier, Emad had headed toward the corner behind the old building, stopping now and then to call Ali to join him.

I felt the urge to stand up, run, and yell for Ali to come to me, but fear held me back. I also wanted to inform the other adults about what I had seen, hoping they would convince Ali to join them instead. Ali was heading toward Emad, though his movements were unsteady, and tension filled the atmosphere. Emad directed Ali from a distance until he slipped behind the building, with Ali still trying to reach him. As soon as that happened, I exited the school and ran to the main street, where I could peer through the holes in the wall. As I sprinted with bare feet, I picked up a few stones. Once I was close enough, I hurled rocks at the ceilings of the houses overlooking the school, hoping they would open the windows to catch whoever was throwing stones.

With immense effort, I threw more stones, and my leg ached from jumping. Peering through a tiny crack in the wall, I spotted Emad fondling Ali, pulling out his penis, and about to sit him on his lap behind the tree.

"You son of a dog! What are you doing?" a woman's voice rang out, altering the situation.

I sat in fear on the wall, my gaze flickering between the west and the east. I anticipated the woman would either leave the house or rush to intervene. When a minute passed and she still hadn't emerged, I was uncertain whether she had yelled at him for forcing Ali onto his lap or because someone was throwing stones at her home. Moments later, I saw Emad exiting the school, heading west. Instead of going home, I took another street east and ran home. For many months, I didn't see Ali, and I didn't encounter Emad either. Years later, Emad became the district leader of one of the Palestinian leftist military groups

For many weeks, what I saw turned into a nightmare for me. I struggled to sleep; my eyes would widen, and I started seeing things that were vast and enormous. I felt unable to share what I experienced, fearing it was expected of me, even though I was a child unfamiliar with these behaviors.

Time seemed to both quicken and slow, and the images of Ali as Emad pulled his shorts down became etched in my memory. Waves of fear flooded me, leaving me anxious about my surroundings. That's when my sleepwalking rituals began. I would wake up in the middle of the night or before dawn and wander the house. My father would ask me what frightened me if someone had beaten me. My reply was always, "No one."

Once, after sleepwalking, my father grew angry and suspicious of my fear. He asked my mother if he should take me to *Qate'i Khoufa* or "Break the Fear", where a respected man pours olive oil between the legs and massages them vigorously. It's known to be one of the most painful experiences, often causing men to scream in agony. The more they scream, the more they seem terrified of something significant.

As we headed south, I remained asleep. My father asked me again if someone had beaten me, and I pointed towards the door of a well-respected religious figure, stating, "Abu Fathi's door." I was hallucinating. My siblings took it as a joke on me, but I recall that day clearly —I had seen Emad sitting at the entrance of Abu Fathi's home.

A few weeks later, I decided to inform the principal about what I had witnessed. Known for his stern presence and formality, he seemed trustworthy. However, entering his office was overwhelming, leaving me anxious and leading to years of regret and a desire to distance myself.

I walked barefoot to his office on a clear, sunny day as school staff returned from vacation. Hearing quiet sounds inside, I entered and saw something unforgettable. No one expected a small child to enter the office and witness what was happening. Perhaps one would wish for a tall man with a shoe that could warn them if someone was coming. The school secretary, seated in a chair, held a child on his lap and caressed his chest and body from beneath the t-shirt. The child appeared to be about five years old, as he was not yet attending school. In less than a second, I transformed into a racecar and sped towards the street. The secretary chased after me, but I had vanished into my home. For many years, I was afraid to look into his eyes or approach him. I would stay near my brother or mother whenever he was around. One day, he came to our class, and our eyes met; I ran to the corner and focused solely on my teacher's eyes, attempting to convey that I was scared.

Years later, that child was killed by an Israeli bullet in his chest. That man was jailed for attempted murder, but I met him many years later in Sweden, seeking asylum. He killed himself in the forest more than twenty-five years after the incident.

# PRISON, PROMISE AND CHICKPEAS, GAZA 1990
## THE SON

My brother-in-law had a Subaru, a Japanese vehicle recognized for its bright white color and four doors. Cars were uncommon in Gaza; most Gazans did not own one. Rather, car-sharing services were prevalent, offering a communal method for navigating the urban landscape.

He had a talent for house painting and was a passionate advocate for Fatah. I was only five years old when my sister became engaged to him. It was a bone-chilling December day when she returned from her teacher's college, her eyes filled with sadness. As a child, I could not fully understand the seriousness of the moment, but I caught snippets of the words *Habis* and *Sijin* – meaning prison and jail—between my mother and another sister as they consoled her.

When my father came home from work, he had little time for himself. After eating lunch and offering his prayers, he seriously asked me if I wanted to join him for an outing. My young heart responded excitedly, unaware of the somber undertones of the day. Without thinking about my shoes, a detail my mother strangely overlooked, I followed him eagerly. As we walked out, I looked back at my mother for unspoken permission. She was wrapped up in her worries, barely noticing our departure.

Rather than heading straight for the main door, my father turned towards *Hakoura*. Curious, I asked him, "*Min han?*" – From here?

He simply responded, "We are going to Abu Nafz's," which brought a smile to my face.

Abu Nafz, the parents of my brother-in-law, lived amid fields in eastern Gaza, renowned for their vibrant green chickpeas – a treat I truly adored. The *Hamla Malana,* as we called the green chickpeas, was my seasonal favorite. I loved sitting in the fields, plucking and enjoying them one by one, their freshness contrasting sharply with Gaza's dry landscape.

My father tapped the already open door, saying "*Ya Sater*"—a traditional way for men to announce their arrival, giving women the chance to prepare.

As he entered the house, I moved closer. Children my age were playing near a frail wooden door that looked as if it would collapse with a hard knock. Looking inside, I noticed a spacious area leading to multiple rooms. These rooms were divided by tall, flowing sheets, creating a barrier between the men gathered outside beneath the open sky around a fire. Nearby, gleaming golden-colored Arabian coffee pots sparkled.

My father chatted with the men, their talks flowing smoothly until he raised the topic of my sister's fiancé, sharing his hope for a quick release with a heartfelt "*Inshalla Yetl'a Besalama.*"

I stood beside him, taking in the seriousness of the moment. That day, my father conveyed a message of steadfast loyalty: regardless of the danger of arrest, my sister would wait for her fiancé.

I later realized that many families cut ties with imprisoned men, fearing both lengthy sentences and the harassment of the Israeli army. However, when my father expressed our perspective, all my brother-in-law's relatives replied with a single word: "*Asil*" – "Noble."

That day imparted a profound lesson in steadfastness and loyalty as true values amid uncertainty and adversity. The idea of self-sacrifice struck a chord with me, a theme I would come to understand deeply throughout my life.

Despite the underlying tension and uncertainty that day, my childlike innocence protected me from the harsh realities I would have faced at Abu Nafz's house.

As several months passed, my sister's fiancé remained in prison. His mother, a farmer, frequently visited us during the late afternoons. She would return home on a cart pulled by a reliable donkey, primarily carrying vegetables. Holding onto the back of that cart brought me immense happiness. Donkeys symbolized patience, laboring tirelessly without ever expressing a complaint.

As she returned from the fields, avoiding the fence Israel had built to the east, she would sometimes drop off green chickpeas or Armenian cucumbers. Those relaxed afternoons spent outside our home, picking and nibbling on the chickpea leaves, turned into joyful tussles with the plants—pure bliss. Yet, I couldn't stand Armenian cucumbers; I found them tasteless, and as kids, we would playfully joke that their strange, sour taste came from the man who had planted them having farted on them.

# Gaza 1990
## The Son

When I first started school, I couldn't read or write at all. My father believed that kindergarten was for those too timid to begin real school. Before classes began, my mother would visit the bustling Friday market, a tradition for families as children prepared to start their own school journeys, following in their older siblings' footsteps. Our home, near several schools, included a small stationery store and cafeteria run by my parents. I spent most of my childhood outdoors, often around the store or our front step, watching people go by.

I observed the scene with attentive focus, noting the diversity of the women who passed by, varying in age, educational background, and socio-economic status. The refugee women, identifiable by their striped white and dark blue dresses, stood in clear contrast to the non-refugee women attired in dark green. I once examined the fabric of the refugee women's dresses to determine whether it was similar to that of garments worn by my relatives.

Young refugee men wore jeans and blue shirts, starkly contrasting with the denim-on-denim look of their non-refugee peers. Even with their school uniforms, I could identify the refugees by their distinct smell—a mix of tuna, fish, beans, and various soups. This particular scent, unlike that of non-refugees who lacked similar provisions, marked their status and was nourished by the UNRWA (The United Nations Relief and Works Agency for Palestine Refugees in the Near East).

When I was five, I first noticed the divide between refugees and *Mwatinin*. I saw a teenager insult a refugee child about smelling like fish—a result of the UNRWA's rule that children had to consume fish oil before receiving food. I didn't question the labels or food distribution; instead, I gradually became aware of social divisions as I grew up.

My mother often tried to keep me at home, but I was always eager to explore. As a child, simple things like people-watching or spotting a new pair of white *Forza* sneakers brought me joy. That brand fascinated me, and eventually, I got my own pair—a small but memorable win. Looking back, I've realized those little victories meant everything in childhood.

Years later, in Italy, I learned "Forza" means "Power", adding nostalgic meaning to my old sneakers. Shopping for school clothes with my mother was a joyful memory—I always accepted her choices, unlike my sisters, who often wanted more. I proudly wore my new outfit, trusting her taste and carrying that confidence into adulthood.

The constant noise would ultimately push my mother's patience to its limits, leaving her tired and frustrated among the remnants of our shopping trip. At her breaking point, she'd exclaim, "Indeed, girls are a burden until death," and "Raising boys is as easy as striking a flint."

The scent of new clothes, the thrill of wearing them, and proudly walking around the house brought me great joy as a child. These genuine moments marked my excitement about growing up. When my older brother stopped by with an analog camera, I changed quickly, posed in my new outfit, and smiled—a moment of happiness now captured in a photo that reminds me of how much I've changed.

I ventured in alone on my first day at school. My father, as stoic as the morning sun, simply stated, "Your teacher is *Ustaz* Omar."

I was already acquainted with Ostaz Omar and his classroom—he recognized me as well. While many children experienced the first day of school like a grand festival, I viewed it as the beginning of a family endeavor to sell stationery, snacks, and sandwiches to my classmates. As my father engaged in a lengthy discussion with the principal, he motioned for me to join Omar in the asbestos classrooms since the ceiling is made from asbestos. Those four old rooms, dating back to the 1950s, welcomed us eager learners starting our first-grade journey.

My teacher had a unique connection with me, strengthened by his relationship with my family. My parents often invited him for tea during breaks, creating a warm friendship. Although he was generally friendly, he did admonish me a couple of times in my early years with him---once for not turning in a homework assignment and another time for failing to answer a question in class. His threat to tell my parents filled me with fear.

The first three months felt like enduring an unending tempest. While my classmates excelled in reading and writing, I grappled with these new abilities. They had the advantage of having gone to kindergarten before me. Omar frequently called on students who hadn't done their homework, wielding a hard black plastic tube—a stark symbol of his disciplinary methods. As he enforced his punishments, I would watch in dread, my face marked by sorrow and my eyes filled with fear. Just the sight of him approaching our classroom sent us scattering like sheep escaping a wolf, only to provoke a grin from him.

Having the same teacher throughout first and second grades felt incredibly monotonous. I longed to move up and explore different subjects with various instructors. However, the thought of landing in the feared "mice rooms"---dark storage areas full of rats and miscellaneous items that we believed were home to many mice—was even more daunting. When I first witnessed a punishment and heard the threat of being sent to the "mice room," my initial excitement for school disappeared completely.

On a specific day when Omar was sick, a substitute teacher filled in for him. This tall man had a prominent nose and curly hair, and he carried a long, thick bamboo cane along with a short, rigid plastic pipe. His deep voice resonated against the classroom walls, filling us with dread. His stern expression only intensified the fear that his words inspired. Unlike *Ustaz* Omar, he had a strained connection with my family and rarely visited our family cafeteria. His intimidating presence seemed to cast a shadow of dissatisfaction wherever he went. He assigned five pages of Arabic sentences as homework, a task that felt as monumental to me as climbing a steep mountain.

When I arrived home, I tossed aside my backpack, feeling the burden of unfinished homework lift from me. I lacked a desk, a place of my own, and even a designated spot for my backpack, which ended up in my parents' room and would be retrieved the next day. Homework became a struggle as I lay on my stomach in the hallway, surrounded by my sisters, who were immersed in their studies. I watched them diligently write their assignments and fervently memorize texts, their voices creating an educational chorus. Still, I never questioned why I didn't share their zeal for studying.

I anticipated Omar's return the following day; however, the substitute teacher appeared once more, and I was reminded of my incomplete homework. In my youth, I possessed a willful disposition, often described by my mother as stubbornness, accompanied by a tendency for blunt honesty that could affect even the most self-assured individuals.

Upon the substitute's entrance, the class rose in unison. His authoritative directive to be seated echoed through the room as he placed his black bag, reminiscent of a modern laptop case, on the desk.

He then issued the command, "*Qiyam*" (Stand Up), with a voice of considerable volume. Methodically, he walked among our desks, scrutinizing us with the precision of a leader reviewing his team.

"Who hasn't finished the homework?" he asked, scanning the room. I glanced left and right, silently hoping I wasn't the only one. Unfortunately, my hopes were crushed; just two others found themselves in the same situation. A sense of dread settled in my chest—not merely from the looming punishment, but also from the idea of admitting it to my parents.

"Come to the front, fools," he commanded with a voice as unforgiving as the blazing desert sun. There was no point in pretending innocence—he would inspect our notebooks. "Should I put them in the mice room or subject them to *Falaka*?" he asked the rest of the class.

*Falaka* was a term that represented our greatest shame. It involved the largest students lifting each other over a desk while the teacher wielded a tube or bamboo stick to deliver punishment. The victim would be referred to as *Abu Falaka* for the entire academic year. I had never experienced *Falaka*; this time, the substitute teacher chose not to use physical punishment. Instead, he focused on me.

"Why didn't you finish the homework?" he inquired, his voice an icy chill in the warm space. My eyes were glued to the floor, occasionally flicking up to catch his gaze before quickly looking away.

"Did you forget to eat?" he continued, unaware that I often went without meals, only consuming food when hunger became unbearable. He left the room for a moment, and I watched him nervously, preparing for what was to follow.

Upon his return, he beckoned me towards him. My steps towards him were measured but drenched in fear. Abruptly, he clamped onto my ears, sending a jolt of electric pain shooting through them. I let out a sharp scream but held back tears. He placed a small stone on my earlobe and ground it in, amplifying the throbbing pain.

Nearly all the teachers relied on physical punishment. They used sticks or hard plastic tubes with a normality that concealed their true intent—some even favored bamboo sticks. As I eventually left Gaza and started to reflect on my school days from afar—a scene filled with suffering—the sheer scale of the violence we endured was not only bewildering but also shocking. It felt like coming across a silent snake in a meadow of wildflowers—alarmingly unanticipated.

---

The final days of the first semester had arrived, bringing with them the looming mid-term certificate. Like an executioner's blade, it represented a verdict for all students, yet I barely thought about it. I still hadn't understood the importance of high grades. Even after several months at school, my parents showed no curiosity about my performance.

A few days before the day of distributing grades, one of my sisters playfully teased me, laughing at me: "We'll see how many *Ka'aka* you'll earn."

*Ka'aka*, the circular Levantine cakes, represented a metaphorical equivalent to the dreaded red circles marking a failing grade on our certificates. This term became ingrained in our minds during our school years, symbolizing failure. These experiences linger with children, as indelible as the craters on the moon.

I clearly remember the day I got my first yellow certificate. It was a cold day in mid-December, with rain that began early and stopped around ten o'clock. When our teacher, Omar, entered the room holding the yellow certificates, a deep silence enveloped us. It felt like we had transformed into a community of moles, deeply buried in the earth, where even our shared breathing was soundless.

The stillness broke only when a student was summoned. Each child moved to the front, collected their certificate, and tucked it away in their bag without a second look. A few bold ones managed to steal a glance, cleverly concealing their results from prying eyes.

When my name reverberated in the room, I stood up and walked towards the teacher. *Ustaz* Omar's face revealed much—a tempest was on the horizon, and I found myself in its midst. He discreetly shielded my certificate from the inquisitive gazes of my classmates and handed it to me. I slipped it into my pocket without a look.

"This is the mid-term certificate. You have an opportunity to improve next semester," he remarked as the bell rang for *Forsa*, our thirty-minute break.

As the classroom emptied, I found myself anchored to my seat, a lingering sense of unease cloaking me. Carefully, I withdrew the yellow paper and beheld my academic fate. A red *Ka'aka* glared back at me. I had failed religious studies. The thought of confessing to my parents filled me with trepidation. I ruminated on a possible solution, and a plan took shape. I would eradicate the red *Ka'aka*.

A sense of quiet dread enveloped me as I headed home. The streets were filled with students proudly displaying their mid-term certificates. When I arrived, I found my mother deeply engrossed in her work at the shop. Seizing the opportunity for privacy, I took my certificate and a blue pen before retreating to the backyard, our private *Hakoura*—an area in the back of our house where we had a huge olive tree.

Using the wall as a table, I nervously erased the red circle around my failing grade with saliva, then added a one to turn it into a 19. I failed because I didn't want to memorize the Quranic verses for religious studies.

While I was focused on my work, I did not notice my mother's approach. Upon noticing the altered certificate, she inquired about my actions and stated her intention to inform my father, underscoring the seriousness of the matter.

The remainder of the day passed in a state of unease. Anticipation of my father's return preoccupied my thoughts and produced a pervasive sense of apprehension. Every noise, including the slightest movement of doors, heightened my anxiety. Upon his arrival at four o'clock, I withdrew to the *Hakoura*, maintaining vigilance over the entrance from a place of concealment.

As my father changed and prayed before dinner, my mother told him what I'd done. His loud call made me emerge from hiding, fearful. In the room, he confronted me with my poor grade and dishonesty, holding the yellow paper.

What followed was a blur. He lifted me and set me on top of a high closet. "Stay there. Let the mice and cockroaches nibble on you," he ordered before leaving, abandoning me to sob atop the closet.

From that point forward, I consistently maintained a high educational standing through to my high school graduation. That experience was a pivotal moment in shaping my outlook and future path. It signifies both the repercussions of failure and the significance of perseverance. Had my father chosen an alternative approach, repeated setbacks might have led to complacency. His decisive response instilled in me resilience—not a fear of consequences, but a determination to always make an effort.

# Education Before Liberation, Gaza 1991
## The Son

I was raised in a family with a complex political background. Although my father was not a politician and did not actively participate in politics, he quietly supported the *Fedayeen*, the freedom fighters. He married my mother, whose family members—including cousins, a brother, and father—were involved in this movement. My father seldom discussed these topics.

One sunny afternoon, after a night of heavy rain, I arrived home from school to a disturbing sight. Typically, I would dash home with my backpack and then run outside again. From a distance, I saw my sisters gathered around my mother, who was seated in a chair. This was unusual for this time of day. My sisters were weeping, while my mother had her face hidden in her hands, fixed on the colorful tiles beneath her. Moving slowly on my small legs, I glanced from one tearful face to another, not even noticing one of our neighbors quietly sitting in the corner. I walked in, placed my school bag down, and stood still, weighed down by the silence. Abruptly, one of my sisters erupted into loud, painful sobs.

My mother sprang from her chair, her voice quivering and sharp as she said, "He wasn't martyred; why are you crying?" She then looked at me, her eyes heavy with unexpressed fears: "Take your bag to the room," she instructed before retreating into the kitchen in her long, rosy dress.

A sense of confusion enveloped me. Who were they discussing? I shifted my gaze between my sisters, seeking answers. I moved closer and settled onto the patterned mattress on the floor. Yet, no one spoke. The atmosphere felt thick, reminiscent of the stillness before a storm. I looked back at their faces, anxiously searching for hints.

The phone rang, the noise breaking the heavy silence. Usually, I would have dashed to answer, but I stood still. All eyes turned as one of my sisters hurried to grab the receiver. The stillness was so deep that I could hear their breathing, tense and irregular.

"Alooo," she said, her voice trembling as she inquired who was on the line. It was my father, calling from work.

"He says he'll be home later, but our brother is doing well. He may be released tonight," she explained to the rest of us. The relief was tangible, like a breath of fresh air blowing through the room. The tension that had surrounded us all started to ease.

"Prepare tea for Um Atef," my mother gently directed one of my sisters. It was at that moment that I started to connect the dots of the story. Someone had been imprisoned—my eldest brother, who was studying around Ramallah. Imprisonment felt like a loss to me, as I constantly worried that the Israeli army might imprison my father and leave us abandoned.

Later, I learned that my oldest brother had been taken from his dormitory near the Birzeit University hills. It occurred under the cover of night, during one of those abrupt raids that leave everything in disarray. The Israeli forces often terrorize people after 2 a.m. Many students were taken in their sleepwear. My brother, who was just starting to find his voice as an activist, had been involved with the student council and participating in political activities. That morning, a neighborhood friend who also studied there called us with the news.

Our home, usually filled with family noises, succumbed to a

heavy silence. My mother, forever haunted by the specter of loss, was seized by a fear that this arrest could derail her purpose: to ensure her children received an education and to become the mother of both an engineer and a doctor.

Fear enveloped us all, shadowing every part of our home and reflected in my sisters' faces. It felt as though the very walls absorbed our apprehension, resonating with the unspoken tension. The only one free from fear was our other brother, an undercover activist in Fatah, who fully understood the fate awaiting every activist.

My father, by contrast, provided a calm and stabilizing presence within our family. Upon returning from work, he consistently maintained a composed demeanor and communicated with my mother in an even tone that concealed any personal concerns.

"He is not the first to be arrested, and he will not be the last," he remarked, his words laden with experience. My father, rooted in rationality and wisdom, appeared certain that my brother would make his way back home. Yet, underneath his composed surface, a subtle change in his demeanor revealed deeper anxieties.

The next two days felt surreal—a blend of anxiety and discomfort. Time seemed to stretch and compress unpredictably, charged with nervous energy. My mother's hands shook as she served tea, with tears silently pooling in the cups. My sisters and I shared worried glances, our eyes mirroring the fears we were unable to voice. The house fell into an unsettling silence, as if the very atmosphere was waiting breathlessly for news. My father, usually a source of strength, appeared more withdrawn than ever. He drifted through the house, praying quietly, his thoughts entangled in depths unspoken.

As the sun sank below the horizon and the call to *Maghrib* prayer resonated through the streets, the phone rang. The sound sliced through the tense atmosphere. It was my brother. My mother, heart racing, jumped to answer, but he wanted to speak to my father.

A look of understanding crossed my father's face as he picked up the phone—my brother had broken his promise.

After whispering prayers for his safety, my mother passed the phone to my father, who spoke with a mixture of love and disappointment: "I sent you to study, not to be a fighter. Once you show me your degree, you may liberate Palestine—until then, please act wisely."

Those words are deeply engraved in my mind, echoing over the years like a silent mantra. My father's conviction was clear, shaped by a lifetime of hard-earned wisdom: "Education is the first step toward liberation."

# School and Rain, Gaza 1991

## The Son

My early years were marked by persistent feelings of envy, which influenced both my memories and interpersonal interactions. I frequently found myself in internal conflict, not only with my own perceptions but also within the context of my family and broader society. I experienced significant jealousy toward classmates who had privileges such as remaining at home during inclement weather or accompanying their fathers on outings, whether at recreational locations or places of employment. I resented those who could enjoy food from sources other than our school cafeteria, which was operated by my family, something that intensified my feelings.

Observing fellow students unveil their well-organized pencil cases elicited an acute sense of longing. The enthusiasm others exhibited for activities like football was particularly perplexing to me. Such moments provoked numerous unspoken questions regarding my role within my family, educational setting, and community. Although the cause of my jealousy seemed apparent, the pursuit of its underlying reasons proved to be complex.

One winter morning served as a clear example of this discontent.

I awoke in my parents' room, layered in two blankets. My mother promptly ended this period of comfort with instructions to prepare for school. I hesitated to leave the warmth of bed as the cold permeated the room. Despite being only partially awake, I proceeded to dress for school, assembled my belongings, and acknowledged my mother's reminder to wash up. While absentmindedly searching for my shoes, I recalled previous discomfort experienced during earlier winters due to inadequate footwear.

Stepping outside, I noticed that my only pair of white shoes was already wet from the rain. Upon informing my mother, she advised a practical solution—wearing socks with the shoes—while she continued preparing falafel sandwiches for sale. The resulting discomfort while wearing damp shoes and socks was unavoidable, and I faced a solitary walk through empty, rain-soaked streets.

Unlike my peers who remained at home, I proceeded to school while my father and the principal were chatting at the gate of the school. After a brief inquiry about my educational progress, the principal announced class cancellations due to the weather. When I requested permission to stay home, my father insisted I attend school regardless of rain.

Reflecting on my twelve years of education, I am reminded of my infrequent absences, attributable to a stringent approach to schooling adopted within my family. This policy, while ensuring consistent attendance, limited my ability to exercise independent judgment regarding attendance.

I developed a sense of maturity at an early age, feeling alienated from the typical experiences of childhood. Over time, these circumstances contributed to a general disenchantment and a sense of lost opportunities for personal fulfillment during my formative years.

# Challenging School, Gaza 1993
## The Son

One cold spring day, I woke up early in the morning to prepare for an exam where I would recite the verses of *Surat Al Qalam*—the 68th chapter of the Quran—to my classmates. My parents noted my early rise, and when my mother inquired about my actions, I replied that I needed to study for the exam. My older sister recognized my tendency to review material at the last minute.

As I wandered through the winding corridor of our home, I began softly reciting the sacred verses like a monk murmuring his prayers. I took each verse one by one, repeating them five times, hoping to weave them into my memory. The chapter spanned fifty-two verses, and I felt like a small boat battling a strong current, managing to grasp only ten of them. The weight of expectations was heavy—I was meant to remember every word.

"Drink tea to warm your body," my mother gently urged, holding the teapot.

I gratefully accepted a small, sugar-laden cup. The sweet warmth enveloped me as I held the sacred book in my free hand, sipping the tea as if drawing strength from its essence. With each tick of the clock, I put on my jeans, shirt, and shoes. Fear crept into my heart like a cat. I clung to a fragile hope that my turn to recite the *Surat* would not arrive today.

A chorus of 36 students was assembled, reciting verses under the diligent supervision of our teacher. We were guided by a distinguished instructor—a modest and empathetic individual recognized for his wisdom, and by his long white beard and hair. His slightly stooped posture appeared to reflect the breadth of his knowledge. Highly regarded within the community, he was often praised by elder members, claiming, "*Ustaz* Abu Tawfiq was the finest teacher." His educational influence extended to my eldest brother and most of the men in the neighborhood.

During that spring, the third session was an Islamic studies lesson taught by Abu Tawfiq. This class was scheduled just before the fifteen-minute break known as *Fursa*. When the bell sounded, I usually went to the cafeteria operated by my brother and mother to assist with sandwich preparation or oversee the snack counter. On this particular day, the teacher decided to hold the lesson outdoors. Students sat on the ground while the instructor remained in his chair, holding a pen, the Quran, and some paper.

As each student was called to recite from the Quran, dread enveloped me. Brief relief washed over me each time his gaze passed by. The ticking clock and my furtive glances toward the principal's room formed a terrifying duet, each tick inching me closer to my potential failure or deliverance.

All my careful planning unraveled when I heard him say, "Ayk, your turn."

My heart raced, sweat dripped down my back, and I felt as fragile as a leaf in the wind. I moved toward him like a lamb walking to the altar. With my right hand over my left in a gesture of respect, I began my recitation from the start. I decided to take control of my fate, and he allowed me to continue. However, when I neared the ninth verse, it felt as though I teetered on the edge of a chasm, poised to reveal my hidden inadequacy. Just as I feared, everything was about to collapse. The bell rang, its victorious chime signaling the end of the session.

A throng of students rushed toward the cafeteria; their thoughts focused on the sandwiches awaiting them. While others hurried, I chose to hold back, feeling a newfound strength swelling inside me. I informed the teacher that I had completed my portion and asked him to record my name; he did so. A wave of relief enveloped me, and I dedicated myself to memorizing that chapter for the impending final exam.

I had been immersed in the essence of initiative that day. I discovered that the most powerful tool is the desire to take control and navigate one's own path, rather than passively following the well-worn trail. It's not about attaining perfection immediately but rather facing the challenges of mistakes and learning to maneuver through them. I understood that success resembled a bird poised to soar, needing just a gentle nudge from the edge of initiative.

---

During our initial training session, the teacher directed us to "turn to the right." I found these instructions challenging to interpret, akin to deciphering ancient hieroglyphics embedded within scouting terminology.

For several years, including my time in secondary school, I faced difficulty distinguishing between right and left turns. This confusion persisted as I participated in the early scouting groups established in Gaza's schools following the arrival of the Palestinian Liberation Organization and Yasser Arafat.

At the age of ten, I became a member of a scouting group with an interest in experiencing aspects of military life. Activities included structured marching, singing revolutionary songs for Palestine, and fostering teamwork among participants. The scouting uniform served as a symbol of unity, and members contributed ten shekels (equivalent to three USD at the time) to obtain patches, a woggle, a scarf, and badges. During the first year, members were instructed to acquire military-style uniforms before the Palestinian Ministry of Education finalized the official scout uniform colors.

We started our journey by learning how to march and taking on the regular task of raising the flag each morning after the first Palestinian national anthem. Abu Ziyad, our sports teacher, supervised our practice sessions.

When I left class for scouting activities, teachers often commented, "Let scouting benefit you in exams," expressing mild concern.

My older brother, mistaking my enthusiasm for foolishness, reprimanded me during a training session and sent me back to the classroom. The impact of his words left me devastated. I walked back to the room, his disapproval casting a long shadow over my happiness. However, this setback couldn't sway my determination, and the scouting uniform continued to be a source of immense pride for me. As I put on the military uniform, grey scarf, orange badge, Palestinian flag badge, and woggle, I felt an unparalleled sense of strength. My reflection mirrored the heroes I had admired in newspapers, igniting a feeling of belonging and purpose within me.

As I stepped out of the house dressed in my full uniform, my father, who was making falafel, looked at me with admiration. He lifted his hand in salute, a cooking spoon still in his grip—an image that will forever remain in my memory. I returned his salute using the traditional three fingers of a scout, while his was a full, five-fingered salute.

He chuckled, saying, "I am big, that's why I use five fingers."

Marching to school in my uniform, I was met with curious stares and hushed questions from those around me. There were whispers that Yasser Arafat planned to change the school dress code to a military style, promoting a stronger sense of nationalism and the fight for Palestine's liberation.

One woman even joked, "Where is your gun?"

Still, with my chest out and steps brimming with pride, I made my way to school like a peacock showcasing its vibrant feathers.

One of my most unforgettable moments was being part of the flag team when we raised the flag on the pole for the first time. Although I wasn't selected as a group leader to raise the flag myself, my role as a guardian on the right side was just as significant, and my enthusiasm remained intact. From this experience, I learned that every opportunity comes with a cost—a disappointing lesson in favoritism that would linger as a bitter memory for years.

The morning school program typically began with either a Quran recitation, a "do you know" segment, a Hadith of the Prophet, a song, or a speech focusing on a particular individual or event. For these sessions, my father helped me prepare speeches about various political and historical topics. His narratives, covering everything from the Nakba to Dalal Moghrabi and the Karama battle in Jordan, informed and motivated us all.

As the announcement, "*Taheyat Al'alam, Ista'ad*" (Flag Salutation, be ready), resonated through the courtyard, the melody of *Mawtini* filled our ears. It began as a soft murmur, progressively intensifying into a powerful flow, carrying us all in its patriotic wave.

*My homeland, my homeland,*
*Glory and beauty, sublimity and splendor*
*Are in your hills, are in your hills.*
*Life and deliverance, pleasure and hope*
*Are in your air, are in your air.*
*Will I see you, will I see you?*
*Safely comforted and victoriously honored.*
*Safely comforted and victoriously honored.*
*Will I see you in your eminence?*
*Reaching to the stars, reaching to the stars*
*My homeland, my homeland.*
*My homeland, my homeland,*
*The youth will not tire*
*Their goal is your independence*

*Or they die, or they die.*
*We will drink from death, and will not be to our enemies*
*Like slaves, like slaves.*
*We do not want, we do not want*
*An eternal humiliation, nor a miserable life.*
*An eternal humiliation, nor a miserable life.*
*We do not want, but we will bring back*
*Our storied glory, our storied glory.*
*My homeland, my homeland.*

[Trimmed: Long street history condensed.] Gaza's streets carried centuries of memory, but for us, they were simply the paths of survival.

We moved in unison, our steps echoing rhythmically off the ground, one after another, like a well-oiled machine. I held my head high, my eyes locked on the back of the second scout's head as if it were a guiding north star. In the center of the assembly, we paused, turned left, and the leader ascended the stairs toward the flagpole. As he began hoisting the flag, I raised my hand with three fingers, symbolizing our united commitment. My foot shot up and struck the ground with a solid thud, a salute to the flag now rising.

Once the flag reached its peak, the leader grabbed the microphone and spoke, his authoritative voice inviting the entire school to echo his words:

*Long Live Arab Free Palestine*
*Long Live Arab Free Palestine*
*Long Live Arab Free Palestine*

And then the last phrase:

*Glory and Eternity for our martyrs*

However, as we learned about the history of the Palestinian Scout movement, I understood that we were reigniting the spirit of the 1912 movement, a flame first ignited at Saint George School in Jerusalem.

*Kun Musta'idan*, echoed in my mind, a motto I had sewn onto my uniform and woven into my being over the years. "Be prepared" served as a personal battle cry, urging me to remain vigilant against adversaries and to alert my fellow scouts. Yet, I felt taken aback when it was clarified that it represented a readiness to support everyone. This insight brought a wave of disappointment over me.

A year later, they changed the motto to "Do your best."

I hadn't even seen ten summers when the Palestinian anthem abruptly changed. We were unaware of the reasons behind it. One morning, during assembly, the familiar tune of *Mawtini* was substituted with an unfamiliar melody. As always, there was no warning; we were just puppets in a play with a script that kept changing.

It was a period of societal upheaval and confusion, and this feeling of uncertainty affected not just us, the schoolchildren, but the whole community. Just a week before the anthem's transformation, ten Palestinians had been killed by their fellow citizens.

I overheard my father say, "They killed him because they are against Abu Ammar."

These were protestors opposed to the Palestinian Authority and the Oslo Accords. My view of the Islamists was tainted with negativity; they were against a Palestinian state and Arafat's return. Nonetheless, the new anthem resonated with strength, igniting a newfound eagerness in me to learn it. As the teacher distributed the lyrics to the new anthem, I eagerly clutched the printed paper, prepared to absorb its lyrical significance.

*Warrior, warrior, warrior,*
*Oh my land, the land of the ancestors*
*Warrior, warrior, warrior,*
*Oh my people, people of eternity*
*With my determination, my fire and the volcano of my vendetta*
*With the longing in my blood for my land and my home*
*I have climbed the mountains and fought the wars*
*I have conquered the impossible, and crossed the frontiers*
*Warrior, warrior, warrior,*
*Oh my land, the land of the ancestors*
*Warrior, warrior, warrior,*

*Oh my people, people of eternity*
*With the resolve of the winds and the fire of the weapons*
*And the determination of my nation in the land of struggle*
*Palestine is my home, and the path of my triumphal*
*Palestine is my home, Palestine is my fire*
*Palestine is my vendetta and the land of withstanding*
*Warrior, warrior, warrior,*
*Oh my land, the land of the ancestors*
*Warrior, warrior, warrior,*
*Oh my people, people of eternity*
*By the oath under the shade of the flag*
*By my land and nation, and the fire of pain*
*I will live as a warrior, I will remain a warrior,*
*I will die as a warrior - until my country returns*
*Warrior, warrior, warrior,*
*Oh my land, the land of the ancestors*
*Warrior, warrior, warrior,*
*Oh my people, people of eternity*

With steadfast determination, I was keen to engrave this mantra in my memory: "I will live as a warrior, I will remain a warrior, I will die as a warrior."

This resonated with the wild call inside me—that was my true essence. I spent a day committed to memorizing the mantra, its words resounding like a persistent drumbeat in my thoughts, their rhythm syncing with my heartbeat.

"You've had enough; we know you're a warrior," my father would gently chide as I chanted endlessly, as if those words held the power to turn me into the warrior I longed to be. Still, my older brother's weary cynicism would sometimes cut through my youthful excitement.

"Stop with your warrior nonsense," he would snap, visibly disillusioned by the political favoritism and corruption pervading the fledgling Palestinian Authority.

I can still recall my father's sighs and soft mutterings about the hopelessness of this warrior's journey, suggesting a grim future filled with poverty and disappointment.

Years later, I unearthed the reason behind the anthem's sudden change; *Mawtini*, as it turns out, is also the national anthem of Iraq. Written by the celebrated Palestinian poet Ibrahim Tuqan, *Mawtini* served as the national anthem for Palestinians from 1938 until 1996, when *Fida'i* was officially designated as Palestine's anthem. Additionally, *Mawtini* held the esteemed title of Iraq's national anthem from 1985 to 1965 and was reinstated following the American invasion of Iraq in 2003.

In my childhood, the powerful mix of words and music inspired my quest for meaning. Like a ship navigating the vast ocean, I followed the light of these lyrical works. Yet, as I grew up, I confronted the disquieting truth that my natural yearning for these songs was tangled with justifications that ultimately did not meet my expectations, leaving me adrift in a sea of disappointment.

# Mutaradeen, Gaza 1992
## The Son

I remember being six when screams and shouting shattered a peaceful late-summer afternoon. The sky was clear, a breeze stirred the trees, and my curiosity sent me racing to the door like a rocket.

As I burst out of the entrance of our home, I was met with the familiar image of my father methodically wetting the dusty road; a custom aimed at settling the unruly sand and transforming the area into an inviting haven for our evening gatherings with neighbors. Nevertheless, my attention was irresistibly captured by the source of the noise.

A procession materialized through a swirling cloud of dust, almost ghostly in its fervor. At its center was a modest yet dignified cart, pulled by a reliable donkey. Surrounding it was a crowd ablaze with fervent emotion, their voices rising with nationalistic chants, a powerful blend of defiance and hope. During this emotional storm, I spotted Naem, our neighbor, who had been a shadow in our community for a year, lost within the confines of an Israeli prison.

Naem, along with three other young men, mere boys aged twenty to twenty-five, had been arrested for painting messages on walls while masked, seeing themselves as Fedayeen. They wielded no weapons, only flags and a shared cause, their identities concealed but their intentions unmistakable.

The sight of Naem's family, their faces glowing with joy and relief, left an imprint in my mind. His mother's tears, blending pain and happiness, alongside his siblings' laughter, a tune of freedom, introduced me to unfamiliar emotions. The incident raised puzzling questions in my innocent, childlike view of justice. *Why are they imprisoned when a simple scolding, like on TV, would do?* I pondered. This moment was more than just an event; it marked the beginning of my journey to understand the intricate fabric of human emotions and the mysterious ways of the adult world.

During the first *Intifada*, the dynamics of Palestinian national movements were compelling, especially in terms of their activist approaches. There were two main types of activists: the Masked activists, who operated anonymously, and the *Mutaradeen*, who were actively pursued by Israeli authorities. Although both groups rarely wielded weapons, their influence was significant

I recall the first instance I inquired my older sister about the *Mutaradeen*. Her answer stayed with me for years: "They are the good guys, the ones who protect us," she confidently asserted, a conviction unique to an elder sibling. As a child, I found this captivating and started using the term regularly, even jokingly threatening to call the *Mutaradeen* on my parents whenever they turned down my requests. It always generated laughter, a moment of lightheartedness amid otherwise somber times.

These activists primarily operated under the cover of darkness, their messages splashed in bold calligraphy on walls, acting as announcements and morale boosters for the public. Their actions, often coordinated by a group known as "The United Leadership," included marches and the distribution of leaflets containing vital information.

The *Mutaradeen*, enveloped in mystery, achieved a near-mythical reputation among Palestinians. Occasionally armed, they sometimes carried out attacks targeting Israeli vehicles, soldiers, and military installations. The only instance when I encountered one was in 1993, during the funeral of our neighbor, Abdelhakim, who had been killed by the Israeli army. This meeting intensified my youthful curiosity, prompting me to question my brother about the hiding places of these elusive figures.

His response, "We do not know," was just as cryptic as the *Mutaradeen* themselves.

As I matured, I became aware of their clever methods of concealment. Rumors circulated within the security forces that they often took refuge in the homes of dancers, who were looked down upon by society. This tactic was astute, exploiting societal biases to their benefit. The Israelis would hardly suspect that these respected activists, known for their stringent values, would seek sanctuary in such places. This discovery provided a profound understanding of the complexities of resistance and survival under occupation, underscoring the art of deception and the resilience of the human spirit.

# More Loss, Gaza 1992
## The Son

Time moved in a strange dance, expanding and contracting to an inexplicable rhythm. I often felt overwhelmed when I witnessed two people performing the sacred rite of naming their child. This moment triggered a deep instinctual urge to either withdraw or find some trivial distraction. My heart would turn cold, creating a stronghold of fear and fatalism. I resolved to never suggest nor support a name for any child, as the weight of mortality became too burdensome to endure.

This naming process felt to me like engraving in stone, with the name acting as a constant reminder that I was the one who granted them these eternal names. A name, like ethnicity or gender, becomes a stable and socially constructed identity within a few weeks of the child's life.

I had only once taken on such a responsibility, and he was taken from us just shy of his twentieth birthday. In 2008, while I was in Italy, far from home, I received the heart-wrenching news. My father's sorrowful voice rang in my ears, saying, "The boy you named has been martyred."

A wave of numbness overwhelmed me, and tears streamed

silently down my cheeks. I clung to the faint hope that this was a mistake, but my father's voice repeated the painful truth and reminded me of my part in determining his fate.

That Saturday was marked by the weekend and a Jewish holiday. Workers from Gaza, on break from their roles in Israeli agriculture and construction, spent time at home or with relatives. My father, neighbors, and family were outside, having tea together in a relaxed setting.

At seven years old, I approached my father's cousin and uttered the words "Abu Ayham," which left him puzzled. I didn't explain my statement; instead, I laughed innocently and ran back to my father, carefree like any child.

My father's cousin then solemnly proclaimed, "I swear if I have a son, I will name him Ayham." He had five daughters and no sons in his family. However, a few months later, a boy was born into his family, and as promised, he named the child Ayham.

Nineteen years later, Ayham was killed by Israel, his dreams shattered en route to his university. His death plunged me into deep sorrow. It felt as if a bright flame I had ignited years ago was extinguished without warning. I likened it to watching a tree I had nurtured for over two decades be abruptly cut down at its roots.

# Games of Gazan Children, 1992-1993
## The Son

Our home was a rectangular building situated between two streets, with a back door that opened onto the road leading to Gaza's highest point and a front entrance facing an old school. The house was surrounded by a few neighboring families, but there were no children of the same age. The layout of the home created uncertainty about social connections and play spaces, as it was unclear with which group on either side to interact. Parental supervision limited opportunities for independent play and forming friendships. Approaching peers felt challenging, though other children frequently offered invitations to participate in their activities.

Growing up in a family that owned a shop selling marbles, I was particularly fond of the game. We would arrange the marbles in a tidy triangle, using either a white or blue marble as our "shooter." Occasionally, we would dig a hole in the sand, and the team that successfully shot the "ducks"—the other marbles—into the hole would be declared the winner. At times, the rules allowed a successful shooter to keep whatever they hit. I remember one instance when my father caught me playing instead of studying. He scolded me, insisting that I focus on my studies instead of wasting valuable time.

One game that I cherished was "The Hole," where we gathered apricot kernels. We would dig a hole close to a wall and shoot from a marked line roughly two meters away. If you successfully landed a shot in the hole, you would receive all the kernels that missed the target.

On a sweltering summer afternoon, my sister introduced a new game she had learned at school called "*Hakim w Jallad*," or "Ruler and Executioner." At the same time, my father was carrying out his cherished summer tradition of inviting guests over for tea and coffee. My ten-year-old sister had the responsibility of serving the tea. Her careful steps, revealing her anxiety about spilling the hot liquid or facing my mother's disapproval, caught my playful attention. I imitated her, raising my right hand as if balancing an invisible teapot, which inevitably led to a playful conflict that always ended in laughter, usually at my expense. The fragile dignity of childhood, as delicate as a porcelain vase, can easily shatter with the slightest provocation, sparking impulsive outbursts and indignation.

As the evening shadows lengthened, a new game of "*Hakim w Jallad*" began. My other sister prepared four slips of paper and a stick, writing "Ruler," "Thief," "Investigator," and "Executioner" on each. Our younger brother, unaware of the roles, was tasked with distributing the papers. Once the roles were revealed, the game commenced, showcasing a captivating mix of deduction, punishment, and redemption. I observed them daily, sometimes joining in. Yet, like any headstrong and spoiled child, I longed to play the executioner, enjoying the authority to punish my friends.

# Political at an early age, Gaza 1993
## The Son

The buses buzzed with teenagers, alongside four adults in every vehicle. Their spirited enthusiasm was displayed on white T-shirts featuring the *Fatah* logo on the back and Palestine's flag on the front. However, the prints were made from a cheap, low-quality material, failing to capture the vibrant intensity of their passionate hearts.

At nine, I was dwarfed by the teenagers around me. My T-shirt, far too big, hung past my knees and made my age impossible to hide. I tried to tuck it into my pants, but that only drew more laughs. Resigned, I wore the oversized shirt and an equally too-large white hat that always slipped down and obstructed my view. I often wished to hurry past these awkward years and earn the respect given to those older than me.

Through the bus window, excitement bubbled up as the engine came to life. Abdelhakim, confident and commanding, stood at the front. "If soldiers ask, we say we're on a school tour in Gaza," he said, his tone serious. He repeated the instructions, making sure we understood. Then, he called out, "Where are we going?"

We replied in chorus, "On a school tour!" But he wanted us louder, stronger. Following his cue, we shouted in rhythm, voices fused and determined.

We were headed to Khan Younes in southern Gaza, a place marked by its history and the shadow of conflict. Three buses crammed with determined teenagers, accompanied by *Fatah* activists whose fates—unknown to us—would soon be changed forever. Some would later be targeted, killed; others among us would not escape the violence of the coming *Intifada* and wars. Even so, we did not let worry diminish our spirit. We closed our windows, turned up the national songs, and lost ourselves in the moment.

---

A few days before our bus trip, my older brother rushed into the house on a hot August afternoon, drenched in sweat and urgency, looking as if something serious had happened.

During all this, I stood just two meters away, leaning against the wall and watching quietly. My mind raced, trying to make sense of what was going on. Occasionally, I looked at my mother, who kept some distance but watched my brother closely, her eyes alert.

The cassette player blared gunshots and shouts of "*Allah Akbar.*" Instantly, relief softened my brother's face, and he managed a smile. My mother did not respond in kind. Her expression remained tense, showing frustration and fear as the sounds continued. There was no argument or explanation. My mother withdrew to the kitchen, focusing on making lunch. She understood that my brother's commitment to *Fatah* was beyond negotiation. The reality of the threats—imprisonment or death—made it pointless to try to hold him back.

A man's voice soon filled the room, reciting Arabic poems that celebrated Osama—Osama Al-Najjar, known among us as the "Fatah Hawks." Israeli special forces would later kill him in a hideout in

Khan Younis. The poem was mixed with the sound of gunfire from the cassette. My brother, tired but smiling with quiet defiance, stood facing the midday sun.

Drawn in by the song and the sound of simulated gunfire, I found the courage to take a few steps forward, crouching my petite frame and casting glances toward the door, the kitchen, and the bathroom. With my fingers shaking, I turned the volume dial to the right, releasing a flood of amplified sound from the speakers. In an instant, I saw my older brother racing toward me, desperately buttoning his jeans, while my mother wielded the mesh skimmer she used for retrieving fried potatoes from the boiling oil. Her face reflected a blend of anger and fear, a mix of emotions I had never encountered before.

With my heart racing and no clear reason, I dashed toward the safety of our backyard. I sensed that something was deeply wrong.

Over the ensuing months and years, I learned that simply owning or listening to such cassettes could lead to my brother or father facing several years in prison. That day, I closely examined the cassette player and identified the specific tape that contained the *nasheed* (chants). It was a plain white cassette with an image of Mecca and the inscription "Quran Kareem." However, in tiny black ink on the right side was the word "Osama." This served as a clever trick to mislead Israeli troops during their raids on cassette shops in Gaza, as they typically targeted nationalist and patriotic recordings. By altering the cassettes to resemble the Quran or featuring images of belly dancers, a layer of protection was provided.

As I matured and eavesdropped on conversations among *Fatah* fighters and activists, I learned that the safest refuge for wanted individuals lay within the arms of suspicious and ostracized women.

As one of them claimed, "The Israeli army would never suspect me hiding in the home of a *Sharmouta* or *Raqassa* (dancer)."

These women, labelled immoral and defying societal norms and values, became the unlikeliest hideouts for renowned fighters. Israeli forces believed that these fighters, highly regarded in the community, would never jeopardize their reputations by seeking refuge in the homes of such women. Yet, unbeknownst to them, many fighters found sanctuary there. Those who employed this strategy managed to evade the Israeli killing machine until 1993.

As the days passed, I would grab the cassette and retreat to the solitude of my room. Lowering the volume to a whisper, I immersed myself in its contents. Sometimes, I listened silently, crafting vivid fantasies of myself as a freedom fighter. Other times, I stood tall, marching with military precision or offering a firm salute. At eight years old, my thoughts were set on a predetermined future, believing that only the course of history could alter my path.

A year later, the tides of history turned, launching my life into a new direction shaped by the Oslo Accords and their repercussions. In that moment, my mind flexed, unknowingly embracing a sliver of patriotism. It never regained its earlier unyielding determination, instead bending and warping repeatedly.

---

We arrived in Khan Younes just as Abdelhakim's voice resonated through the microphone. Towering green trees lined the road, their leaves and branches swaying in a rhythmic dance.

Beneath a tree, an elderly woman sat, her weathered face peeking out from behind wooden boxes filled with ripe figs. As a fig merchant, she symbolized the resilience of Palestinian women, shouldering the burdens of their society's challenges. My eyes were drawn to the fresh fruits, making my mouth water and my senses awaken with craving. However, my view was blocked by a white Peugeot 404 parked in front of her, disrupting my gaze. It felt as though I had lost something captivating or been jolted awake from a beautiful dream.

A few moments later, our buses came to a halt alongside the others. The senior members, our leaders, stepped off, gathering numerous bags from the storage compartments. It was lunchtime. The bus buzzed with lively conversation, children breaking into revolutionary songs, guided by their elders. I sat quietly, engrossed in the scenery outside the window, searching for intriguing details to distance myself from the communal atmosphere inside the bus.

A plastic bag was placed at my feet, ending my peaceful moment. When I picked it up, I observed what others were carrying. Our lunch included two Mortadella sandwiches, orange juice, and an apple. Next to me, a teenager unpacked his meal: a *Zaatar* sandwich, a tomato, a banana, and an orange. His food had a noticeably stronger aroma than the Mortadella sandwiches.

"Now, eat quickly," one of the leaders said, "then we'll visit Osama Al Najjar's funeral home to honor his martyrdom."

At that moment, I understood our purpose and destination. Excitement surged through me, amplifying my eagerness. I yearned to witness firsthand the scenes I had previously only heard described on the cassette.

As we exited the bus, we formed straight lines, resembling soldiers marching deliberately. We marched toward the funeral hall, our voices echoing with chants of sacrifice and dedication to Palestine.

"Our blood, our soul, we sacrifice for Palestine."

"Our blood, our soul, we sacrifice for Abu Ammar (Yasser Arafat)."

Fifteen minutes slipped by within those walls. One of the *Fatah* leaders, holding the microphone, delivered a passionate and revolutionary speech against Israeli occupation, gathering support for the cause. Among his words, a phrase lodged itself in my mind, haunting me whenever I heard the name Khan Younes or the first Intifada: "If they killed Osama, one thousand Osamas will sprout. Look at the children we have brought. They are our next Osamas." Occasionally, I would reflect on these words and smile, pondering whether I was truly meant to become Osama.

As I rose from the plastic chair where I had been resting, my thoughts flying around, I noticed all the children forming a military-like line and marching back towards the buses. I realized that I had been deeply engrossed in contemplating my role as the next Osama.

Climbing the bus's steps, I overheard the guides and *Fatah* activists discussing their next destination—where his "martyrdom", or his assassination, happened. From that moment, I understood that every child harbored a blend of excitement and fear, signaling the onset of adulthood or, in other words, the plunge into the abyss of relinquishing childhood. I oscillated between two emotions—excitement at witnessing the scenes I had longed for and fear of the potential dangers that awaited us.

During the 15-minute bus ride that followed, I mentally prepared myself to confront that place. However, as we arrived and lined up to enter the home, darkness seemed to descend abruptly upon my vision, only to realize that I had closed my eyes. As we proceeded, I surveyed the faces of the individuals gathered in the neighborhood. It resembled a pilgrimage; men, women, elders, and children congregated with a common purpose.

A *Fatah* activist shouted, urging us to stay in an orderly line and warning us not to tread on the sacred blood of Osama. We proceeded inside, letting the details around us register. The walls were marked by bullet holes, stark reminders of the clashes that took place and the number of weapons used to end Osama's life. Light filtered through the asbestos sheets, casting a soft glow that turned the room into an artist's canvas. As I glanced at the light source, I saw openings and holes—evidence of countless bullets striking. I felt increasingly isolated, as if I were drifting through space alone.

Whispers around me became indistinct, especially as my eyes fell on the extensive bloodstains embellished with scattered stones and palm leaves. The air carried a hint of musk, lending an almost otherworldly quality. People gathered around these areas, their eyes glued to the stains. I found myself staring at those spots and others a few meters away, contemplating who decided which blood belonged to

Osama and what came from Israeli soldiers. I pondered the reason for simply standing there. Years later, I learned that some had sprayed musk over the bloodstains.

These memories carry me across continents, making me reflect on my solitude and the understanding that growing up in occupied territories deprived me of a true childhood.

# Scenes of The Occupier, Gaza 1993
## The Son

Each day, the sight of military jeeps became intertwined with our childhood fantasies. They were so entrenched in our lives that we began to name these intruding vehicles of occupation after animals, drawing inspiration from their strange shapes and distinctive sounds.

"The Cockroach is coming," we would declare as the powerful hum of the engine approached from afar. Silence would descend upon the room, and like a deer in headlights, I'd widen my eyes and rush for comfort near my mother or sister. The Frog, the smallest of the creatures, posed much less of a threat than the Cockroach. I stood firm against it unless it had its larger companion or the chilling sound of gunfire echoed nearby.

The most terrifying moments occurred when they disrupted our sleep at midnight, or in the eerie silence of three in the morning, startling the entire neighborhood awake. Initially, I responded with fear as a child, but gradually I learned to numbly ignore their interruptions.

Years later, my mother revealed that she would wake me at the first sound of engines in the distance. She lived in constant fear that, should they invade our home, I would be so terrified that my heart might stop. She had heard stories on the radio of a child in Rafah whose heart froze in horror when Israeli soldiers crashed into his home while he was deep in sleep. My father vividly described how the Israeli army would invade the area in their jeeps, turn off the engines, and wait silently for hours. Their stillness became their weapon, sowing seeds of fear and dread.

Sometimes they launched their alarming campaigns, abducting youth aged 17 to 30. When they arrived, every young man would quickly get dressed, collect their IDs and pack a small plastic bag with underwear and a change of clothes, ready for detention. The mood was one of despair, with entire lives paused temporarily. They resembled a ship adrift at sea, battered by waves of uncertainty.

The last room in our house remained a mystery. It was sealed tight, holding the remnants of my uncle's life, who had left Gaza in the early '80s and never returned. It was odd that no one dared to enter the room, fully aware he would not come back. He died in exile in 1999 without saying goodbye. Strangely, the rooms in our house were named after their original occupants. Any attempts to change these names always failed. It felt as if the rooms were imbued with nostalgia, longing for the people they once held.

# Whispers of Resistance, Gaza 1993
## The Son

Suspended within the tumultuous timeline of the first *Intifada*, a palpable figure of a man flowed through its essence—a man marked by suffering. He represented the collective experience of every Palestinian.

My father, a professional administrator, usually finished his workday around 2:30 PM. However, he often arrived home later, between 3:30 and 4:00 PM. As a child, the countless moments I spent waiting for him, caught in the suspense of his return, felt as numerous as grains of sand on a beach. Upon seeing him, I would spring into a joyous run, meeting him halfway in our shared excitement.

On a crisp autumn day, a playful wind danced through the streets, though it refrained from bringing rain. Its influence was apparent in the graceful movements of the surrounding trees, whose branches swayed rhythmically. The rustling leaves created a fleeting symphony, leading me to believe, as a child, that the trees were putting on a show for the wind. However, today my mother imposed her decision, stopping me from waiting for my father.

Inside our home, the tension filled the space like a thick fog. My mother sighed deeply, as if trying to release a heavy thought from her heart, and whispered, "When will your father be home?"

Her question was met by the sound of the door creaking open and my father's voice resonating down the hallway, "The Israeli soldiers are here."

His voice resonated with both anger and concern. He called for my mother, saying, "Come here for a moment."

She quickly left, only to rush back, her anxiety stirring the calm of the room. In a flurry, she put on her headscarf and *Dayyer* before urgently gesturing for me to follow, saying, "Come with me."

I let her lead, her intense grip guiding me as we hurried toward the group of young men and teenagers throwing stones and shouting at the Israeli soldiers.

As we entered the swirling chaos, my mother was a whirlwind of emotions, continuously whispering a fervent prayer, "*Allah Yustur! Allah Yustur*".

Upon reaching the front lines, she rushed into a nearby shop, urging the shopkeeper to alert the youth about the soldiers advancing from the fields. Unaware of the looming threat, the young protesters resembled deer oblivious to a lurking lion. A small child was sent to deliver the warning.

"Give me two packs of cigarettes," my mother asked the shopkeeper, promising to settle the payment the next day. I briefly left her side, drawn by the sudden silence that enveloped us. The once noisy and crowded area now felt eerily deserted. In the distance, I noticed two jeeps and a battalion of soldiers, a foreboding sight that compelled me to return to my mother and take her hand.

The empty street seemed like a blank canvas, leaving only my mother and me as the final touches of a forgotten artwork. As we made our way home, a storm of questions swirled in my mind, driven by the unsettling silence. We were alone—why exactly? What had ignited the fear in the protesters that made them flee? Where were the soldiers my mother mentioned?

Once we arrived home, we discovered my father focused on

cutting and hammering wood. He gratefully received my mother's cigarettes before she disappeared into the kitchen, softly uttering another "*Allah Satar*" while preparing tea.

Seeing my father work on a door, despite having quit smoking months earlier and with cigarettes available in our shop, bewildered me. I made my way back to the street, trying to understand what was happening. My heart raced like a drum as I noticed the soldiers approaching, and I felt my fear deepen.

"They are coming, they are coming!" I exclaimed, my foot anxiously tapping the ground. But my father simply held me close, whispering words of comfort.

He spoke to the officer in Hebrew while I held my breath, frozen in fear. Then, he went inside the shop and came back with two cans of Coca-Cola. Soldiers surrounded us, closing in. "*La la,*" the officer refused. My father put the cans back and offered a pack of Imperial cigarettes instead. My mother watched the scene unfold outside, her expression a mix of fear and anger.

Unexpectedly, the officer burst into laughter, a contagious sound that swept through the ranks, transforming the tense moment into a display of odd humor. With a nonchalant wave and a cheerful "*Khalas,*" he signaled my father to cease. As the pressure lifted, the reverberation of their laughter lingered in the air, serving as an unusual conclusion to an inexplicable day.

Years later, my father would tell that day's story numerous times, each recounting filled with evident pride. On his way home that pivotal day, he caught a snippet of a conversation on the military channel. The officer, speaking Hebrew, was devising a plan to ambush the defiant youth from our neighborhood, who were expressing their frustrations by throwing stones and shouting insults at the soldiers.

Grasping the officer's words, my father rushed home to inform my mother about the situation. She quickly took action, warning the unaware youth of the looming danger. When I later questioned her about her odd decision to buy two packs of cigarettes and bring me along, she offered a straightforward explanation: "If soldiers had stopped me, I would've said I was bringing you to your uncle. On the way back, I could have explained my trip by claiming I was getting cigarettes for your father."

As the soldiers approached my father, his understanding of Hebrew was put to the test. The officer asked, "*Ata Midaber Ivrit?*" inquiring if he spoke Hebrew. Each time my father told this story, a broad grin would spread across his face, as if the memory was as vivid as fresh morning dew.

With a touch of drama in his voice, he would say, "They thought they could fool me!" accompanied by hearty laughter. He continued, "When they first asked, I brought them Coca-Cola. The second time, I offered them cigarettes."

His actions reminded me of an adage I once heard: *What's the purpose of life if not to ease the burdens of others?* My father was willingly placing himself in danger to shield our youth and their families from potential imprisonment or death. "Those sons of dogs thought I was an idiot," he would chuckle.

Neither of my parents surrendered that day, as in their hearts, they could not fathom the idea of defeat. This resistance shone brightly in their hearts, lighting a path of defiance against overwhelming odds. Their bravery resembled a sturdy ship facing a raging storm, steadfastly holding its course.

# Between Excitement and Fear, Gaza 1993

"Do you want to come to work with me?" my father asked as he buttoned his old beige suit. It was early summer, the sky a light blue. I woke up refreshed and excited to visit his workplace, something I always enjoyed during school breaks, exploring the city and sharing snacks. But this time felt different.

"If we encounter soldiers and they question us, just hold your stomach and pretend to be sick," he said. I nodded, my heart racing with excitement as I changed into my spare jeans and crisp white shirt. Until I was nearly ten, my wardrobe was limited to just two pairs of jeans and one set of training pants. I wore the spare pair on special occasions, like when my parents took me out.

As we stepped outside, my father's colleague, our neighbor, joined us, and we headed west. My eyes remained fixed on the road ahead as I walked between the two men, ready to grasp their hands at the sight of soldiers. Fear curled within me, like a sleeping serpent, and I dreaded the thought of encountering soldiers. This fear transformed into a lasting aversion to uniformed police and military personnel that would persist for decades. The streets echoed with an eerie silence, as desolate and still as a graveyard. Only a handful of heads poked out of homes, their eyes scanning the area, and a few men dared to smoke cigarettes outside their dwellings.

Twenty minutes into our journey, excitement surged in my heart as I saw cars and people ahead. But that joy quickly faded, replaced by a chilling sense of dread. My small hand instinctively found my father's, while my other hand reached for his colleague. The lively scene around me dimmed, as if the sky had rapidly clouded and unleashed a rainstorm, distorting my view. All I noticed were the two soldiers standing guard in the middle of the road.

My breath caught in my throat as I whispered in terror, "*Jaish. Yahud.* [Army. Jews]." My fear had taken shape before me.

On other occasions, the Israeli soldiers treated the school like a toy, swaying it side to side while we remained frozen in our classrooms, our teacher stuck in a harsh limbo of indecision: to keep us inside or let us out. This was my initiation into chaos, my first experience with the sharp smell of tear gas. I was just seven years old.

The day remains vividly imprinted in my mind as a somber turning point. It marked my second year of school when a swarm of Israeli soldiers invaded our school, saturating the hallways with an array of stinging tear gas canisters. Panic surged through us like a shockwave, transforming the formerly orderly student body into a frantic crowd of children---crying, shouting and scrambling. I felt as still as a statue, a smile plastered on my face as I gazed at the door, anticipating the inevitable.

As the white clouds of tear gas started to seep into our classroom, the stench became suffocating. Students coughed and cried, yet I remained seated, anticipating the rescue I believed would come. I thought my mother would rush in, scoop me up, and take me to safety. But she never did. I hoped my brother would come to defend me. But he didn't show up either. The chaos of voices and cries grew around me, transforming into a deafening roar that resembled a distressed radio signal. Then, the teacher came in, delivering an unexpected remedy: an onion. He placed it on the floor, lifted his foot, and smashed it down with the force of a dinosaur's stomp.

He distributed a piece of onion to each of us, and the classroom filled with sharp intakes of breath as we inhaled its powerful scent, reminiscent of desperate heroin addicts. We had discovered that the smell of onions could alleviate the effects of tear gas. And it truly did help. We felt calmer yet still overwhelmed with anxiety.

After the teachers and headmaster had negotiated with the soldiers, they carefully approached each classroom, instructing us to grab our bags, raise our hands and proceed to the football field one class at a time. The scene looked like something out of a Hollywood movie, with hundreds of us children appearing from a distance like a line of prisoners, marching with our hands on our heads. The only exception was the school bags we carried.

Being third in line, I attempted to steal glances at the soldiers positioned in the distance, but the teacher promptly stopped me, insisting that I look straight ahead. It wasn't so much fear that gripped me as it was a sense of being shattered. Their expressions instilled more fear in me than their weapons ever could. We endured a painful two hours of silence until the soldiers left, and we were eventually dismissed to head home.

Later that day, I heard my father wondering if the stone-throwers were children from our school. This incident, the sight of children with their hands raised, is etched into my memory like a scar—an enduring image that shapes my view of the world and symbolizes my painful rite of passage. It sparked the first flicker of defiance within me, a resolve not to let them claim victory over me. From that day onward, life and death felt intertwined, with both being equally possible at any moment.

The following year, news of Arafat's plane crash in the Libyan desert ignited widespread protests, clashes, and street closures. The city was in turmoil, with neighborhoods filled with young people ready to throw stones at the Israeli soldiers' vehicles.

Israel was ill-prepared for the scale of the protests erupting in the Gaza Strip. It was the first time I heard Israeli soldiers speaking in faltering Arabic, pleading, "We did not kill Abu Ammar [Yasser

Arafat]," and, "We want peace. Please do not throw stones at us." This marked the beginning of the peace process, which remains devoid of actual peace.

The headmaster of the school instructed us to evacuate that day as the skies darkened from burning tires, while the youth readied themselves for confrontation.

"*Awoulad Al-Manyuka* are coming," proclaimed a man on the street, carrying bags filled with vegetables, his voice full of dread. The soldiers, adorned in their menacing purple and maroon berets—the *Golani* and *Givati*—were the specters that plagued our community nightmares.

I noticed the fear in my parents' eyes whenever they spoke of these elite soldiers, which led my young imagination to envision them as monstrous beings, even cannibals. As I matured, I realized they were the skilled professionals of the Israeli army. My personal experience with them during a curfew made me feel as if my body had twisted in knots, with my heart racing in my throat.

The memories linked to *Golani* and *Givati* starkly remind us that life is not an abstract idea, but rather a concrete, tangible reality. Therefore, whenever *Golani* or *Givati* faced losses in military actions, those memories would reemerge, haunting me and softly suggesting that the pursuit of meaning in life is a continual journey.

# Whispers of the Intifada, Gaza 1993
## The Son

I grew up in a politically vibrant family environment where activism was a constant presence in our daily lives. My father shared his wisdom in secrecy, urging us to stay hidden and avoid the spotlight. His message was a call to resist from the shadows, protecting us from the dangers of arrest. In contrast, my brother operated quietly within *Fatah*. He took a risky route as an undercover activist engaged in media and logistics efforts. Frequently, he came home long after dark, leaving my parents anxiously waiting within our walls.

I remember one night when he was very late, filling my parents with deep worry. The eight o'clock curfew heightened their fears. When he finally snuck into our unlocked house, my father's anger boiled over.

"Will you liberate Palestine?!" he said. Those sharp words reflected my father's frustration and unwavering belief in the importance of education. "The Japanese succeeded and rebuilt their nation because they valued education. Victory can only be achieved through knowledge," he would often declare. His statements became legendary in our home: "Your *Kalashnikov* is the university degree."

My aspirations set me apart from other kids who dreamed of becoming engineers or doctors. Whenever someone asked about my future, my answer always prompted laughter. "I want to be Yasser Arafat," I would confidently proclaim.

My ambition was reflected on my walls, where I drew a man in the iconic *Kufiyah* and wrote "I am the president" in pencil. I celebrated the vivid images of freedom fighters, as their passionate slogans filled every aspect of my life. Politics, Palestine, and *Fatah* became the threads that intertwined to shape my existence.

My father's assured words echoed among the men: "The *Intifada* will be stronger." I was captivated by their spirited discussions. It was then that I first learned about the term *Intifada*—the uprising. I found myself drawn to my father and his friends, engaging in conversations that animated the political landscape. Politics began to weave into the fabric of my life, influencing my upbringing in ways words can hardly describe.

More than ten years later, my father and the neighbors resumed their talks, now centered on the *Intifada*. "Do you recall when I mentioned that the *Intifada* would grow stronger?" my father reflected.

However, a neighbor's views had evolved and provided a contrasting insight. "Yes, it was, but then Arafat undermined it with the Oslo Accord and the Peace process!" he declared.

This dialogue reflected a change in the man's outlook. Once affiliated with *Fatah*, he had distanced himself and embraced a different political movement in the early 2000s. Many activists turned against Arafat's choice to endorse the peace accord, especially after its collapse in 1999. The generation that ignited the first Intifada also sparked the second *Intifada*. They were passionate nationalists, ready to fight fiercely. To us, Palestine represented not just a cause but a sacred mission entrusted to us by a higher power. The burden of oppression only intensified our resolve to resist. With nothing left to lose, we approached the second *Intifada* with a sense of renewal. Nonetheless, we soon recognized that our strength was rooted in the experiences we had gathered—the experience of oppression and the experience of living as warriors.

# Against the Wall, Gaza 1993
## The Son

On a cold, rainy night when I was five years old, I lay curled up in my parents' bed, comforted by a heavy blanket as thunder echoed outside. Half-asleep, I barely noticed my mother's gentle attempts to wake me, dismissing them as part of a dream until she abruptly pulled back the covers. The chill and the distinct scent of the Israeli military woke me fully. My mother quickly gathered me and my brother, leading us from the room. I glimpsed my sisters, one of whom hurried me away from the soldiers who briefly entered before leaving for the street.

As they left, my sister muttered "*Allah Yakhdkum*," in frustration and someone spat in their direction. Exhausted, I returned to a room thrown into chaos—mattresses displaced, clothes scattered, and muddy boot prints on my bed. My mother, angry and upset, hurried toward the door, cursing. My sisters immediately began cleaning up. I asked about my absent father and brother, concerned, but my sister reassured me quietly, saying they would come later.

At that moment, my sisters entered and worked diligently to restore order. I sensed my mother's thoughts wandering to my father. Worried, I asked again about my brother, but my sister silenced me.

She looked deeply into my eyes, grasping my arms tightly, and whispered, "Habibi, he will come later." The tension of our conversation hung in the air, and I gently freed my hand from her hold, placing a finger against my lips to signal silence. Her wry smile spoke of an understanding beyond words.

As the chill of the night clung to my trembling body, I directed my attention towards the doorway, where my mother stood, cradling my little brother. I positioned myself beside her left leg and peered through the doorway, eager to witness the unfolding events. Dozens of men lined the walls, their backs turned towards us. Amid them, I recognized my father, his hands pressed against the wall while four soldiers trained their guns upon the men.

Three jeeps, their engines clamorous, emitted an aura of military menace. To my young ears, the sound of those jeeps served as a macabre symphony, the discordant notes of death and fear. Women emerged from their homes, taking their places before our home, their men merely fifty meters away, separated by only a few soldiers. Every few minutes, a soldier bellowed, "*Roukh Al beit*," with their broken Arabic, urging the women to return home.

Their response was an unequivocal cry: "We want our men," or "I want my husband." The air swelled with their pleas.

An officer, holding the men's IDs, examined each one closely. The men, tense, turned to face him. I strained my eyes to catch a glimpse of my father's face. The officer gestured toward the walls before pointing at the tallest tree in the area. A heated debate broke out, with voices rising in defiance.

One man even had the audacity to speak in Hebrew, forcefully stating, "*Lo Lo Lo*." They stood firm, resisting the officer's commands and engaging in an argument that lasted for hours. As my sister gently pulled at my sleeve, urging me to step back, I resisted and clutched my mother's dress instead. After a few minutes, the soldiers finally relented, permitting the men to leave. A smile appeared on my face as I realized my father would soon be back.

"Give me the hand broom and a bucket of water," he instructed my mother.

The soldiers insisted that the men strip the walls of our neighborhood of national slogans and graffiti. These walls represented the essence of political parties, freedom fighters, announcements and orders. The punishment involved covering the walls with darkness and filth. One by one, the men advanced, armed with brooms and buckets. Under the soldiers' vigilant gaze, they gathered the ashes of burned tires, mixing them with water before each was assigned to a different wall to clean.

The scene resembled a film, as their synchronized efforts to erase the painted words unfolded with fluidity and intent. As I watched them, searching for distinctive traits, I discovered only a torrent of hatred. My slight frame trembled, not from fear, but from the icy air that enveloped my skin as I anticipated an unforeseen conclusion to this dramatic display. It felt as if this moment of anguish and chills would last forever, an endless pause in time. All I desired was my father's comforting presence and the peace of sleep.

The next morning, I woke up with swollen eyes, as if I had been crying all night, possibly in my dreams. An intense day of anger arose from the news of a young man's death that morning, not far from our home. It was a day of fury and protest. My mother prepared fried potatoes, made falafel, arranged white cheese and cooked eggs with onions, placing everything on the floor next to the portable fireplace we lovingly referred to as the "Cannon." Bread toasted over the glowing coals, while tea steeped nearby, its scent mingling with the snap of the fire.

"They wanted us to take down the flag," my father said as he ate. The soldiers had asked the men to climb a tall twenty-meter tree to remove a Palestinian flag. His laughter echoed as he continued, "Are they crazy? We're all old men, our bellies full of fat. Climbing stairs is no easy task for us."

# Rajamma, Gaza 1993-1994
## The Son

"Hide! Hide! Hide! *Rajamma* is here!" My mother's fearful voice rang out as she hurried inside from the street.

It was a July evening when chaos erupted in the neighborhood. The smell of burning tires mingled with the sharp odor of tear gas, saturating the air. Dark clouds from the fires mixed with the white trails of gas canisters, creating a haunting scene above us. Everyone covered their mouths, hands pressed against their noses to block the choking fumes. A woman on a donkey-drawn cart covered her face with a white headscarf, clutching an onion to provide some relief with its strong scent.

As the sounds of *Rajamma* drew near, the terrified crowd disappeared like shadows. The sound of *"TOK TOK TOK TOK TOK"* echoed for a moment before stopping. Sometimes, it would halt for ten minutes, only to start up again.

A man rushed by, his sandals slapping against his feet, raising a cloud of dust behind him as he shouted, "It is going to load again!"

*Rajamma* was one of the most terrifying and ruthless machines used against people. It served as a mechanical symbol of violence, filled with stones of various sizes. Once activated, it would fire a stream of projectiles, wreaking devastation on neighborhoods and destroying solar panels and water tanks. Many sustained serious injuries, their heads cracked open from its onslaught. I still recall the day our solar panels were obliterated by *Rajamma*. My father chose not to repair them, fearing they would suffer the same fate again. For many years afterwards, we depended on a Primus stove, lovingly named "Babur," to heat water for our showers and laundry.

# Young Fighters, Gaza 1994
## The Son

As the evening progressed, teens from every corner of the neighborhood gathered at a familiar spot on the street. From a distance, I could hear their excited conversations and feel their vibrant energy pulling me in like a moth to a flame. As I approached, a middle-aged man walking next to me left a captivating scent lingering in the air.

He held a bag of falafel in one hand while balancing a plate of hot "Foul" in the other. The rich scent of beans and spices wrapped around me, igniting a deep craving. I felt a powerful urge to turn back, ask my father for a single Shekel, and savour the delightful taste of Foul.

Our culinary landscape featured four prominent shops: *AlHelou*, *AlTuhami*, *Alzaeem*, and *Akila*. Each had its specialty: *Akila* offered the finest Falafel, *AlZaeem* prepared the creamiest Hummus, and *Al-Helou's* Foul was unmatched.

In Gaza, we enjoyed Falafel, Hummus, and Foul for both breakfast and dinner, a routine that changed when I left its borders. I recall laughing at my Lebanese colleagues as they chose Falafel for lunch.

Fast forward a few months, and I found myself ordering a salad for my midday meal.

Blending into the crowd, I found comfort among the young. Drawn by conflict and excitement, my bonds formed on a street alive with resistance, shaped by the political climate. Embracing these realities, I realised I could transcend them.

"What are we going to do?" asked a young voice, piercing through the noise.

"Let's grab black plastic bags," replied Rami, the oldest among us, confidently.

His suggestion prompted an immediate response. We returned home quickly and efficiently. I proceeded to the kitchen and selected four plastic bags from the designated storage area: two black, one white, and one blue. My selection was purposeful, aiming to maintain both distinction and discretion. After gathering the bags, I departed without drawing attention.

Like migratory birds heading home, we returned to the meeting spot. Some carried thick sticks, while others wielded kitchen knives. Our plan was to sneak into the school, don our plastic bags, and march solemnly down the street in a line; twelve of us, the oldest being 12 and the youngest only seven.

I felt an exhilarating sense of fulfilment at that moment. I fashioned the first black plastic bag into a vest, while the white and blue bags became our shoes. The last black bag was transformed into a mask. As we emerged, cloaked in anonymity, we imagined ourselves as the most wanted, leaving no evidence of who we were. Our procession was marked by a rhythmic chant: "We die to live in Palestine."

People gathered along the streets watched us with amusement. Like my own, fathers leaned back, smoking casually by the door, chuckling at our antics, while mothers encouraged us with shouts of "Our future fighters."

For that brief moment, we were not just children; we were warriors on the edge, sacrificing our innocence for a cause we scarcely understood.

As the day ended, we tossed aside our plastic disguises in school, our faces glowing with triumph and the promise of more such adventures. Yet, we never repeated this act. Upon entering my home, my father remarked, "Did you see the children? You should play with them and be like them."

Little did he know, I had just uncovered my knack for stealth and deception as a clandestine freedom fighter. If my own father couldn't see through my disguise, then who could?

# 28 March, Gaza 1994
## The Son

As I held the well-worn copper teapot, its surface marked by the scars of frequent use and rare cleaning, I was engaging in a kind of ritual. The pot, heavy with boiling tea, made my young back arch as if I were emulating the figure of a wise old man. Its warmth seeped into my hands, prompting me to keep it at a careful distance from my body. Leaning forward, I made the brief walk toward the house door.

As I stepped outside, my brother-in-law's voice pierced the crisp air: "Here, here, bring it here." I obediently crossed the street, setting the teapot among my brother-in-law, his brother, and another tall man. As these gatherings occurred more frequently, I discovered that these men were members and activists of *Fatah*, with some even involved as freedom fighters in the resistance against the occupation. My nine-year-old innocence concealed the significance of their involvement.

My brother asked me to bring the teacups, known as Gaza's signature cups. While washing dishes, my sister guided me to the teacups on the third row of the metal shelf. Using a small wooden stool for support, I meticulously stacked six teacups, holding them gently as if they were a small child. Her voice hovered in the background, reminding me of our mother's anger should any cup break. A wave of triumph washed over me as I delivered the delicate cargo safely to its destination.

After finishing the task, my brother, maybe sensing my intrigue regarding their whispered meeting, sent me away. Even though I was young, I had a feeling that their gathering had political significance. My interest deepened when I realized that two men who had been there earlier were now missing. I settled on the steps of our house across the street, quietly watching passersby.

About twenty minutes later, the two men approached from the east. Abdelhakim gave me a quick high-five before joining everyone. His voice resonated in the small shop, catching my mother's attention and interrupting her work. She welcomed them cheerfully.

As the March sun set, I fell asleep at nine, unaware of what the night would bring.

That night, I was enveloped in Morpheus's embrace, sleeping as soundly as if sharing a bowl of rice with angels—an idiom in Palestinian culture symbolizing deep sleep. Snuggled under a thick brown blanket in the expansive corridor, my senses were lulled into oblivion, barely registering the soft chatter of the small black-and-white television murmuring away in Hebrew.

As I drifted in and out of sleep, my sisters' voices and my mother's gentle tapping roused me. Her repeated calls of "Wake up!" pulled me from my haze into a life-changing moment.

Shaking off the last traces of sleep, I looked around the room. My father and older brother were noticeably missing, while my sisters and mother were glued to the small television on a modest wooden desk.

Folding my legs up to my chest to fend off the encroaching chill, I listened as my mother, filled with emotion, announced, "Wake up. Abdelhakim was martyred!"

It felt like I was jolted awake by a splash of icy water. Gradually, reality crept in, accompanied by the distressing scenes of chaos and despair relayed by Israeli television. It was the Israeli Arabic language news. My sisters sat, tears welling up in their eyes, silently expressing our grief.

"Where is my father?" I managed to ask.

My mother replied gently, "At Abu Nafez's house." Our father had gone to visit Abdelhakim's grieving family. The memory of Abdelhakim's high-five from that morning lingered in the air like a haunting ghost. The man who had undergone a medical procedure just weeks ago was gone.

"How did they kill him?" I asked, my voice barely above a whisper.

The answer was curt, "In Jabaliya. The Jewish army killed six."

The murder of Abdelhakim and his comrades seemed to have inflicted a mortal wound on the steady march of time itself, slowing it to a crawl as if it were navigating through a landscape carpeted with debris.

Although I was able to sleep a few more hours, the night was interrupted by my mother's departure, wearing a white headscarf and black dress as she left for Abdelhakim's home. That evening, I noticed a lack of fear. My perception of courage shifted, making a previously intimidating concept easier to understand. In Gaza, death gradually became less associated with terror, particularly when connected to the pursuit of freedom. For those engaged in resistance, death came to be viewed as an act of bravery rather than solely something to fear.

Within hours, I was speeding through the lively neighborhood, the day's events leaving a lasting impression. The area bustled with people—some cleaning the streets, others painting walls, and a few standing in shock, their disbelief plain to see.

As the ambulance arrived, anticipation hung like a heavy cloak. I expected to see Abdelhakim's body, but it was his father, Abu Nafez, who emerged. The crowd's chants echoed off the surrounding buildings, a fervent chorus.

"*Allah Akbar.*"

"Oh martyr, rest in peace, we will continue the struggle."

"With our blood and souls, we will sacrifice ourselves for the martyr."

"With our souls and with our blood we will free you, Palestine!"

I joined in, lending my voice to the swell until my throat was raw, the words grinding to a halt. The departure of the ambulance signaled Israeli policies; the Israeli army had seized the bodies of the six martyrs, forcing hasty, early morning burials without the customary ceremonies, funerals or gatherings.

Before long, the atmosphere brimmed with nationalistic melodies. One song stood out—a ballad named "*Wein El Malayeen*," which poignantly asked about the lack of Arab unity while the wealthy slumbered peacefully, leaving millions to endure hardship. This question was filled with sorrow: "Where are they?"

An elderly man, appearing from the opposite end of the street, shattered the collective trance by asking, "What happened?"

In response, a young man replied, "Abdelhakim is a martyr."

The old man's face, marked by sorrow, drew him towards the crowd that had gathered around Abdelhakim's father. A deep silence enveloped the area, broken only by the gentle scratches of a painter's brush as he painted nationalist slogans on the walls. Seeing Abdelhakim's name in bold letters made me contemplate whether my name might one day share the same fate on such a wall.

A lump of grief tightened in my throat as the crowd parted, revealing Abdelhakim's portrait alongside his companions. One of the faces belonged to a tall, fair man with gentle, flowing hair. I learned his name that day: Majdi Obeid, a regular visitor to our home, a name I will never forget.

The melancholic melody of a song dedicated to the mothers of martyrs filled the air, its refrain a moving plea for strength amid the struggle. Abdelhakim's mother, Um Nafez, a tall and courageous woman, stepped onto a chair, her words a passionate testament to her sacrifice in losing her son and her readiness to sacrifice even more for Palestine. However, as her speech concluded, she broke down, using her white scarf to wipe her tears.

In that defining moment, my childhood appeared to vanish, leaving behind a deep emotional vulnerability. As the crowd gradually scattered, I turned to a secluded spot, allowing my tears to flow. It was then that I understood that my life had changed forever. The gentle nature of my soul was overshadowed by a harsh reality, and tenderness transformed into a scarce presence in the story of my life.

# Hope and Fear, Gaza 1994
## The Son

A few weeks after the Madrid declaration, my brother-in-law visited us, bringing along a large bag of sugar. It appeared almost empty, except for something mysterious hidden inside. Being a familiar face in our home, he made his way to the back room, left the bag there, enjoyed some tea with us, and quickly departed. The bag gave off a subtle sugary scent combined with a hint of something strange and intriguing.

As a child, curiosity often got the better of me. I focused on the bag and the door, but my mother's wary look warned me away. She explained that the sugar bag was full of street-cleaning brushes. Despite her caution, I hung around the backyard near the room, pretending to be a street cleaner, until schoolyard games pulled me elsewhere.

Our neighborhood had a teenager named Masa'ad (He was murdered in the Gaza genocide in 2025), a tall figure with sun-kissed skin and a slender build. I was a newcomer in school while he was already in the fifth grade. Despite his age, a sense of unapproachability surrounded him, a tangible barrier that kept everyone but his relatives at a distance. As I matured, I learned that his father's rumored link to *Hashish* had cast a pall of social isolation over the entire family.

Looking back at those days, the memory of the neighborhood plays like a reel of heartbreaking stories, a macabre showcase of executions, tortures, and unjust killings. Innocent lives were lost, snuffed out under the guise of revolution, societal values or norms, orchestrated by factions like Fatah, Hamas, the Palestinian Front for Liberation of Palestine, and the communists.

As a child, my mind was filled with questions that lacked simple answers, and I longed to take on challenges beyond my abilities. I recall asking my father why revolutionary figures, brandishing guns and axes, chose to conceal their identities with masks.

"*Jawasis*," he would respond. They feared collaborators. Ironically, despite the masks, everyone recognized them. Still, the mask endured as a representation of fear and power.

Masa'ad began an apprenticeship as a blacksmith, where his keen intellect quickly mastered the craft of shaping slingshots from olive wood. Having experienced being shot with a rubber bullet, he was familiar with the pain inflicted by the enemy. He would lift his shirt to reveal his scar, confidently proclaiming, "I will make them pay for this."

Masa'ad showed a group of teens his new metal slingshot at school, his soot-stained clothes proof of his dedication. He demonstrated how using metal increased its impact against soldiers. Standing apart, he aimed and hit a soldier, prompting laughter that quickly shifted to fear when the soldiers retaliated. Chaos erupted as stones flew and everyone scattered.

Looking back, we were never taught to harm soldiers; as youths, we acted independently. Mosa'ad, humble yet determined, vowed revenge. We saw the soldiers as invaders and responded instinctively. Children and teenagers have little grasp of land or politics—we either copied revolutionaries or defended ourselves by impulse.

# Facing the Soldiers, Gaza 1994
## The Son

As I darted towards home, my mother shouted, "Come here, go inside, the soldiers will come!" She knew the secret that the sugar bag held.

That day, clashes flared between the youth and the Israeli soldiers, turning our quiet neighborhood into a battleground. The signs of my mother's worry were all too evident. When she donned her full black and white attire and started gazing west and east in anticipation, I knew she was waiting for someone, her anxiety bearing the weight of a mother expecting a son from a battlefield.

A group of soldiers, numbering in the dozens and equipped with two jeeps, stood firm at the entrance of our street as the youth hurled stones at them. Simultaneously, others confronted the Israeli soldiers positioned along a nearby street. The atmosphere was tense and on fire, and my mother consistently blocked my efforts to leave the house. Finally, I reached a compromise: I could lean my head outside while the rest of my body stayed inside. This arrangement was accepted.

The scene developed rapidly. The young people moved in different directions. I went indoors quickly, joining three others.

They proceeded to the backyard, aiming to reach the fields and trees. One person, appearing frightened, turned toward the last room, opened the door, and entered. I remained motionless.

My mother's screaming crescendo from outside was interrupted by her outstretched arms, a futile shield against the soldiers surrounding her. The uproar intensified. Instinctively, I pressed my hands over my eyes and huddled against the wall. Time felt stretched, and in that prolonged moment, I became acutely aware of the soldiers' distinctive odor. I felt their heavy footsteps and heard the escalating noise outside.

Gathering my courage, I opened my eyes and saw the soldier who had entered the last room. My mother appeared, gasping like a tired engine, her face reddened and dripping with sweat. I moved forward, the ground seeming to sway beneath me. I observed the soldier directing his gun at Shareef, the boy hiding beneath the bed, and shouting a command in broken Arabic: "*Ta'al*," his voice laden with menace.

As the chaos unfolded, my mother charged into the room like a force of nature, her screams desperate for the soldier's attention. I noticed her brief absence as he left with Shareef. When it dawned on me what she had accomplished, I was in awe. She had swiftly relocated a pile of clothes from her room to the last one, strategically hiding the "sugar bag" beneath a blanket of fabrics, just before two other soldiers could barge in.

I returned to my corner, adopting the stance of a silent statue, watching the soldiers retreat. The wailing of the women crying, "My son, my son,"—their desperate efforts to reclaim the detained youth—filled the air. They did all they could to rescue the arrested young men, but it was futile. Once the dust settled, my mother walked into the house and collapsed onto the floor. The sounds, the scene, and the soldiers remain engraved in my memory, serving as a constant reminder of the bravery of the women who stood as the first line of defense during the First *Intifada*.

A few hours later, a man knocked on our door, asking about the sugar bag. When my mother heard him, she hurried to get the bag. After she returned, he politely asked, "Can I enter a bit here, *Khalti*?"

He glanced around nervously before placing the sugar bag on the floor. Opening it, he revealed its contents to me, an intrigued onlooker. I had anticipated brushes, but instead, he pulled out a *Kalashnikov* machine gun. My childish curiosity got the better of me, and I moved closer, touching it with both awe and excitement.

Years later, I learned that if the soldiers had found the gun, my father and older brother would have faced a twenty-five-year prison sentence. I often reflect on how someone can accept their own death sentence or imprisonment so willingly. Why would my family choose to act as a stash for weapons, aware that even a small mistake could result in lifelong incarceration or death? How does human instinct balance pride and the fight against an oppressor? These are the enigmas of survival and resistance.

# Blood and Birds, Gaza 1994
## The Son

Childhood in Gaza felt like an accelerated film, swinging between chaos and calm, where life's outlines frequently faded into confusion. The maze of uncertainty I traversed pushed me to the edge of losing my identity countless times. Certain moments lingered in my mind, like lasting tattoos, plunging me into deep reflection for days.

On a sunlit day, the fragrance of spring filled the air as birds serenaded from the trees. The warm sunlight against my skin felt like a comforting embrace, shielding me from the chaos surrounding me. Sitting with my little brother, we were like two still figures in a peaceful scene.

Hearing a sound, I hurried barefoot to the door. My mother, busy in the kitchen, called out that she was frying potatoes and making sandwiches for me. Her words faded into the background as my curiosity about our visitor took over. On Fridays, when there was no school, I often got scolded for trying to open the door, but my mother's distraction gave me the perfect opportunity to satisfy my curiosity and answer the knock.

"Is your father here?" a woman asked. Her voice echoed in the stillness as I stood, silent and unmoving.

When she repeated the question, I redirected the conversation, asking her about the creature she was holding by its feet. It was a chicken, unsettlingly calm, as if it had accepted its fate. Her expression soured with dissatisfaction as she once again repeated her question. Finally finding my voice, I called out for my mother, wondering if my father was at home.

The woman raised her eyebrows in disbelief, taking a step back as she responded, "You do not know if your father is not at home?"

My father was not at home.

"What's happening?" my mother called from the kitchen, her head appearing as she noticed our neighbor. "Oh, please come in, Um Asim," she gestured, walking towards us. The sound of her flowing black *Dayer* skirt and the flip-flop of her green and black plastic sandals resonated in the room.

I stood firm, a still figure until my mother arrived. I had expected a crisis, but our neighbor was merely looking for someone to kill the chicken. With my father and older brother away, my mother proposed asking another neighbor nearby.

Excitement bubbled within me at the prospect of witnessing the chicken's demise. It was an amalgamation of anticipation and apprehension, a macabre dance of morbid fascination. I stared at the chicken, its vacant eyes staring back, and the gleaming blade the woman carried.

"Haram," I whispered, my voice a gust of wind carrying the unsaid words to the woman.

"Not Haram. They are for your stomach", she chuckled, injecting a dose of humor into the somber atmosphere.

The man arrived as my mother retreated to her culinary canvas, and my three-year-old brother, as quiet as a shadow, slithered towards the doorsteps. The chicken's fate was sealed as the man gripped its neck and wings, transforming it into a squawking bundle.

"*Bismillah Allah Akbar*," he muttered as he brought the knife down.

The world seemed to freeze as the crimson fountain erupted, while the chicken writhed in a gruesome death dance, resembling a marionette with its strings cut. I stepped back a few paces, mesmerized by the eerie scene, momentarily losing track of my little brother.

Then, a scream shattered the momentary stupor. "The boy's head. The boy's head!" echoed the words, a horrifying chant in the stillness. I ran towards the sound, my heart pounding against my ribs. I arrived just in time to see my little brother's face, painted red with blood, a horrifying tableau against the backdrop of the slain chicken. A terrifying cocktail of avian and human blood filled my vision, indistinguishable and terrifying. My brother fell on his head and hit a sharp metal object.

As I raced toward my mother, I called out her name in a wail, "Yamma! Yamma! Yamma!" She was already running, her face painted with fear, as she hurried to us. She scooped my brother into her arms and quickly ushered him inside.

At the same time, the woman shouted, "*Kahwa! Kahwa!*" Her call for coffee felt oddly incongruous amid the gruesome scene. I observed my mother applying her long white scarf to my brother's injury. His face slowly appeared from the crimson tide, his dark skin fading to a lighter hue than normal.

My sister rushed in with ground coffee. My mother removed the scarf, quickly applied coffee to the wound, rewrapped it, and pressed down to stop the bleeding.

"I believe it needs stitching," my mother murmured, her voice a faint echo in my hazy mind. She swiftly pulled on her long black skirt and sandals, her feet kicking up clouds of dust as she hurried toward the clinic two kilometers away.

I remained there, switching my eyes between the motionless chicken, a victim of an unintentional sacrifice, and my mother's rushing figure, a woman racing against time. The memory of that day, a complex mix of fear and curiosity, blood and birds, still haunts me. It acts as a vivid reminder of the unstable balance between life and death, a constant dance dictated by fate.

As my mother searched for a ride to the clinic, I kept her in view while crossing the street. Matching her pace, I followed, driven by the urge to stay close to her and my injured brother, never taking my eyes off them.

They turned right into darkness at the street's end, moving through black dust left by protests. My mother disappeared for half a minute, and I anxiously searched for her when I reached the corner.

Finally, the square appeared before me. On the opposite side, I noticed my mother was still searching for transportation as she continued heading west. What caught my attention, however, were two Israeli jeeps surrounded by armed soldiers. For several moments, my focus shifted between the soldiers and my mother.

I observed two soldiers approaching her while another returned to the jeep. As they neared and addressed her, I became concerned about the potential outcomes, including the possibility of my younger brother being separated from her. The square was largely empty, resembling an abandoned area, as people tended to avoid places where military presence might result in questioning, identification checks, or extended detention.

The tallest soldier took hold of my brother and moved quickly toward the jeep, with my mother following. Although the soldiers were armed, on this occasion, they were not acting against the people present. This was an uncommon scene.

I stood in the center of the square with my hands behind me, observing what was happening. I saw my brother being taken to the jeep and my mother attempting to reach for him from a distance. Motivated by concern and interest, I approached to watch more closely. My brother was shouting, and each time my mother tried to go closer, a soldier prevented her, which added to my uncertainty about the situation.

As I continued to watch, time seemed to stretch. Eventually, my brother was returned to my mother. They hailed a car and compelled the driver to take her to the clinic. Later, I discovered that among the soldiers was a medical doctor who had provided first aid to my brother. They found the coffee on his head both amusing and puzzling.

I remained a few more minutes, a solitary figure gazing westward, hoping for my mother's return. A neighbor noticed me near the soldiers and yelled for me to go home. I didn't reply. She set her basket down, approached, and inquired about my mother's whereabouts. I informed her that she had gone to the hospital. With a gentle nudge, she encouraged me to walk ahead as she resumed her path home.

As I walked, my mind swirled with thoughts of armed soldiers, often perceived as heartless killers, attempting to display their humanity. To me, the Israeli soldiers resembled men traveling through a desert who had buried their hearts long before reaching Gaza. This contradiction—the paradox of a soldier helping my brother and mother—ignited questions that would remain unanswered for many years to come. The Gaza genocide has revealed that those soldiers are no less than monsters. They have filmed and helped people in front of the cameras, then shot them directly.

When my brother got back home, his head was wrapped in a bandage, and his arms were laden with sweets and desserts. A few weeks later, as his wound healed, it turned into a scar we affectionately called "the chicken," serving as a lasting reminder of the turmoil and contradictions of that day.

# Forbidden, Gaza 1994
## The Son

I witnessed how soldiers and armies could strip away life's most essential and beautiful aspects. This realization extended beyond times of conflict to moments when I longed for the simplicity of a peaceful day by the sea.

One day, my eldest brother returned from university, and his announcement brought me immense joy; he promised to take me to the sea with a group of volunteers dedicated to beach cleanup. It was my first opportunity to volunteer in Gaza.

That Saturday morning, I awoke brimming with anticipation, having struggled to sleep the night before, my mind racing with thoughts of the beach and a day filled with purpose. Dressed in my new jeans and white sneakers, I eagerly took my brother's hand as we left. His long strides easily outpaced my shorter ones, his height still towering above me in adulthood. A shared taxi took us to the port of Gaza, where I sat on the seat next to the driver, gazing at the world outside. My brother shared stories about Gaza's landmarks while the driver laughed.

"Is he going to be a tour guide?" the driver joked.

With unwavering optimism, my brother replied, "Maybe! One day, Gaza will be a tourist destination."

The driver's cynical response sliced through the air, "I will shove my ass on the wall if Gaza becomes a tourist destination."

My brother fell silent, choosing not to engage for the remainder of the journey.

We met with Dr. Iyad Sarraj, a highly respected and well-known figure in Gaza, who is the director of the NGO responsible for organizing the volunteer day. Brooms, brushes, and buckets were packed into two Italian Peugeot 404 cars. As the vehicles departed, we heard insistent honking from the second car, indicating something was wrong. Dr. Iyad, taking on the role of driver, pulled over.

"We forgot the plastic bag," a man from the other car called out. In a rush, we turned back to get it. Dr. Iyad then decided to take the beach road, hoping it would be a faster option. Instead of the detour that would add twenty minutes, this route was estimated to take only five. While unaware of the stakes involved, I listened to their heated discussions.

Growing more frustrated, Dr. Iyad returned to the car and began driving with evident anger, as the second car followed close behind.

"I will take the sea's road, whatever happens," he declared.

It was only a few minutes later that I realized we were trapped with four Israeli soldiers. This checkpoint complicated the lives of the people in that neighborhood even more.

A dialogue began: "Where are you going? What do you have?"

The soldiers then began to inspect the car. Dr. Iyad got out, showing the soldiers the passengers' ID cards and NGO credentials. "Go back," the soldiers ordered loudly as Dr. Iyad tried to convince them, presenting his case repeatedly.

One soldier raised and loaded his weapon, shouting at Dr. Iyad. In that moment, I covered my face with my hands, seeking shelter under the car seat while others urged Dr. Iyad to get back inside. He returned and attempted to find an alternate route, but our access to the beach was firmly blocked. It was off-limits to us.

That day surpassed my ability to understand and cope as a young, hurt child. It loomed larger than life, and I felt as if the world had crumbled around me, leaving a profound sense of loss. I had anticipated going to the beach for two days, only to end up returning empty-handed. Since then, my relationship with the sea has evolved into a complicated bond. I visited only a few times a year, seldom immersing myself in its waters or spending extended moments nearby. It felt as though the sea did not want my company, as if it conspired with the soldiers.

# THE LAST KITE, GAZA 1994
## THE SON

Summers offered a welcome respite from daily responsibilities; free from early mornings assisting my parents and schoolwork, they provided an unparalleled sense of freedom. These months allowed for immersion in play, whether running through the neighborhood with peers or enjoying moments of solitary recreation, which, in retrospect, provided a particularly meaningful source of personal fulfillment.

Among my preferred activities was climbing the walls surrounding the school grounds. These structures, standing two to three meters high and only 15 to 20 centimeters wide, presented a formidable challenge. Running along their narrow tops became my personal benchmark for agility and courage. While I never experienced a significant fall, there were occasions when I stumbled, sustaining injuries that resulted in lasting scars on my feet—tangible reminders of my formative years.

The summers in Gaza were marked by remarkably clear, deep blue skies and intense, golden sunlight. Although I generally welcomed the warmth, periods of oppressive heat and humidity occasionally diminished my enjoyment.

Seasonal fruits such as watermelon and cactus fruit were highlights of this period. My parents would purchase large quantities of watermelons, their varied sizes neatly stacked at home. While I was initially apprehensive about the prickly cactus trees, I found the harvesting process intriguing. Ultimately, I relished eating the fruit, often consuming so much that my mother cautioned me regarding the risk of overindulgence—a warning I rarely heeded.

I only flew a kite once, and even then, it lasted less than an hour. However, that wasn't what I anticipated most. The highlight of my summer was the rare opportunity to accompany my father to his office. This occurred only a few times over those three months, but each time felt like a special gift. My father was more than just a parent to me; he was also a teacher and mentor. He introduced me to geography and history long before I encountered them in school, guiding me around the city and sharing the stories of Gaza.

The walks were lengthy; after a few kilometers, my legs would tire, yet the journey was always rewarding. A treat awaited—either a Kebab sandwich or a cup of Nescafé from his office. On the best days, I'd enjoy a *Barrad*, a slushy unique to Gaza, whose yellow color and distinctive flavor remain etched in my memory.

On a sunny Friday in June, a light breeze set the tone for the day. Children and teens gathered excitedly near our house, while my father shared tea with neighbors. The street smelled of wet sand, evoking a sense of history. Noticing the teens' excitement, my father asked where they were headed as I sat barefoot beside him, listening quietly.

One of the boys shouted over the group that they were heading to Fras Market to buy supplies—*Khitan Masess*, thin polypropylene ropes, wood, and colored paper. He waved his hand, displaying a dozen shekels, the orange currency glinting in the light. Once my father heard this, he realised they were all set to fly kites. The excitement was infectious, with the boys calling out to each other as they checked on who was running late. Clearly, this was not a last-minute plan; it had been arranged in advance.

Fras Market was one of the oldest and most significant markets in Gaza City. It offered a wide variety of goods—groceries, meats, fruits, fabrics, second-hand clothes, animals, and cigarettes. If any market in Gaza had historical importance, it was undoubtedly this one. However, I despised it. The odor lingered in the air—damp, stale, and unpleasant. Even as a child, whenever I walked past with my father, I'd scrunch my nose and say, "Someone made a poop here."

While my father conversed with the neighbors, he frequently glanced over to watch the boys. As the group began to move, their laughter and happiness radiating, my father shouted to them, asking if they could also purchase some materials for him. The neighbors laughed, assuming he was referring to himself. He laughed too, but after checking his pocket, he took out 10 shekels and handed them the money.

Just as they were on the verge of vanishing from view, he shouted once more, "Buy the red, green, white, and black papers!"

Rami, being the eldest in the group, turned and shouted, "*Tayeb, A'am!*" This translates to "Okay, uncle!" In Gaza, the term "A'am" signifies "uncle," reflecting respect for elders.

Just before noon, as people made their way to Friday prayers, someone knocked at the door. My father was out, and my mother was busy cooking on a loud gasoline stove in the kitchen. I was the only one who heard the knock. During the day, we never locked our door, only securing it after the *Isha'a* prayer at night. This quiet strategy ensured that if any teenagers or young men fleeing the Israeli occupation needed a safe place to hide, they could slip into our home and exit through the other side.

I approached the slightly ajar door and poked my head out. Rami was there, sweat glistening on his face, holding a black plastic bag filled with paper and rope. "Give this to A'am Abu Akram," he instructed, handing me the bag along with a bundle of long wooden sticks.

I eagerly seized the materials, my excitement overflowing. "I'm going to fly a kite! I'm going to fly a kite!" I exclaimed, bouncing with joy as I dashed back into the house.

My mother, with her hands still damp from cooking, stepped out of the kitchen, her gaze inquisitive. "What's all this?" she asked, noticing the bag I was holding. I opened it and displayed the ropes, sticks, and colorful paper with pride. But rather than sharing in my joy, her expression shifted to anger. Her voice was stern as she warned, "If the army sees this, they'll arrest you," her words hitting me like a bucket of cold water.

I didn't completely grasp her meaning, yet her fear overshadowed my happiness. She took the bag from me and concealed it in one of the rooms. The items remained there for days, untouched, and they were never spoken about. I didn't inquire about them, nor did my father mention it.

A few days later, my father sat outside after watering the street at sunset. Seeing boys flying colorful kites, he remembered our forgotten kite and told me to get the bag from my mother. When I asked her, she refused and angrily confronted my father.

"They'll take you away!" she cried, her voice filled with fear. For a brief time, they engaged in a quiet argument, her worry evident. At last, she raised her hands in frustration and declared, "*Inta Hurr*," which translates to, "You're free to do as you wish."

My father had never made a kite before, but that didn't deter him. He reached out to our neighbor, Mohamed, for assistance. "Let's create a kite in the colors of the Palestinian flag," he said with a smile directed at me. My excitement surged again, and I rubbed my hands together, eagerly anticipating the moment we would fly it.

Mohamed began working in the storage room, the door open as he laid out the sticks and arranged four sheets of colored paper—red, green, white, and black. He mentioned needing flour, which he combined with hot water to create a paste, a simple glue that would hold everything together. I watched in amazement for the next hour as he cut and shaped the paper into the kite's design, crossing the sticks and balancing the ropes perfectly. When he was done, the kite stood almost as tall as I was. I could barely lift it.

I rushed to show my father, who welcomed me with a smile and examined the kite closely. He leaned it against him, eager for everyone passing by to admire it. However, dusk had fallen, and there was no time left to fly it. That night, I went to bed with the kite hovering above me, its ropes firmly held in my hands.

I woke up early, eager to run outside and fly the kite, but my mother intervened. "Wait until the afternoon," she said firmly.

I understood her concern—mothers tend to be overprotective and cautious. She had witnessed so many people getting arrested or hurt simply for displaying a flag or a kite. Her brother had even been imprisoned just for carrying his portrait from his time in the Egyptian military.

Later that afternoon, my father finally permitted me to take the kite and fly it. The wind was gentle, so I ran, dragging the kite behind me. Barefoot, my feet struggled to keep up with the wind. One of our neighbors noticed my difficulty and offered assistance.

"Let's go to the school," he suggested. "It's a better spot there."

Upon arriving at the school grounds, the kite started to ascend, rising higher and higher into the Gaza sky. The Palestinian flag waved proudly, its tail dancing like a snake in the breeze. However, in our excitement, we overlooked something important—the Israeli military occupied a position in the building directly ahead of us.

Without warning, the sharp sound of gunfire pierced the silence. They targeted the kite. Soon after, tear gas was released in our direction. One. Two. Three. Four canisters filled the entire football field with a thick, white haze. We dashed away, fear consuming us as the gas attacked our eyes and lungs. Tears streamed down my face as I sprinted, my eyes burning and my chest constricted.

Before I reached home, I spotted my parents rushing toward me. They had heard the gunshots and witnessed the tear gas.

"I want to retrieve my kite!" I shouted, still gasping from the fumes.

My mother, with a resolute tone, replied, "Forget about the kite. Come indoors."

That was the first—and last—time I ever flew a kite.

# COUNTING COINS, COUNTING TIME, GAZA 1995
## THE SON

Each morning, my parents operated a *Falafel* and snack stand outside our home. My father prepared the food before changing into his work clothes. This routine remained steady, with any deviations creating a noticeable difference in the day.

As I grew older, my mother occasionally left me to manage the stand, entrusting me with responsibilities such as handling customers and managing the proceeds. She would take the coins with her for security reasons.

Customers, typically children, sometimes saw another child acting as a shopkeeper and waited until my mother returned. During these times, I observed people passing by, noting their appearances and behaviors, and often asked them questions.

This approach continued until I was fifteen, when the stand closed permanently. Regularly, I accompanied my mother to the wholesale market; sometimes I went alone, carrying ingredients like sunflower seeds and vegetables. I once carried a five-kilogram bag of sunflower seeds over a long distance, after which the seeds were divided into small bags for sale.

Transporting large mortadella sausages from the market was

particularly challenging due to their weight. I used various methods to carry them. In later years, when asked about my height compared to my siblings, I attributed it humorously to carrying heavy loads at a young age. In 2002, my father decided the shop was no longer necessary. Observing students pass by the now-closed shop marked a change in daily life, aligning my routine with other adolescents.

The time spent working in the shop had a measurable impact on my development. The school's two shifts meant I assisted in the shop during afternoons or mornings, depending on the semester. At thirteen and fourteen, I studied while attending to customers.

On one occasion, while struggling with a mathematics problem, a regular student offered assistance and explained the solution. That was the last interaction; she likely continued her studies or married, but it is possible she recalls helping a young shopkeeper with math years later.

# Fatah, Gaza 1995
## The Son

It was the same week that Israeli forces pulled out when my brother-in-law and his friends started celebrating with marches, waving Palestinian flags, and displaying portraits of Yasser Arafat. I stood outside, struggling to contain my excitement while waving at them as they walked by. That day, the Israeli soldiers intervened, attempting to arrest them for raising the flag. However, instead of facing the severe punishments of the past, the soldiers were confronted with cries of, "We have peace now. You're leaving soon!"

The soldiers wavered, ultimately deciding to let them go. Just a few weeks or months before, such an act of defiance would have resulted in immediate death.

As the sun dipped below the horizon, its glow softened, and the streets buzzed with unexpected activity—the curfew had ended, and people moved west, embracing a newfound freedom. My brother-in-law advised me to sign up at the *Fatah* office for *Tala'a Al Fateh*, a program for teens aged 12 to 18. Although I was not even 10 yet, I embarked on the journey anyway, barefoot as always, heading west. The cemetery was to my left as I ascended, playing with the metal barriers along the way, savouring the last rays of daylight.

When I arrived, the sun was starting to set. I walked up to Ahmed Massani. "Basem sent me to you," I said.

He inquired about my name, wrote it down, and smiled, "Pass my greetings to your father." Then, he gave me a yellow cap featuring the *Fatah* logo and a Palestinian flag. I could hardly believe it—a flag and a cap! My heart raced with excitement, and my legs felt ready to take off.

By the time I left, it was dark. The cap was far too large for my small head, slipping down and obscuring my vision. I found it amusing, tilting my head to see the road beneath the oversized cap. As I got closer to home, the exhilaration of the moment overwhelmed me, and I burst through the door exclaiming, "We die for Palestine! We die for Palestine!"

Frustrated by the commotion, my mother shouted, "Enough!"

Yet, I remained unfazed. I swiftly tucked the flag away in a cupboard, treating it like a precious treasure. That flag and that moment—my initial experience of belonging to something greater than myself—lingered with me for years until I turned 25, when I distanced myself from *Fatah* and all political parties.

# Hope, Gaza 1994
## The Son

Outside, life continued unchanged. The night brought jasmine scents and calm streets under moonlight, contrasting with our home's turmoil. Indoors, emotions ran high—fear, hope, and my father's unwavering resolve.

However, my experience was different. I became politically active early on, without the direct presence of the Israeli military. The soldiers had exited Gaza in 1994 when I was only nine. The constant fear had dissipated, allowing my father to let me explore, as he believed the risks were minimal now.

One spring morning, I recall my mother awakening me. Her face radiated with joy as she exclaimed, "They've left! The Jews have withdrawn!"

In Gaza, the term "Jew" referred to the Israeli soldier. It was a straightforward association—no distinction was made between Jewish individuals and Israeli soldiers. For us, the two terms were interchangeable. This belief persisted until the early 2000s, when young Palestinians began traveling and returning with fresh perspectives. They had met Jews opposed to Israeli policies, or those who were not Israeli at all. Gradually, people started to prefer the term "Zionist" over "Jew."

I was ready for that moment. I had listened for months to conversations among my father, my brother-in-law, and my older brother, all excitedly discussing the potential for a Palestinian army. They spoke of Yasser Arafat being in Gaza. Just thinking about it made me feel like something significant was on the horizon.

I sprang from my bed that morning like a horse released from its reins. Barefoot and determined, I washed my face at the tap near the entrance and declared to my mother, "I'm going to see the Palestinian army!"

I was only eight, but my feet were restless, itching to run. My mother didn't try to stop me.

As I ran westward, the wind led me, my arms extended and feet sinking into the sandy streets of Gaza with each exuberant leap. I resembled a kangaroo, hopping to the rhythm of the earth beneath my feet. My mind was inundated with scattered images—like old, faded photographs—recollections of the Hamas protests that once filled our neighborhood, where protestors shouted, "Gaza-Jericho is a scandal!" condemning the peace accords as disgraceful. I recalled the Israeli soldiers firing at us, chasing us down. For a fleeting moment, I could almost sense the residual smell of tear gas, a haunting echo of those confrontations.

A sudden, loud car horn jolted me from my thoughts, while the sounds of celebration pulled me back to reality. I glanced down at my dusty feet, coated in the fine soil of Gaza, before sprinting toward a nearby donkey cart. Without hesitation, I grabbed hold and jumped on as it clattered along the street. The man driving the donkey smiled, allowing me to ride alongside him.

My legs dangled from the edge, swaying like branches tossed by the wind. I watched them, entranced by their motion, pondering whether they could carry me away quickly if the soldiers ever came back. Would I be fast enough? Could I escape the past?

As we got closer to the market, people moving in opposite directions resembled a living current—some heading west, others east. Smiles adorned faces, brightening the atmosphere like sunbeams piercing through a cloudy sky. In the distance, I noticed Um Nafez, who had lost her son a year earlier. She stood by her vegetable stall, her voice resonating across the market: "Long live Palestine! Glory to the martyrs!" Her words exuded a defiant strength, a melody of resilience amid the crowd. She remained steadfast until her death two decades later, even after losing another son and several grandsons to violence from Israel.

I jumped off the cart and stood beside her, enchanted by her songs as she chanted the nationalist slogans. My thoughts returned to Abdelhakeem, her son. Just a year prior, he had been outside our home, enjoying the tea I had poured him mere hours before he was taken—murdered by Israel. On that day, I wept for the first time in my life, or at least the first time I truly remembered crying over someone's loss. His image remained vivid in my mind, and the sorrow of his absence weighed heavily in my chest as I looked at the lively market.

I glanced to the right down the street, and my expression froze; my small smile vanished as if it had been stolen. The long cement-filled barrels that the Israeli forces had used to block the street remained in place. For a brief moment, I believed I saw soldiers hiding behind them as they used to.

Then Um Nafez handed me a wild cucumber, pulling me out of my reverie. I accepted it with a smile and began to eat, enjoying its sharp flavour as I wandered through the market. As my feet brushed against the asphalt, I recognized my deep dislike for it. The earth and sand beneath me felt much more familiar and comforting. This time, however, I wasn't rushing; I simply relished the cucumber as I strolled, hoping for a donkey and cart to pass by.

Time flew by as I took each bite, and soon I found myself in front of what used to be the Israeli police station. It had transformed completely. Now, Palestinian flags waved in the wind, and familiar faces greeted soldiers armed with AK-47s—who were now Palestinians. A mix of disbelief and curiosity washed over me as I approached. I maneuvered past the first barbed-wire fence, then the next, until I climbed over a small wall. Once I was on the other side, I found myself standing behind one of the soldiers.

I reached out my small hand, hoping he would notice me. Initially, he didn't, absorbed in conversation with others. So I lingered, my gaze fixed on his AK-47. It was an impressive sight, a device I had only encountered through news broadcasts and photographs. And now it was right before me. My fingertips tingled with the urge to touch it, yet I hesitated, uncertain of the consequences. The soldier took a few steps forward, and I followed, still entranced by the rifle. When our eyes finally connected, a wave of fear washed over me—what if he thought I intended to steal it? But instead, he smiled and promptly shook my hand.

The handshake was quick yet felt like a small triumph, a mission fulfilled. I dashed toward the main gate, my heart racing with anticipation. Outside, the area had been cleared, and people were sifting through the dirt. Confused, I questioned their actions. Then it dawned on me—they were looking for bullet casings left by the Israeli soldiers who had recently left. I joined them, digging with my hands until I found two empty casings and a solitary, rusted bullet; another mission achieved.

Everything felt surreal. Just weeks earlier, an Israeli soldier had fired tear gas at us from the same spot. Now the streets were alive with a newfound energy, a sense of freedom. I climbed one of the remaining walls to gain a better perspective. Thousands of people had gathered, celebrating what felt like our first taste of liberation.

After a few hours, the initial thrill started to fade, giving way to boredom. I decided it was time to head home. I didn't worry about whether my mother was anxious for my return; she hadn't crossed my mind. With the occupiers gone, a new sense of safety enveloped the city, accompanied by a collective sigh of relief.

As I sprinted eastward, the wind became like whips, striking my face, while my feet hit the ground with a rhythm that oscillated between joy and fear. At that moment, I understood that the meaning of life varies, its essence shifting from person to person and from one moment to another. What truly mattered wasn't life itself but its significance at that instant.

I mused that the wind was carrying the hope and promised future I had heard discussed in the news and family conversations. My arms were surrendered to the wind, soaring like a bird just freed from its cage. It represented years of hope, and my youthful heart was repeatedly reminding me, "Hope! Hope! Hope!"

# Grieving a Tree, Gaza 1994
## The Son

My father, eyes sparkling with wild delight and an easy smile on his lips, gestured for my brother as he stepped out of the shower, a yellow towel still wrapped around his head. When my brother got closer, my father signaled one of my sisters to place two plates in front of us: one heaped with rice and the other topped with *Bamiya*, garnished with plenty of onions and green chili.

"We believe it is time for you to get married," my father stated, his words floating in the air like a butterfly.

Surprised, my brother quickly asked, "To whom?"

There was a brief silence as my father's eyes moved to my mother, whose expression remained stoic and unreadable. He then looked back at my brother and, after thinking it through, replied, "We haven't made a decision yet, but we'll start looking soon."

"Where will we live?" my brother asked.

As a child, I was overwhelmed by curiosity, especially with unfamiliar faces coming into our home. The thought of my older brother leaving to live with his future wife felt unimaginable. Children have a remarkable way of envisioning what seems impossible, often revealing truths hidden in their dreams.

The stillness was broken when my father answered, "Your second uncle's room. We will build a new shower and toilet and renovate the kitchen." My brother went quiet for a moment before asking about the old trees. "We will tear them down," my father said.

My eyes widened, a storm of emotions rising within me, as I exclaimed, "And the *Siddra* tree?" The grand, decades-old *Nabak jujube* stood proudly at the center of our home. I had ascended its strong branches countless times while my mother and sister draped wet clothes over its twisted limbs. We savored its delicious fruits, and I pursued the birds that nested high above.

"We will cut it down," my father repeated, his voice resonating in the room.

Overwhelmed with excitement and sadness, I suddenly got up and ran to one of my older sisters, shouting, "They will cut the *Tammora!*" Unfortunately, my words went unheard, and she dismissed me.

Feeling dejected, I found comfort by the tree, circling its sturdy trunk, holding it close as if saying goodbye to a beloved spirit. I sat by the tree, pondering how such a grand entity could be taken down. A flicker of hope emerged within me as I thought that its immense size and strength would withstand the hands trying to sever it. My father's stories about the resilient tree resonated in my thoughts, blended with the memory of him, tears rolling down his cheeks, mourning his mother's death under its guarding branches. I tried to rationalize that my father's choice was fueled by vengeance against the tree, though it held no guilt for his mother's loss. Even in my imagination, I had never wielded a weapon to harm a tree or any creature. The only human bloodshed I had ever envisioned was from falling war jets—and even in those dreams, I spared the pilots.

The next day, clouds swirled above the city, moving from the southwest to the north and bringing a chilling breeze that seeped into our home. Classes were cancelled due to a national strike protesting the occupation, initiated by the death of a Palestinian fighter. Two relatives working in construction came by to discuss plans for demolishing and rebuilding our house. A flicker of hope filled my heart, wishing my father would save the tree. When they asked about it, my father opted to uproot it. One relative proposed keeping it for its shade and the gentle winds it provided.

But my father retorted, "Where would we park a car if we had one?" Even though we never owned a car, the tree was lost to us forever.

Months later, our home showcased a new shower, toilet, and a renovated kitchen, built not from concrete but with roof profiles—metal pieces nearly twenty years old, many showing signs of rust. My mother asked for a small area where the tree used to be, to grow mint and basil for our cooking needs.

# The Hakoura, Gaza-No Time
## The Son

I have always loved plants and animals. Although we didn't keep pets, our neighbors had chickens, a rooster, and cats that sometimes visited our home. Behind our house was the *Hakoura*, a small plot with a large storage room and fragrant mint, once a source of peace but left unused after 1992 due to difficult times.

The storage room, dark and isolated without electricity, stood among two olive trees—one especially captivated me. As a child, I found comfort under its branches, imagining conversations with it. My mother, worried about my visits, warned me of a giant black snake nearby, instilling a lingering fear that stayed with me into adulthood. Only when accompanied by my siblings did I feel brave enough to return, though often my requests for company went ignored.

For over a year, my mother grew anxious twice a week at twilight, always checking our cherished *Hakoura*. She would quickly move between the window and the *Hakoura*, dressed in a covered head and a black skirt. After a few tense minutes, she'd sigh with relief, sometimes helped by my eldest sister with whispered conversations and silent gestures.

As a young boy, when I tried to peek into the *Hakoura*, my mother stopped me and told me to sleep. It took years before I finally learned its secret: hidden behind the twisted face of the old olive tree, freedom fighters and activists masked their identities, wearing uniforms before launching their secret missions. The *Hakoura* and the olive tree served as their sanctuary, a discreet center where they found shelter and readied themselves for nighttime marches or their mission objectives. As a child, I devoted my full attention to that olive tree, which in turn gained a cryptic and vibrant charm, revealing its beauty in countless forms.

At just six years old, a relative blocked my way while I walked alone, barefoot, a kilometer from home. He called me over and asked, "Where are you headed?" I remained silent, unable to reply. "Where is your mother?" he continued.

I looked around and soon spotted her in the distance, struggling with a box of chickens balanced on her head. He tilted my face toward him, examining me closely, and repeated his question.

"Home," I finally answered.

"Where do you want to go?" he pressed on. I pulled my right hand from my pocket, revealing a single coin—a shekel.

"I want to buy a tree," I proclaimed.

His laughter filled the air as he told me I needed my mother to do that. Taking my hand, he guided me halfway home, stopping only when we reached our house. With an authoritative voice, he told me to run the rest of the way. I felt betrayed; my plans to buy small plants at the market the next day seemed dashed. That night, I tucked the *Shekel* under my pillow, dreaming of a world full of leafy plants. The next morning, filled with resolve, I made small basins from sand in the *Hakoura* and carefully filled them with water from an empty Pepsi bottle, my determination tinged with defiance.

"May water and plants vanish," I whispered angrily to myself, hurrying to escape my mother's watchful eyes as she approached to take the precious bottle away.

That section of the house became my playground, a space where I would care for imaginary plants, even without real greenery. Connecting the green pipe to the tap, I would eagerly pull it over, positioning it over the planting basin, ready to unleash a flood of water.

My father, exasperated, would shout, "Where on earth are the plants to be watered?"

With childish pride, I would reply, "I'll buy them next Friday."

Many Fridays passed, yet I never made the intended purchase. Still, an idea took root in me—I longed to plant something. Although my parents didn't give me a daily allowance like other children, they never denied my request for a shekel or two. They thought I didn't need an allowance since I could have sandwiches from home, while other kids relied on their allowance for store-bought meals. Yet sometimes, I grew tired of our falafel and mortadella sandwiches and would return home for an alternative.

One Friday morning, I woke up early and ventured into the *Hakoura*. Spring was awakening, and I had started sleeping in the corridor, having given up my room during winter. This routine continued for two years, regardless of the season. On this day, I aimed to tend to a small area of the expansive planting basin, equipped with a rake and a crocodile steel hoe head, ready to prepare the soil. For a long time, I had desired to cultivate this overlooked part of the *Hakoura*, and today, I decided to turn that aspiration into reality.

"What are you doing?" my mother asked, her voice reflecting curiosity and concern.

Without pause, I answered, "I want to plant today."

She watched me sitting on the floor as she listened intently to the radio, her legs elegantly extended, a cup of tea in hand. Eagerly, she anticipated updates from Israeli radio, BBC, or Monte Carlo. A half-hour later, I found myself inching closer to her, each step deliberate, my mind racing with what I would say. Finally, I approached and stood against the wall, pondering my words. I moved closer, letting the radio's voice wash over me.

*"The peace process is in jeopardy,"* the radio announced, resonating with a sense of foreboding. Those words echoed within me for decades. Just as I was about to speak, my mother quickly silenced me with a gesture resembling a rocket launch, pressing her finger to her lips. She leaned in close to the radio, intently listening, her gaze shifting between me and the device. When she finally lowered the radio, I took it as a cue to make my request. Seizing the moment, I nestled beside her, playfully messing with her feet, cherishing those moments of connection.

"I want five shekels," I stated, locking eyes with my mother and ensuring my gaze landed on the mole beside her right eye.

Naturally curious, I had often inquired about its meaning, and she would reply, "It is the sign of God. I sense within it a glimpse of the future." To me, that mole represented an antenna—an ancient link capable of observing, interpreting, and foreseeing what was to come.

As I spoke, I noticed her take a sip of her steaming tea, with fragrant green mint floating on the surface, its aroma wafting through the liquid.

"And what do you plan to do with five shekels?" she asked, her eyes fixed on me.

Momentarily flustered, I stood silent like a statue, considering my desires and what I wanted. Uncertain about the price of plants, I raised my hand to request a pause in the playful caress of her feet and placed it on my head. With childlike pride, I finally said, "I want to buy a tree."

A broad smile spread across her face as she answered, "So, you want to buy plants? Is that why you were tending to the sand?" I nodded eagerly; my head filled with excitement.

Without any further hesitation or adult negotiations, she smiled and clarified her decision. "I will give you five shekels, but you must write down what you plan to buy," she said.

I eagerly agreed, my heart filled with joy, and I set off on the adventure with a piece of paper in my hand, barefoot. I dashed like a rocket, exactly as she suggested.

As I strolled toward the Friday market, I carefully sidestepped my relatives' homes to avoid a repeat of past experiences, when they stopped me and returned me home. I wanted to protect my joy and maintain the happiness that belonged to me.

With one hand holding five shekels in my pocket and the other grasping my shopping list, I navigated through a lively crowd. Many were oblivious to my presence as I skillfully maneuvered through the throngs, darting effortlessly between large trucks. The main difficulty was finding the section dedicated to plants. At the Friday market, each item had its own space—poultry, jeans, second-hand goods, clothes, electronics, etc. I knew the plant area would come right after poultry. Spotting the first cage of chickens nearby confirmed I was getting close to my goal. The dream of having a garden felt tangible now, and excitement coursed through me. At last, I saw a tall, slender figure holding a tray of seedlings.

"I want trees," I declared, handing him the paper. He gave it a quick look before passing it to one of his assistants, instructing him to fulfil my request.

The assistant began reading slowly, then turned to the vendor and said, "He wants mint and basil seedlings."

I felt pleased, but a hint of disappointment remained since mint didn't exactly qualify as a tree. As he collected the items on the list, my attention shifted to a miniature rose that was nearly as tall as I was. Lost in thought, I daydreamed about numerous trees, roses, and plants—an endless array of varieties, shapes, and colors.

The man's sharp tap on my shoulder brought me back to reality, and he said, "*Ishaa Ya A'ami*," (Wake up, uncle), his voice laced with impatience.

After handing over five shekels, I looked into the plastic bag now containing five seedling cells. Just as I started to enjoy my excitement, he called me back and placed two and a half shekels in my hand.

An opportunity arose—I had the money and the freedom to buy. I asked about the price of a large tree that had captivated me, longing to own it.

The man replied, "Three shekels." It weighed four and a half kilograms and was half a meter tall.

With disappointment, I said, "But I only have 2.5 shekels. I can give you the remaining half shekel next week."

The man laughed and said, "Alright, hand me the money."

As I approached that beautiful plant, its delightful fragrance filled me with joy and a hint of sadness, not knowing it would flourish in Gaza while I wouldn't be able to see it grow. Carrying the heavy load with the plastic bag firmly in my grip, I walked a hundred meters from the market and found a neighbor's donkey cart. I placed the tree on it and walked alongside, turning down the offer to ride.

# The Mosque and Ramadan, Gaza 1995-6
## The Son

"Don't you dare go there again, understand?" my father said in a low yet intense whisper.

I had just come back from the mosque, filled with joy and smiling because of the *Siwak* they had given us. How had he noticed my trip to the mosque? The strong scent gave me away, and he inquired about my whereabouts and why I was holding a *Siwak*. *Siwak*, a natural toothbrush made from the Salvadora persica tree, is commonly used by Imams and the pious as a *Sunnah*, a practice that emulates the actions of the Prophet.

"Alright," I conceded, but the persistent sparkle in my youthful eyes revealed a different perspective. I relished being in the congregation with the man clad in white, discussing Islam, Muslims, and the heavenly contrast of *Janna* and *Narr* (Heaven and Hell). I followed my agreement with, "All boys attend the mosque too."

With a sideways glance, he replied while retreating into the room, "Only when you come with me." His words were conclusive, leaving acceptance as my only option.

The day before, I had been caught up in street games outside our home when unfamiliar faces, religious young men from Saudi

Arabia, approached us, inviting youngsters aged eight to 15 to join their circles. These gatherings were called *Halakat*, literally meaning circles, as they would sit in a ring. One of them handed me a booklet that clearly explained the significance of prayer in Islam. I attended their gathering for *Asr* prayer the next day, a meeting that would turn out to be my last.

My first experience at a mosque happened with my father's guidance. At just four years old, he took me and my older sister to his workplace several times each summer. One day on our way home, it was time for *Asr* prayer, and he decided to take us with him. Until that day, I had never entered a mosque before. The only glimpses I had of it were from my father's regular Friday visits, when he returned home in the afternoon with fruits, sweets, or even vegetables.

Upon entering the Grand Mosque of Gaza, I was immediately struck by its remarkable architecture. The soaring ceiling and intricately designed mosaics adorning the floors and carpets exemplified a high degree of craftsmanship. Pillars extended upward, drawing attention to an impressive crystal chandelier. Although I attempted to point out the chandelier to my father, he did not notice it at the time. I had previously believed that such architectural grandeur was unique to prominent mosques; however, my subsequent visit to a church in Italy at age 21 revealed that this level of aesthetic refinement is a common feature among various places of worship.

The atmosphere was notably tranquil, characterized by the orderly and respectful gestures of prayer performed by the congregation—a coordinated act of devotion observed collectively. I found this display intriguing, as it reminded me of my father, whom I regarded as devout, performing similar practices in our home.

My sister and I stood watch by one of the immense pillars, guarding our plastic bags filled with belongings as we awaited our father. I began to pray, and my sister's laughter rang out in reply. This marked the only instance in which my father insisted that I enter a mosque.

He never inquired whether I had prayed, asserting, "If you pray, it is for you, not for me." He prioritized good morals and values over religious practices.

Fast forward to the future, and I learned that my father harbored resentment towards religious figures. He would claim, "They are deceivers," adding, "They cultivate fear and hatred rather than love and admiration for Islam."

His assertions struck a chord because the only time I participated in the circle, the Wahabi sheik conjured images of a gargantuan serpent that would torment us and cast us into the earth for seventy years. The specter of that snake haunted my dreams. To this day, any sight or depiction of a snake awakens the image of that monstrous reptile ready to mete out punishment.

On another day, a respected Sheikh introduced himself at our home during the dusk of an otherwise typical day. As I opened the door, I was captivated by his imposing stature, his outfit harmoniously matched by a stylish, contemporary vehicle and an attentive chauffeur. A wave of reverence overcame me.

"Where is your father?" he inquired.

"Dad!" I shouted from the doorway to my father, ignoring the dignified man. Later, I learned he was a respected judge and Sheikh seeking my father's help with loan documents. He chose the privacy of our home over the scrutiny of his office, wanting to evade the public perception of a respected Sheikh taking a loan, an act viewed as taboo in Islam.

Years later, rumors emerged that tarnished the Imams' reputations with allegations of child abuse. The thought alone made my skin crawl with disgust and fear. Walking past the mosque turned into a dreadful task. At one point, mosques evolved into cultural and political centers for Islamist parties, and the derogatory phrase, "You play tennis at the mosque," became common. I didn't understand its meaning until I left Gaza. Playing tennis at a mosque became synonymous with children being molested by Hamas activists. This is untrue but was used by Hamas opponents to undermine and do reputation harm to Islamists.

Much of my education came from observing my father's behavior. During Ramadan, he isolated himself in the mosque until *Asr*, and on Fridays, he would arrive early to claim a seat in the front row for prayers. In this sacred month, he frequently invited my younger brother and me to accompany him for *Fajr* prayers after *Suhoor* (the pre-dawn meal before sunrise). These Ramadan traditions were so captivating that I longed for them until adolescence shifted my life.

One remarkable Ramadan practice is praying *Fajr* early morning at the mosque. The journey home after prayer was more captivating to me than the prayers themselves, particularly with our elderly neighbor, an English-speaking devout man who once collaborated with the English colonizers.

"You are destined for greatness," he frequently told me, a mantra he has shared since I was five.

My father held his words in high esteem, urging me to trust him, stating, "He can foresee the future. He is a man of God."

Following the old man's death, my attendance at *Fajr* prayers diminished, leaving me nostalgic for his wisdom. His lessons struck a profound chord within me, highlighting the importance of learning from elders.

During the nights of Ramadan, I observed that I did not have friends. At ten years old, I watched groups gather for *Taraweeh*, a night prayer involving extended Quran recitation. Some classmates formed circles while others remained alone. On one occasion, my father asked me to go home. Upon later reflection, it became evident that excessive protection may have resulted in long-term negative effects.

While growing up, I came to understand that *Laylat Al-Qadr* is the holiest night in Islam, during which we must endeavor to stay awake and pray throughout the night. Nearly all men would remain awake, gathering at the mosques to partake in continuous prayer until the *Fajr* prayers.

This revered night, which occurs annually on the 27$^{th}$ night of Ramadan, is known as the 'Night of Decree,' commemorating the first revelation of the Quran from heaven to earth. The month of Ramadan is divided into three segments of ten days each: the initial ten days symbolize Allah's mercy, the next ten represent forgiveness, and the final ten promise protection from hellfire. As a child, my motivations were driven more by fear than by faith, with my primary focus being on avoiding hellfire and seeking forgiveness.

Unlike the common practice during Ramadan, my father remained steadfast in his routine, only increasing his Quran readings. On *Laylat Al Qadr*, he would go to bed after *Tarawih* and rise an hour before *Fajr*.

"If you seek Allah's forgiveness, you must pray throughout the year, not just one night," he frequently said.

His message emphasized the pointlessness of worshipping Allah for merely one day or one month each year while the rest of the time is spent in sin, gossip, and theft.

"Allah exists throughout the year," he would often remind me.

During my eleventh and thirteenth years, we occasionally looked for mosques that provided a good *Suhoor*, and we consistently chose *Al-Omari* (the grand mosque). The first mosque's Imam, Wael Alzard (murdered in the Gaza genocide), had a soothing voice that made Quran recitation a pleasure.

On one of those occasions, I sat in the mosque waiting for the meal. The community gathering was as engaging as the ritual, and I gradually became more involved with my peers before ultimately deciding to step back.

My last *Laylat Al-Qadr* experience at *Al-Omari* Mosque was disappointing. After the *Fajr* prayers, we were forced to wait for an hour with many other worshippers.

"Where are our shoes?" one queried.

"Mine are missing," another voiced.

Around a hundred worshippers, both men and boys, moved

anxiously from one end to another, searching in vain for their lost shoes.

"May God curse them!" one man shouted, his face contorted with rage.

In response, the crowd burst into chaos, many yelling at him to leave the "house of God." A few of us chuckled at the man's ridiculousness – how could someone who was just worshipping God curse Him over missing footwear? While I sympathized with their worry about our boots and potential parental discipline, I found the humor in this moment. It underscored our tendency to place material possessions above spirituality, rendering it insignificant in moments of material. loss.

After an hour of unsuccessful searching, we lost hope of finding our shoes and assumed they had been stolen. With my home three kilometers away and the roads grimy, I and my neighborhood teenagers exchanged glances and chose to wear the bathroom sandals. Constructed from a wooden base and a single leather strap, they appeared like artifacts from the tenth century.

As we made our way through the streets and neighborhoods toward home, the heavy, ill-fitting sandals clattered loudly in the pre-dawn silence, waking several people from their sleep.

An old man peered down from a balcony and yelled, "Curse your father who failed to teach you how to respect mosques!"

We hurried past him, keeping our heads down, but my father's words echoed in my mind: "Respect people, and they will respect you back."

Even with the obstacles and setbacks, the mosque's charm and its mysterious teachings continuously beckoned me, profoundly influencing my views on spirituality and existence.

# Part Three
# Intergenerational Echoes

# Silent Tears, Defiance, Gaza 1980s
## The Mother

I have consistently taken a supportive role, closely monitoring your development in a way that nurtures growth within an organization. Each day, I ensured your well-being and progress with careful attention. Over time, as your responsibilities increased, I found myself adapting to the demands of raising nine children before the age of forty. When your sister approached her secondary school graduation, we encountered a significant decision point regarding the direction of her future.

Due to ongoing family obligations, I often experienced limited autonomy, feeling unable to freely express my perspectives. Attempts at communication frequently went unheard within the household, leaving my concerns unaddressed and fostering internal frustration.

One evening, I felt a rush of power surging through me. With your grandmother away, I seized the moment and took your sister's hand gently. I led her into the backyard, where our confessions were hidden beneath the protective canopy of the old tree.

"Listen, they want you to marry. I urge you to refuse," I whispered, my voice barely a breath stirring among the leaves.

"I know. My grandmother wants me to marry my relative," your sister confessed.

This tradition of cousin marriages often ignored the need for a dowry and was known derisively as "Dogs' marriages," reflecting the commodification of women. Women had no say and were forced to comply with patriarchal rules.

"Please say no to that," I implored her. "Dream larger. Share your aspirations to become a nurse or a teacher."

Your uncle's wise and compassionate wife entered our hushed conversation as if she had been waiting for the right moment. "Say you want to be a teacher," she advised. "There's a new teacher training institute in Gaza. Your future can start there."

"But how will we gather the fees?" I questioned, my voice quaking on the verge of tears. She comforted me, assuring that she would find a solution and that your sister must stand firm, as steadfast as a boulder against a storm.

Every day felt like a gamble, with my heart racing in anxiety each time your grandmother called your sister. It was as though we stood on the edge of a chasm, and the smallest misstep could send us plummeting into darkness.

I wished for mercy—not out of despair, but to protect my children from life's hardships. I hoped they could pursue education and grow into strong, independent women, unlike myself, whose dreams of teaching were lost to poverty and social pressure. Contrary to the saying, *"The shadow of a man is better than the shadow of a wall,"* I believe that learning within safe walls is far better than relying on a man's presence.

One day, while I was preparing our meal by crushing *Moloukhiya* leaves for the following day, your father came home, worry written all over his face. His once-thriving cement factory now stood as a decaying symbol of lost dreams. He took a seat, lighting one cigarette after another, each puff appearing to steal a piece of him away.

I offered him tea or coffee, a modest comfort in the chaos. "No, may God be pleased with you," he refused, absorbed in his thoughts.

Later that evening, he summoned me under the ancient *Ziziphus spina-christi* tree, its branches stretching like an open hand against the sky. My heart raced; I worried he might announce he was marrying off your sister.

"She won't be married," he said, his voice gentler than the evening breeze. A wave of relief enveloped me as tears streamed down my cheeks like rivulets after a storm. I understood this decision was a challenge to the traditional customs, yet he remained resolute, prepared to defy even his own mother.

When your sister came home from school, still wearing her achievement badge, I shared the news. "You won't be married. Your father has decided that you will continue your education."

She beamed as brightly as the sun emerging from behind the stormy clouds. "Swear by God?" she inquired, hardly able to fathom her luck.

I watched her—strong, independent, and respected by all. It would have been a loss if she hadn't pursued her education or become the remarkable woman she could be. I realized then that life-changing decisions can result from a single act of defiance or even a silent tear. I was ready to support her education, but your father began what would be a long battle.

---

On a calm Friday morning, our home was disrupted by knocking as our relatives arrived. Your father welcomed them and asked me to make tea.

Entering the kitchen, I focused on making tea, the fragrant leaves twirling in the pot. Their voices echoed in the living room, loud and rough like waves crashing against a peaceful shore. Your grandmother stayed in her room, opting out of the intense conversation. I asked her a question about our guests, and she frowned, whispered a prayer, then returned to her quiet solitude.

Closer to the room where the discussion was going, I was hit by a remark that roared: "But we have no girls to meet men."

It felt like an enigmatic puzzle; the girl's name wrapped in uncertainty. I called for your father twice, but the moment my voice filled the room, a hush descended over them, as if a snake had slithered into the garden or a bird had settled upon a branch above their heads.

When your father brought the tea, I observed his expression. His brow was furrowed, and there were deep lines on his face. He had a cigarette in his mouth. There was some displeasure in his expression while he looked at those around him. He picked up the copper teapot and five clear cups and entered the room. Shortly after, the conversation continued.

Positioned by the kitchen door with my back against the cool cement wall, I struggled to grasp the essence of the conversation. A sense of worry stirred within me, suggesting that a significant problem was being addressed. Minutes passed, each one more agonizing than the one before, feeding my curiosity like a seed sprouting in the spring soil.

*Why is he silent?* I wondered within the maze of my thoughts, trying to decipher his strange quietness. The sole indication of his presence was the sound of matches scraping against the box as he lit his cigarette, a noise I had come to recognize.

His silence finally broke, shattering like glass, his voice resonating with authority. The words rang in my ears – "She is going to be a teacher."

A realization struck me: they were discussing your older sister. Their tone reflected discomfort regarding her choice of becoming a teacher and her dealings with men at her workplace or school. Their abrupt exit felt like an unfinished symphony, leaving me concealed in the kitchen, waiting for your father's return.

When he came, I observed that he appeared content, with an expression suggesting accomplishment.

"They are questioning sending the girl to be a teacher," he said, responding to my silent inquiry. Your sister's presence at the institute and her interaction with men caused concern, but your father responded to their questions calmly. His final statement was, "I told them what they must know."

In the aftermath, I learned about the language he employed to address their concerns. His responses were firm and direct, which caused some discomfort within the group and led to their withdrawal. He underscored the importance of education for her future and advocated for her potential as a teacher. He affirmed that engaging in dialogue and debate with men is an ordinary aspect of her academic and professional experience. He concluded by stating, "My daughter is equal to hundreds of men, and I trust her."

He retreated to his mother's room, where their argument quickly escalated. Aware of the visitors' intentions, your grandmother, upset by our refusal to arrange your sister's marriage, rallied support to convince your father not to send her to the teacher training institute. The conflict grew tense, and I was struck by fear that, even if he won this round, he might ultimately lose.

Amid the commotion, your father stepped out of the room, grabbed a wooden chair, and settled in the corridor. He lit cigarette after cigarette, the smoke drifting away from the turmoil inside. His mother trailed behind him, the remnants of their argument lingering in the air.

"She has tainted your mind," she charged, her eyes piercing into me. I gasped in disbelief, letting out a strangled cry at her baseless accusation.

"She is not involved at all," your father countered.

"No, she encourages all the boys and girls to pursue careers as engineers and teachers instead of focusing on marriage and family," she shot back, her anger evident in her tone.

With a lump in my throat and unshed tears stinging my eyes, I left her in a storm of accusations, seeking refuge in our room. Once inside, I held you close; your innocent presence soothed my troubled soul.

Soon after, your older sister came home from the institute, a daily trip of over 20 kilometers. The fatigue on her face reflected her determination. As she entered our house, your father asked her about her day, a trace of worry in his usually serious tone.

"Good. We had an exam, and it went well. I rushed back to sell these vegetables at the market," she replied, her resolve unwavering. The vegetables she sold came from our small backyard and the neighboring land we owned.

Upon hearing her, he offered his blessings: "May God guide you."

His statement indicated the end of the conflict and demonstrated his support for her goals. On that day, the discontent among the women was apparent. I considered how many women had encountered similar difficulties. In this situation, your sister received encouragement from her father, who remained unaffected by his mother's opinion. It is an intergenerational differences in understanding life.

# Sweat, Stone and Study, Gaza 1988
## The Mother

Every day I watched intergenerational difference on sister's dedication to her studies. Outwardly calm but inwardly anxious, my main concern shifted from myself to fears about your future and how my inner turmoil could impact your sister's education.

Your brother graduated from high school a year later, and his grades reflected his dedication. I felt a mix of joy and anxiety; a rollercoaster of emotions balanced on the brink of uncertainty.

*How will he pursue his studies?* The question lingered in my mind like an echo in a deserted hall. I recalled his conversation with his sister from the year before, his aspirations of studying overseas and soaring like birds. This understanding weighed heavily on me, intensifying my worries. A deluge of questions loomed large, threatening to engulf me.

When your eldest brother was born, I held him and told your father, "I want him to be an engineer."

His simple reply, "*Inshallah*," gave me hope despite my worries.

However, your grandmother ridiculed the idea, asking, "Why

engineer? Do you want to be known as *'Um al Mohuandis'* [the mother of the engineer]?"

I stayed quiet, yet deep inside, I realized that progress unfolds slowly. My responsibility was to arm our children with the strength and bravery to become independent beings, able to fly high as they entered adulthood. They must be resilient enough to forge their own paths, rather than simply conforming to the trends set by societal expectations.

During those times, the idea of him becoming an engineer or a doctor felt as unattainable as a mirage, given our conditions. We struggled to sustain his education right up to high school. Yet, change was looming. Many were fleeing to Egypt, escaping the brutality of the Israeli army that seized Gaza after the Naksa in 1967.

Eighteen years later, we stood at the brink of the moment when I promised he would become an engineer. He should leave, but questions of *where?* and *how?* rang in my mind. We lacked both the financial resources and a local university to support his journey. I cried that day, not tears of joy for his achievements, but out of despair for his uncertain future.

Life rarely presents us with the option to confront challenges boldly or to yield over time. We must either endure the storm with courage or give in to societal expectations. When clouds suggest a coming rain, we often hesitate, anxious about being soaked until the first drops fall on us. I found myself at the edge of such a storm, determined not to surrender, eager to live and dream free from the so-called "laws of life," or societal conventions.

When your father returned from work, his happiness was obvious. I thought someone had told him about your brother's success, but I was wrong. He had visited the school to learn the news himself. He brought with him a large parcel of *Gullac*—a pastry distinctive to the Levant region. Crafted from wheat starch, this delightful dessert surrounded walnuts within its fragile, crisp layers. It evoked pleasant childhood memories of the vendor who sold it outside our school.

One day, your father shared a funny story about how *Gullac* was referred to as *Kuluhum* in Gaza, which means "Eat them." A man from *Sheja'iyya* misinterpreted the vendor's enthusiastic calls of "*Kuluhum! Kuluhum!*"—often seen as an invitation for free food—and ended up eating five servings before leaving.

That day, your father exuded happiness, and his joy was contagious. He relished the *Gullac*, enjoyed tea, smoked his cigarette, and greeted guests in the *Diwan* - the room he set aside for entertaining. Pride shone in his eyes, celebrating his son's remarkable achievement. As evening fell and the streets quieted in preparation for the curfew, we congregated in the center of our home, illuminated by moonlight and enveloped in the sweet fragrance of the surrounding trees.

Without any introduction, your grandmother spoke directly to your elder brother, "When are you going to work with Abu Mohamed?". Abu Mohamed was a construction contractor.

I was astonished, my reaction driven by disbelief and indignation: "But he will study!"

Throughout this interaction, your father and brother stayed quiet. Your father finally spoke up, saying, "He will study and also work."

This statement angered your grandmother, who stubbornly prioritized work over education, insisting, "He should work, get married, and be a man."

---

Every sunrise brought the painful truth of my son starting his day before dawn, compelled into the world of construction and cement work. Each evening, he would come home as a weary figure, drained from a day spent laboring under the harsh sun, his body marked by the physical toll of his work.

His quiet routine exemplified his commitment. He would immerse himself in the refreshing tap water and consume any meal prepared before vanishing into his bed, without a word. His routine was like a mechanical performance, a dull ballet repeated daily.

One day, your father, wearing a light beige jacket with double pockets over a blue t-shirt, inquired about the specifics of his work. He responded, lacking enthusiasm, "I sometimes work with sand and other times with crushed stones."

Your father quietly lit his cigarette and walked away, his silence speaking volumes. The sadness in his eyes reflected my own pain. His sorrow filled the room, its heavy presence stifling in my summer dress. My voice wandered in my mind, and I watched your father as he paced back and forth, occasionally pausing to stare into the void as if trying to solve an impossible equation. His anguish was evident, and it hurt me to witness him struggling with such burdensome thoughts.

Your brother was deeply involved in the often-overlooked field of concrete construction, starting his day at four in the morning. His employer would come to get him, bringing along the loud cement mixer, and drive him to the job site. He operated the hydraulic cement mixer, a large machine typically linked to buildings being erected. They constructed multi-level buildings, sometimes reaching three floors but never exceeding that limit.

His responsibilities included filling a 10-kilogram bucket with sand, swiftly unloading it into the machine, and repeating this task three times each minute for several hours. This exemplified manhood in our culture—to work tirelessly, marry, and raise a family. Unemployment was seen as a scarlet letter, a disgrace that tarnished the family's reputation.

One evening, your brother sat next to me on a cotton mattress known as a *Janbiya*, enjoying his tea after finishing a bowl of *Mouloukhiya*. During this ordinary moment, your father came over to him, his command clear and resolute: "You will study to become a nurse."

This evoked a blend of emotions in me. Joy mingled with disappointment since I had envisioned him as an engineer.

Your brother, as stoic as always, replied, "I will work," keeping his gaze firmly away from our father. Meanwhile, your father elaborated on his vision, passionately constructing castles of dreams in the air.

A sudden surge of defiance overcame your brother when he interrupted your father, asserting, "But I don't want to get married. I want to study like Nafez and Basem." Nafez and Basem, your brother's friends, wanted to study overseas, attracted by the promise of scholarships and opportunities. The Soviet Union became a popular option, supported by the communist leader in our community who offered scholarships to family, neighbors, and party members.

His words struck me like a bolt of lightning, full of excitement. This was the first time he expressed his desires. I longed for him to become an engineer. The atmosphere was charged with tension.

Your father's expression masked his disbelief, while from another room, your grandmother's voice resonated, upholding tradition: "Why do you want to be like the others? Help your father and the family."

With one arm extended, your father leaned forward, turning his head toward your brother as he bellowed, "They only want to go to the Soviet Union for the girls!"

While his statement contained some truth, many were drawn by the romanticized image of the Soviet Union, captivated by its free education and the promise of a new culture. However, we found ourselves with few choices: either send him to the Soviet Union on a scholarship, have him study in Gaza, or try to facilitate his study in Western Europe. Our financial limitations and absence of connections rendered the last option an unlikely aspiration.

Dressed in tattered, faded jeans and a casual blue and white shirt, your brother confidently declared his resolution: "I will find a scholarship. I won't need money from you. Tomorrow, I will go with Nafez and Basem to get a passport."

With restrained calmness, your father replied, "As you wish."

In that moment, I felt a surge of pride, quickly followed by pity for my husband. He had shown wisdom by letting your brother forge his own path, trusting that experience would lead him to make the right choice.

The next morning, the house was filled with the scent of a fresh breakfast—eggs from our backyard chickens, olive oil, potatoes, and the salty white cheese from the woman who sometimes visited our neighborhood.

Your brother got ready for the day, dressed in his finest clothes. "I will take photos for the passport," he declared while counting his hard-earned money.

I communicated your father's request, urging him to stop by before heading to the Israeli army office for his passport. Your father intended to assist with the passport expenses and provide him with his saved earnings. He recognized that experience teaches best and that grasping life's realities would help us make wise choices.

On that day, I came to understand that the most valuable things we yearn for are worth fighting for. I aspired for my son to become an engineer and be well-educated, and deep down, I knew it was worth every effort.

———

Several weeks had passed since your brother applied for a *laissez-passer*, a key to travel outside Gaza. Each morning, he would rise at the rooster's crow, go to work, and he wouldn't return until the sun began to set, usually around four or five in the evening. His work was relentless, yielding little financial reward, barely enough to scrape by in life.

On a sweltering mid-August day, with humidity thick in the air, he stumbled home, soaked in sweat and wearing a distressed expression. Without speaking, he retired to the *Hakoura*.

When your father arrived, exhausted from his second job, he looked for him. I responded not with words, but with a quiet gesture, my hand silently directing him to the *Hakoura*. As my hand fell back into my lap, his loud voice reverberated through the house, calling for your brother—a cry that likely reached our neighbors' ears. He believed your brother had gone to the next street, waiting for the Communist man from whom he expected a scholarship.

Your brother came, his skin radiant with a bronze hue from the sun's heat. He wore light blue pants that flowed like the sky, complemented by a striking black shirt. With a slow gait and his head bowed, he walked toward us.

"As we agreed, we cannot squander this year on the uncertain prospects of an Israeli passport and a scholarship. Wagering on either option is not possible," your father stated, his tone resolute.

"But I don't want to be a nurse. That's not my path. I'm drawn to engineering," your brother admitted, his tone revealing a mix of frustration and stubborn determination. He stole a glance at your father's eyes, reflecting a deep concern and longing for influence. This was a familiar discussion, a recurring struggle where your father aimed to persuade him to consider the recently opened nursing school.

"Your cousin is set to be a nurse too," your grandmother interjected with a voice as firm as bedrock.

I struggled with this idea, picturing him following his cousin to nursing school like a tail trailing behind a comet. It bothered me, leaving an uncomfortable sense of acceptance. The fear loomed like a shadow—the possibility of my dreams for your education crumbling was a haunting presence that felt like it could break me. Your father appeared conflicted, caught between his personal doubts and the necessity of making sound choices.

With a mustache as grand and wide as an eagle's wings, your father suggested a compromise: "You can sign up for nursing school. It's only two days a week. Use the rest of your time to work until your *laissez-passer* and scholarship are set. We can't afford to waste this year."

He appeared to have convinced himself that this was the best temporary solution, eager to avoid conflict. Drawing strength from an unknown source, I proposed a different approach: What if he went to Egypt to study with his paternal uncle? Your father silently disagreed, turning his head as if to ignore my suggestion. At the same time, your grandmother shot me a sharp, uneasy look, her stare intense like that of a falcon.

"His uncle has no time or money and can't take care of him," she retorted. Her reaction was expected; she always had an excuse ready.

---

As August drew to a close, I began to contemplate whether one of my brothers might offer guidance to your brother. In Israel, Saturday is a holiday for workers. This break also started to influence our own lives, tinting our holidays and days off. As Israel's hold on Gaza intensified, Saturdays, along with the brief respite of Friday afternoons, became our weekends. We organized family gatherings, enjoyed beach outings, and even scheduled doctors' visits on these days.

With the joyful company of you and your one-year-old brother, and after making sure your oldest sister would supervise the two older girls, we left home. From our door, we turned right, heading east along the well-worn path I had explored since childhood. A few minutes later, we took a left into the narrow, steep alley. As always, you were full of energy, bouncing around like a squirrel freed from a cage. After a brief walk, we reached your uncle's home, where I gently knocked, pushed the door open, and softly announced our arrival with a quiet "*Ya satter*"–a call to God, letting the inhabitants know we were there.

My brother recognized my voice and greeted us warmly, saying, "*Tfaddali, Ahla W sahla Ya akhti*" (Come in, my sister).

We sat facing one another, with a feast laid out that included steaming tea and *Feteer meshaltet*, a delightful Egyptian cushioned pie made by my sister-in-law. My brother received us with a friendly smile, and we became part of their small gathering.

As he poured the tea, he asked about your brothers and sisters. His innocent inquiry triggered a wave of nausea within me, clearly evident on my face. Noticing this, he took the children to another room. Once we were alone, he questioned what was bothering me. I expressed my worries about your sister and your brother's working conditions, which had kept me awake at night, along with my strong desire for him to pursue engineering. He nodded in agreement without hesitation, promising to take your brother to work and requested him to be ready by four that following Sunday morning.

"We have an engineer from the West Bank. I'll ask him about engineering and how to apply," he promised.

An hour later, I made my excuses, needing to go home to cook for your father. We backtracked to our home. As we emerged from the alley, you darted away like a liberated sparrow, excited to get back home. Meanwhile, your father was outside chatting with others. Inside, the sounds of your grandmother and her friends filled the house, thick with gossip and stories.

"Where have you been?" your grandmother asked, her tone unaccustomed to being left out of the loop.

"I went to visit my brother," I replied simply.

"Why didn't you tell me?" she questioned, her eyes not leaving mine, her demeanor slightly put off.

"I told my husband," I stated, walking to my room.

"Where are you going? Call Nabila. We want her to read our future," she commanded, her voice a rising crescendo.

"I need to prepare dinner for the children. They're hungry and waiting," I replied, my voice heavy with the weight of her expectations. Her demand lingered in my thoughts, and I couldn't shake the feeling of being at her beck and call.

After my excuse was accepted, she requested that your other brother summon Nabila, your uncle's wife, who was known for her skill in reading coffee cups and interpreting omens. The group would drink their coffee and then place the cups upside down for several minutes before Nabila analyzed the resulting patterns to offer insights about the future. Even into their sixties, your grandmother and her sisters maintained this tradition with notable enthusiasm. I observed with interest as they discussed predictions from the *Fattaha*, or fortune teller. References to a snake frequently led to conversations about certain women, since this symbol was commonly understood to denote someone regarded as malicious.

On Sunday, your brother went to collect his *laissez-passer*, but his application was denied by the Israeli authorities. As a result, he could not travel. He chose to enroll in nursing school, following your father's recommendation, and continued to look for other ways to obtain his travel documents. His friends were able to secure their documents. That evening, I made tea and spoke with your brother about future options, encouraging him regarding his studies.

In the days that followed, he focused on finalizing the necessary paperwork for nursing school and attending several classes. During this time, my thoughts were consumed by him. It felt as if his future was intertwined with mine. One day, he came home beaming with a broad smile.

"There is an engineering school in Birzeit. They've set up a new engineering department," he announced, his voice resonating with the excitement of a long-sought discovery.

A wave of breathless joy washed over me. My thoughts formed a straight beam of light, illuminating the possibilities of his dreams being realized.

"When will you apply?" I inquired, my voice mirroring the hope within me.

"We will head to the West Bank tomorrow and return in the evening," your father responded, concluding the day with happiness.

In the '70s and '80s, taxis were readily available from the center of Gaza to anywhere in Palestine. Ramallah was only a two-and-a-half-hour ride from Gaza. The following morning, they rose at five. Your brother dressed in his finest clothes, looking like a groom on his wedding day, while your father put on his jacket, meticulously packed his bag of documents, and straightened his proud mustache. Their adventure was about to start.

Love in general is often difficult to understand, and our feelings towards your brother were similarly unclear. Your father and I had different goals for him, much like two separate approaches to the same objective. He hoped your brother would stay in Gaza, become a nurse, work diligently, marry, and start a family. Your grandmother shared this perspective and strongly supported your father's wishes.

My aspirations for him were different; I wanted him to pursue a career as an engineer, and I actively encouraged this path. They went to Birzeit, leaving behind a household with certain expectations. In the evening, I checked the time, aware of their absence. I found it hard to relax, pacing around the house and watching the far western end of the street.

As the clock struck five, the father-son duo was still nowhere to be found. Anxiety started to accumulate in my heart like water in a puddle after heavy rain. Your grandmother grasped her stick and approached the doorway. You appeared as a delicate silhouette against the concrete bunk, while I stood as a shadowy figure by the doorway next to the toilet, an uninviting sentinel at the entrance of our home.

"*Elfar Bada Yela'ab fi E'abi*," your grandmother whispered, meaning she was starting to worry.

I held back my words, anxious they might provoke her anger. She left, setting off on a journey to the west. A school, quietly watching, stood on her right, while a landscape of cemetery and trees stretched out to the left. The sky wore an almost surreal blue, and a cool breeze, infused with the aroma of the streets and their emerging life, enveloped us. The fragrant olive trees swaying softly in the wind entranced me, offering a brief escape from my worries.

As night fell, unease marked the faces of your older siblings. Our watch at the house entrance heightened the growing anxiety. In contrast, your other older brother leaned against the wall, looking eastward with one foot on the sturdy mix of brown sand, rocks, and dirt. It wasn't until 1999 that we finally had a proper paved road.

As the clock's hands neared seven, tears started to flow. The cries of your sisters, a sign of our collective fear, echoed around us. A storm of worried questions surrounded us: *Where could they be? What had happened to them? Were they still alive? Had the Israeli army captured them? Were they in prison? Were they victims of an accident?*

Gathering my resolve, I put on my white headscarf and *Dayyer*. I directed your eldest sister to retrieve my ID and prepared myself to step into the unknown. My destination was the *Sekka*, the train station; the transportation center in our town. As I set out on my journey, the sound of crying grew stronger. Your sister held onto my clothes, her tears marking the fabric.

"Watch over your sisters," I told your older sister as I walked through the doorway. Your other older brother's anxious voice echoed after me. When he learned where I was headed, he urged me to come back to the safety of our home, cautioning me about possible dangers from the Israeli military.

As I walked halfway down the street, I encountered our neighbors, Um Ibrahim and her husband. The concern in their eyes was tangible.

"*A'asakum Bekhair?*" *We hope you are fine!* They asked, their words heavy with meaning.

When I admitted that your father and elder brother were still away, the man encouraged his wife to join me. I will always cherish such moments of unspoken solidarity, where neighbors created a rich mutual care, and women stood together like resilient vines, supporting each other in times of need.

As I walked alongside Um Ibrahim, I felt like a puppeteer with severed strings; like a wounded animal moving forward, bleeding but resolute. My thoughts spiralled into an uncontrollable web. *Had they been killed? In prison? Who could I seek for help?*

Upon arriving at the sacred cemetery, we saw your grandmother sitting on a grave, her figure matching the quiet solemnity of the surroundings. She disregarded Um Ibrahim, making her seem as unseen as a ghost, while anger and annoyance built up within her.

"You sought an engineer? You want to be *Um Al-Muhandis*?" she taunted.

I silenced my response, holding back the tears that nearly fell. A wave of despair surged within me, a tiny storm I had to endure alone. At that instant, I craved divine intervention and wished for my husband and son to return. As Um Ibrahim attempted to console me, her eyes sparkled with understanding, and I could see that we were more than just the same age; we were reflections of each other's suffering.

Just as Um Ibrahim and I were about to head to the main square, your father and brother appeared as suddenly as a lightning strike.

"What are you doing here?" your father asked, his gaze shifting among his mother, wife, and neighbor.

I was so stunned I could only stammer a few questions, inquiring about their location and what had happened. Um Ibrahim and your grandmother quietly stood beside us, taking in the tension of the moment.

Your father described the challenges they encountered at the university, including the early gate closure and the registration delay. He noted that your brother was accepted because of his outstanding academic achievements. His words offered a glimmer of hope amidst my overwhelming fears. Pride swelled in me. Even though powerful emotions threatened to reveal my vulnerability, I remained steadfast. It may have been a small victory, but it was a victory regardless.

In the days that followed, a more complex situation emerged as your father struggled with the challenges of funding your brother's education. The next two weeks felt like a harsh test, with every moment feeling like acid slowly eroding our resolve. Your grandmother's taunts rang out constantly, reminding me of my goal to be recognised as *Um Al-Muhandis, the mother of the engineer.* Through all this turmoil, your brother remained resolute, working with your uncle and diligently gathering every bit of savings, much like a squirrel hoarding nuts for a tough winter.

After what felt like an eternity, the beige telephone, with its clunky headset and old-fashioned dial, rang, its nostalgic ringtone shattering the quiet. Your delightful habit of dialling random numbers and engaging in friendly chats often filled our home with laughter, your innocent "Aloooo" perfectly mimicking adult conversations.

As I picked up the receiver, cradling you in one hand and pressing the cool plastic against my ear with the other, a stranger's voice came through asking for your father. A surge of fear pierced my heart, my thoughts racing with the dread of it being the Israeli army or intelligence. However, the subsequent news acted as a soothing balm for my frayed nerves: the university was calling to confirm your brother's official admission.

After the call ended, I found myself engulfed in a whirlwind of emotions. The intense joy clashed with relief, leaving me as breathless as a deep-sea diver coming up for air. I released your hand, pressing my palm against my chest as a surge of happiness flooded through me. While my victory may have been minor, it was still mine.

However, that excitement faded quickly when your grandmother insisted on knowing who had called. I told her a fib, claiming the nurse training center was inquiring about your brother. The more she remained unaware, the less she could criticise endlessly.

I returned to the kitchen with a lighter heart, preparing *Bamiya* and rice for the family. Joy invigorated my senses, and in my excited state, I made you a sandwich filled with Gaza's fiery red chili and offered you a ripe tomato. You've always loved chili, even at one year old.

When your father returned home from work, the atmosphere felt heavy with unspoken words. He ate his meal in silence, sipping tea as if it soothed his concerns. Without a word, he floated out of the house, a figure lost in his reflections.

Your brother returned home later, his clothes marked with the signs of a day's hard work - cement dust and oil stains clinging to him like a warrior's armor. With cautious optimism, I shared the news from the university. His face brightened, determination igniting a strong resolve within him. For him, life was not an abstract concept; it was real and filled with tangible tasks, each serving as a stepping stone toward his dreams. His commitment to funding his education reflected his unwavering spirit.

Your brother, much like you, started working at the age of eight. From an early age, the journey of life came clearly before him, and every struggle instilled in him the resilience to carry on.

When your father returned, a somber smile appeared on his face, his demeanour marked by an unmistakable weight. He performed his *Maghreb* prayers. After the prayers, he called your brother and me over, showing us a small amount of borrowed Jordanian dinars. His voice, heavy with sorrow, painted a vivid picture of how we would manage your brother's upcoming departure and his life at university afterwards.

In the haunting stillness of dawn, your father grappled with the unknown ahead. His concerns poured out while I made his tea and breakfast after his *Fajr* prayers. The weight of supporting our expanding family hung heavily on him. I gave minimal solace, murmuring "*Allah B Yorzoug*" and beseeching divine assistance. I concealed my sorrow, with tears quietly saturating the fried potato in my grasp.

Lost in his thoughts, your father proposed selling a piece of land to fund a small shop. "He also has been working hard and saving money! He can work too, and we give a hand", your father replied. This came as a surprise, yet I swiftly expressed my support, offering to run the shop while he was away. His first reluctance, influenced by societal expectations, was countered by my unwavering resolve. In the end, he consented, finding encouragement in my determination.

A week later, when the taxi arrived at our house, I felt a surge of emotions. I observed your brother, a part of my heart, getting ready to depart. I couldn't tell whether my tears were due to happiness for his future or sadness over his leaving. Thoughts swirled in my head, surrounding his new life away from us.

That evening, your father came back, a shadow of his former self, exhausted from the emotional upheaval. His eyes, reddened and weary, reflected my own sorrow. His fatherly instincts drove him to want to bring your brother back, yet his heart struggled with the painful truth of having to let go.

Two weeks later, I began selling in the shop. I decided to face the challenges to help support our family's survival. While many women found solace in their homes, I remained steadfast, absorbing the harsh sunlight and overseeing our watermelon stock while your father sourced more produce. Sweat trickled into my eyes, bending the light, causing the world to feel like it was exploding around me for that fleeting moment. Still, I welcomed it, as every drop of sweat represented my resilience.

# "Istambul" 1995
## The Son

The first time I noticed him, I was just five years old. He seemed like a wizened figure, navigating through life as if he were orchestrating a slow, careful symphony with his movements. His legs appeared to be part of a continuous experiment in walking, creating a gentle, choreographed ballet. These unhurried walking marathons were a daily ritual, unaffected by the winter's chill or spring's warmth, always beneath the friendly gaze of the sun.

Abu Ameen was a puzzle, a living artifact from another era, and the age gap between us exceeded seventy years. He entertained us with stories of past empires, filled with memories of the Mecca train, the lively bazaars of Damascus, and his preference for calling the city "Istambul" rather than "Istanbul."

My youthful gaze persistently followed him, like a camera lens searching for meaning in the slow, rhythmic pattern of his walks. He would set out, then return, taking a moment to soak up the sun, lifting his hands and shielding his eyes as if trying to see the distant horizon, forever chasing the sun. His presence was formidable, and his frame was both wiry and robust. His eyes were strikingly green. After each walking marathon, he'd sink into a small chair without armrests, gripping a weathered brown stick that he would wield playfully to frighten his grandchildren. Then, without fail, he'd reach for his cigarette box.

He referred to his unique cigarettes as "Arabic cigarettes," resembling crumpled green leaves and emitting a peculiar, lingering aroma. Yet, appearances can be misleading; these were a powerful concoction, a true test of strength. It was believed that only the toughest of men could resist their intoxicating charm.

As his cigarette extinguished and lost its vibrant glow, he would pull a lighter from his pocket, flick it on with a graceful movement, and place it back. A sip of tea would follow, providing a brief pause in his routine. I counted, and he repeated this elaborate ritual over 30 times in just an hour. At the young age of eight, I found myself captivated by this odd behavior. However, the most peculiar aspect of these cigarettes wasn't their look or strength, but their surprising result. It was widely acknowledged that indulging in these Arabic cigarettes would lead to an orchestra of loud flatulence, much to the delight of those around him.

Abu Ameen was a storyteller, weaving enchanting tales that far surpassed the drudgery of daily life. His youth resembled a tapestry of bold adventures, highlighted by legendary chicken-culling escapades that became family lore. However, the most enthralling of all was his whimsical trip to the mythical city of "Istambul," as he would describe it, filled with vivid imagery and fanciful meetings with exotic characters.

In his stories, Abu Ameen embodied more than just an elderly relative; he represented a living time capsule, rich with history and whimsy. His relationship with my father was characterized by recurring conflicts. At times, they would engage in conversation, but at other moments found they were avoiding each other entirely. I vividly remember a summer day when, as a teenager, I stood next to my father while Abu Ameen cast a piercing gaze his way. He donned a *Galabiya* in faded gray adorned with brown stripes, rolled up at the waist, along with a pair of tattered, white pants. Clutched in his hand was a timeworn walking stick.

As the late afternoon breeze started to rustle, my father asked Abu Ameen to join us for tea. The elderly man appeared surprised, his face reflecting uncertainty. After what seemed like forever, he gradually made his way over. For reasons I couldn't explain, a wave of happiness washed over me. Eager to serve him tea, I stepped forward, yet he stayed quiet, a mysterious figure of old age.

Seated between Abu Ameen and my father, I sensed his intense gaze. Eventually, he broke the quiet, asking, "Who are you?"

I responded, "I am Ayk."

His expression tightened, and he sat up straighter to scrutinize me. "You are my grandfather," he asserted. I was aware that I had been named after my great-grandfather. He continued, "The Ottomans killed him. They executed him." His words faded, and we remained silent for what felt like an eternity.

Then, suddenly, he exclaimed, "Ah! Your father named you after him. Why did he rebel against the Ottomans?" Once more, he lapsed into silence, ensnared in his thoughts.

"When states clash, necks are lost," he eventually remarked mysteriously.

I was puzzled by his words. In an effort to comprehend, I asked if he recalled the Ottomans.

Abu Ameen fixed me with a piercing, nearly accusatory gaze. He then looked to the east, lifted his cigarette to his lips, and released a cloud of smoke that merged with the delicate wisps in the blue sky.

"I remember the Ottomans," he said. "I recall when men would cut their fingers to avoid being conscripted to fight alongside the Ottomans against the English." With that, he silently rose from his seat and left, leaving me with a sense of mystery and a desire to uncover the stories and secrets concealed within Abu Ameen's enigmatic history.

On a rainy November day, the persistent downpour drove Abu Ameen back to the safety of his home. The streets had turned into streams of water, making his once-pleasant stroll uncomfortable.

His *Galabiya*, the traditional robe he wore, soaked up the rain, its ends becoming wet as he fought to light his cigarette. With every drop that hit the matchstick, his patience dwindled, prompting him to rush inside his modest home, silently passing those huddled together, seeking shelter from the stormy weather.

That day, my father shared Abu Ameen's story—a narrative rooted in the turbulent history of Gaza. This was during a time when the British Empire had seized control of the city following a year of unyielding battles and three fierce assaults. At just 18 years old, Abu Ameen was caught in the British's interrogation net, like many other men throughout Gaza.

In March 1917, the British military made its first attempt to capture Gaza by utilizing air power and gathering more than 31,000 troops. Nonetheless, despite their significant firepower, they were unable to take the city. At that time, Abu Ameen was far from Gaza; he had escaped Northern Palestine and was making his way back to his home in Gaza. Many people outside the city assumed Gaza had succumbed—yet, to their surprise, it remained unconquered.

When Abu Ameen returned home to *Sheja'iyya*, he chose to stay inside during the second battle of Gaza. The British faced catastrophic losses in this battle, with almost half of their troops defeated and their cutting-edge armored vehicles, which had once been the pride of their military industries, left in shambles. This significant defeat sent shockwaves to London, where newspapers confidently proclaimed, *"We are being defeated in Gaza."*

But come November, Abu Ameen emerged among the local youth. He played a crucial role in defending Gaza during the onset of the third battle. The British Empire's army unleashed a horrific arsenal, including chemical weapons, wreaking havoc from the skies and the ground, reducing the city to ruins and extinguishing thousands of lives in the process.

After the conflict, Abu Ameen was at the mercy of British soldiers, held captive for several harrowing months, enduring unimaginable suffering. When he was finally released, the scars he bore were deeper than just physical, as his mental stability had been profoundly affected. He started exhibiting strange, disturbing behaviors that went against the expectations of adulthood.

One peculiar day, he wandered to *Hakoura*, a small area of the land where his mother kept her precious chickens and lamps. There, a strange spectacle unfolded. Abu Ameen gathered the hapless chickens and strung them up on a clothesline, their frail bodies swaying in the breeze. He watched them with a burst of eerie, haunting laughter as they gasped for their final breaths. When his mother confronted him, her anger rising like a tempest, he explained, "They are happy."

Later, in a somber conversation with his brother, Abu Ameen revealed a chilling truth that sent shivers down the spine. He recounted witnessing British soldiers committing horrific acts, hanging Palestinian men in full view of all prisoners. It was a horrifying ritual that occurred several times, etching itself into the collective memory of those who bore witness. Abu Ameen, a reluctant participant in these macabre affairs, was forced to bear the grim task of carrying their lifeless bodies and burying them.

As my father recounted this haunting story, his expression changed, his face marked by age, tension, and seriousness. Listening to this chilling narrative, I experienced a storm of emotions, confronted by the burden of eighty years of history. It is a vivid reminder that humans, much like clay molded by the relentless forces of hardship, carry the lasting imprints of their struggles.

# THE OLIVE TREE, GAZA 1990
## THE SON

In the *Hakoura*, there was an olive tree, which had a unique charm for me. My siblings affectionately called me "the monkey" because I was unable to resist climbing its twisted branches. Repeatedly, I would sit on one of its strong limbs. I envisioned creating a little house among the branches—a dream that, though unfulfilled, always stayed in the back of my mind.

Nonetheless, a shadow hung over our *Hakoura*, constantly reminding us that it wasn't genuinely ours. Whispers drifted in the air, telling of ownership belonging to the *Al-Arishya*, residents of Arish in Sinai. As I matured, my father revealed the complete narrative; *Hakoura*, along with another section claimed by our relatives, belonged to his cousins who had been compelled to flee to Sinai in 1948. Israel prevented their return to their ancestral lands in Gaza when 1967 came, as they had no IDs to verify their Palestinian heritage.

Over time, *Hakoura* became my personal playground. It was a place for carefree days of play, where I sowed seeds of imagination that flourished alongside the crops, and where I raised sheep each year for *Eid Al-Adha*. Although it also served as a makeshift laundry drying area, its true importance was its closeness to the expansive fields beyond. The young people in our neighborhood utilized it as a hidden passageway, allowing them to escape the vigilant gaze of Israeli soldiers.

One Friday morning, I woke to my father at home—a rare sight, given his usual work routine. The sun rose, casting a golden glow over everything.

He sat on a small wooden chair without arms, basking in the warm sunlight, his white *Gahalbiya* billowing softly. My father was a man who found fulfilment in hard work, and when he remained idle, he became restless, as if life itself had lost its rhythm. I thought it was Friday, but even on this day of rest, my father would usually take his chair outside to the street, where he would warmly greet passersby, offering them tea, engaging in conversation, or giving advice.

As I rubbed the sleep from my eyes and wandered into the kitchen to make a sandwich, my mother, her voice laced with concern, asked, "Do you think this curfew will last longer?"

My father, lost in the pages of an old newspaper called *Alquds*, remained silent for a while, his thoughts elsewhere. After a brief pause, he replied thoughtfully, "I do not know."

Half an hour later, we heard the sharp calls from the neighboring street. It was our neighbor, Abu Ibrahim, inviting my father to join him for tea. In response, my father offered an invitation to sit in the *Hakoura*. He was not one to visit others' houses; he preferred to host. I trailed closely behind, peeking out beneath his *Galbiya*, eager to see what was happening on the street.

"Hurry," my father urged Abu Ibrahim, his eyes darting anxiously in every direction for any signs of approaching soldiers. Once we were safely inside the *Hakoura*, a *Hassera*, or plastic carpet, was spread beneath the old olive tree while my mother prepared tea.

It didn't take long for me to learn about the reason behind the curfew; it was *Al-Ard* Day, or Land's Day. This significant occasion commemorates the anniversary of protests against Israeli colonialism. In March 1976, Israel violently suppressed these protests, resulting in the deaths of six Palestinians holding Israeli citizenship. These protests were triggered by Israeli laws aimed at seizing and expropriating extensive Arab lands. Palestinian citizens of Israel took to the streets in protest, but their pleas for justice were met with harsh force. Six lives were lost, and hundreds sustained injuries. March 30th has since been permanently engraved in the collective memory of Palestinians, serving as a day to honour the resilient spirit of a community caught between colonization and indigenous resistance.

As time went by, masked fighters appeared, tossing pamphlets into the air and marching through the streets with intense resolve. Unable to hold back, I rushed out the door, my feet pounding against the ground. I ignored my father and his guest. I snuck away until I found myself among the masked individuals who were handing out papers featuring the Palestinian flag. In my eagerness, I grabbed two, each displaying the bright colors of green, red, and black.

As I reentered *Hakoura*, I encountered an unexpected twist of events. My father, after looking at the posters, took a lighter from Abu Ibrahim and set them ablaze, the flames consuming the rebellious symbols of Palestinian identity. Only later did I grasp the seriousness of his actions; if the Israeli authorities had found those posters with him, he likely would have faced years in prison.

Israel often imposed curfews in the early morning hours, a dreaded proclamation that shattered the tranquility of dawn. I remember numerous instances when I was jolted awake at the dreadful hour of 4 a.m. by the resonating calls of Israeli jeeps announcing the terrifying "Curfew." In my youthful mind, I grappled with conflicting emotions; while part of me relished the prospect of being excused from school, another part trembled with fear, understanding that soldiers were violating the sanctity of our home.

# Between Sport and Politics, Gaza 1990s
## The Son

E ven during dark times, there were always bright days when our community united, pushing away the looming shadows. As a child, I eagerly awaited *Eid Al-Adha*, not merely for the thrill of receiving sheep, lanterns, gifts, or money. My heart truly soared with another expectation—the much-anticipated basketball championship among the *Fatah* activists in Gaza.

Hiteen school became a lively center for three days, attracting activists from throughout Gaza. The air was filled with the scent of food vendors. Hundreds of lively youths and children gathered, their excitement evident. The school yard was animated with older men chatting and sipping tea, shouting and joyful kids, highlighted by a stall selling Palestine flags and hats featuring the flag.

The school was founded as a primary institution in the late 1940s, took its name from the historic Battle of Hattin. However, during the memorable days of the basketball championship, it transformed from a mere educational establishment into a place for the community.

The Battle of *Hattin* stands as a pivotal moment in Islamic history, occurring on Friday, July 15, 1187. This confrontation was between Salah ad-Din al-Ayyubi (Saladin), the Muslim leader, and the Crusader forces led by Raymond III, the King of Tiberias. I've often pondered whether the name of the school is just a coincidence; some theories propose that the region's inhabitants were originally Salah ad-Din fighters and warriors who stayed in Palestine.

The battle ended with Saladin's victory, paving the way for liberating Jerusalem from the Crusaders. Following the Battle of Hattin, hostilities persisted between Crusaders and Muslims throughout the area. *Hiteen* occupies a significant place in the hearts of those who were raised in Eastern Gaza. Until the late 1970s, it was the only school in the area, welcoming nearly every child from East Gaza. During my years there, the school featured a vast backyard, where we discovered agriculture—learning to plant and harvest as curious children. It became the most cherished hour of my week.

The expansive, shaded roofs provided shelter to classrooms, each filled with dozens of pupils. I spent my initial two years in the school's older classrooms located on the northern side. Hiteen also boasted a spacious front field, serving as a playground where local youth gathered after school for energetic football matches. This was a setting where friendships blossomed and connections strengthened under the sun's warm glow.

While many gravitated toward football, I was captivated by basketball's possibilities. Unlike football, whose rules I learned quickly, basketball intrigued me but proved harder to grasp. Hiteen School served as the backdrop for my unique path.

I also noticed a clear divide in the world of sports. Football seemed to be more of a social activity preferred by those sympathetic to Hamas. This might explain my lack of interest, as they tended to stick to themselves, mainly mingling within mosque circles. Conversely, others were more connected to clubs that emphasised our ties to Palestine.

Basketball typically drew individuals associated with Fatah, leftist groups, and Communists, but these games happened less frequently than football matches, which took place every day. I never felt fully accepted by either group—the football teams tended to form around members from particular mosques, while basketball squads, although somewhat more varied, still split along regional or political lines. At that point, I was unaware of the level of this division. Yet, as I matured, I began to realize that there were more significant divisions among Palestinians than I initially thought.

On a particular sunny spring day, two matches were set, one for basketball and the other for football. The football players wore white shirts and green hats, without any Palestinian flags. In contrast, the basketball teams and their supporters showcased black and white caps featuring the Palestinian flag or the *Fatah* symbol. As an innocent child, I was drawn to the football stands and tried to grab a green cap, only to be reprimanded by a bearded man, our neighbor, who often visited the nearby mosque.

I swiftly informed my father, expecting a negative reaction. To my surprise, he calmly approached the stands adorned with caps featuring the Palestinian flag and the Communist symbol, asking for one for me. My excitement soared as I received a cap, although it was too big for my small head. I dashed around, waving it proudly and frequently checking the Palestinian flag.

Looking back, I recognized the importance of symbols in our society.

The basketball matches served as a venue to observe the variety of political parties and activists who united in their chants for Palestine while fiercely competing for the basketball championship. It was here that I discovered the role of sports in nurturing nationalistic feelings and building strong social unity.

Over time, these community-organized events faded as many activists transitioned into positions within the Palestinian Authority's security forces. It became evident that to undermine grassroots community activities that benefitted the people, the most effective approach was to institutionalize and formalize them or to offer activists paid roles, which distanced them from the community.

# Um Nafez and Hebrew, Gaza 1990s
## The Son

U m Nafez was regarded as an influential figure whose stature had only been strengthened by the passage of time. Her appearance remains unchanged—her commanding presence and steadfast features were readily apparent. Known by a name predating her own, she was recognized within the community as the "mother of the wanted fighters," a title that carried considerable significance.

Her actions were deliberate, each movement indicative of her life experiences, as she proceeded through the streets with purpose. Clad in a black dress and a meticulously clean white head covering that extended to her waist, she presented a distinguished appearance within the community and was consistently met with respect.

My first meeting with Um Nafez remains memorable. She arrived on a donkey-drawn cart, as was customary. Upon reaching our home, where my father and other men were present, she greeted them before securing the donkey and joining the gathering. Unfolding a simple grey sheet, she exposed a supply of Armenian cucumbers. With a welcoming gesture, she offered the produce to those present, balancing her authoritative demeanor with hospitality. The exchange was marked by mutual appreciation and cordiality.

In the following years, I understood the source of her esteemed reputation. Her family's sacrifice was woven into the fabric of her identity—two brothers killed at the hands of the Israeli army; two sons branded as wanted men for their resistance against the Israeli occupation, and a third languishing behind bars.

She manoeuvred through the challenges of life in Palestine with poise and resolve, embodying the strength we all carry within, poised to be unleashed in the quest for justice and freedom. Laughter filled the street as Um Nafez infused her conversation with Hebrew phrases. Her captivating smile and strong voice, touched by a hint of defiance, mesmerised us all. I sat next to my father, and one of her sons (who was murdered by Israel in 2021), as he asked her about her Hebrew language skills. She answered his question with a blend of amusement and defiance.

"How would you address the Israeli soldiers?" he asked, a mischievous glint in his eyes.

Her laughter rang out before she replied, "*Beit Holem, Beit Holem,*" repeating the Hebrew word for "hospital" with a playful sparkle in her eyes. She then effortlessly listed more words, each symbolising resistance and strength.

As her words remained in my mind, I observed her actions during the first *Intifada*, a period marked by Israeli curfews that restricted movement in our community. Um Nafez did not remain indoors during this time; she found ways to navigate the environment with determination. She chose to learn some Hebrew, which served a practical purpose in overcoming language barriers. The words she used became a notable part of my daily experience as I walked to school.

One incident that stands out in the community's history occurred during a Friday market in *Sheja'iyya* while Yasser Arafat was at the mosque for prayers. During this time, Um Nafez publicly displayed her disagreement by waving her shoes, an act recognized as a symbol of dissent toward the leadership. This event highlighted a form of resistance and illustrated how expressions of dissent can take various forms within the community.

At eleven, I entered upper intermediary school, traveling two kilometers east each morning with classmates after leaving home at 6:30. Early in the semester, a new instructor joined our faculty, introducing an unfamiliar language into our daily routine. He communicated with us in Hebrew, eliciting initial reactions of surprise and amusement.

Greeting us with *"Shalom,"* she initiated our first lesson in Hebrew. She then guided us to say *"Ani Katan,"* meaning "I am a child." At the time, Hebrew felt unfamiliar and carried connotations of authority and historical conflict, representing both a means of education and reminders of military encounters.

Hebrew instruction was briefly incorporated into our curriculum, providing us with exposure to the language spoken by those perceived as adversaries. Yet, this initiative was soon withdrawn, and the subject was removed from our studies by the Palestinian authorities. Despite ongoing political discourse and calls for resistance, there remained a prevailing belief in the strategic value of understanding the language of the opposition within the context of the liberation movement.

During this period, figures such as Um Nafez and my Hebrew teacher made a significant impact on me. They served as vital connections to a language both foreign and somewhat familiar, revealing its complexities and nuances. My Hebrew teacher eventually transitioned to a role as a sports coach, while Um Nafez's resolve seemed only to intensify following personal tragedy attributed to Israeli actions.

# Between Games and Vision, Gaza 1990s
## The Son

Throughout my childhood, I often found myself alone in a quiet house, my footsteps the only sounds in the silence. Contrary to common perceptions of large families fostering close relationships and shared experiences among siblings, my reality was marked by significant age gaps that led to generational divides and limited interaction.

My inclusion in my siblings' activities typically occurred out of necessity rather than genuine invitation, leaving me feeling peripheral. While such moments brought fleeting enjoyment, this sentiment rarely lasted, resulting in my withdrawal or observant participation from a distance.

Our play evolved with the seasons, adapting spontaneously to changes much like deciduous trees. Winter gatherings included games such as *Khemir Al-Ajin*, engendering laughter and lively engagement within the household. These activities fostered a sense of cohesion among us despite underlying individual differences.

Nevertheless, parental guidance and household expectations inevitably curtailed our play, with regular prompts to maintain order and decorum. Information and news in Gaza, particularly among women, traversed households rapidly, underlining the immediacy of communal awareness.

My mother regulated my access to sibling interactions, generally permitting participation only during special occasions or when her attention was diverted. One notable memory involves my grandmother's funeral, when I joined relatives in playing *Homes and Homes*.

The olive tree served as the central setting for these imaginative endeavors, symbolizing the continuity of familial stories that have endured over time. Such memories, though sometimes tinged with discomfort, evoke nostalgia and highlight the enduring influence of formative experiences. On occasion, I observed younger relatives recreating similar games, underscoring the lasting impact of tradition.

Games once thought unique to our community—such as *Hide and Seek* and *Get Together*—were later recognized as universal. My preferred hiding spots, including closets and under beds, were constrained by practical limitations and parental intervention.

My mother generally discouraged hosting non-family children in our home, though exceptions occasionally occurred, allowing for memorable group play experiences. These rare events stood out as highlights in an otherwise solitary routine, prompting reflection on what constitutes typical childhood activities.

Attempts to construct makeshift play spaces inside the house met with mixed reactions from my mother, ranging from amusement to irritation. Her comments often hinted at potential career paths, weaving encouragement into daily interactions.

Evening routines involved the preparation of traditional mattresses known as *Tanjid*, reflecting a link to the past and the gradual introduction of modern alternatives. This process cultivated a desire for involvement and underscored the physical challenges faced in early domestic tasks.

Toys, emblematic of childhood, were notably absent from my personal experience. Although I participated in the sale of toys during Ramadan, ownership eluded me. Requests for toys were typically dismissed due to concerns about durability and finances, contributing to a growing sense of detachment from childhood pursuits.

The birth of my nephew marked a shift, as he received numerous toys that seemed inaccessible to me. This disparity highlighted broader socio-economic constraints impacting family life in Gaza and shaped my understanding of privilege and deprivation.

Over time, these cumulative experiences fostered an internal struggle characterized by feelings of loss and unrealized potential. Ultimately, the pursuit of providing for a large family came at the expense of certain aspects of childhood, shaping both identity and perspective in enduring ways.

# Gaza Toys, Gaza 1993
## The Son

At eight years old, I developed an interest in constructing toys, inspired by observing other children with commercially produced plastic trucks and bulldozers. Due to limited resources, I employed alternative materials—notably Coca-Cola cans—to pursue this passion.

One June afternoon, seeking respite from the heat, I watched workers at a construction site operate a semi-manual lifting machine linked to a concrete mixer—an activity that further motivated my creative process. With Coca-Cola cans at hand, I began assembling a miniature version of the machine, manipulating the metal lids until they were open, and proceeded to source a sturdy rope.

Recalling the ropes sold for kite flying, I acquired both rope and metal wire, carefully boring holes into the cans and threading them together. This process fostered innovation and personal fulfillment.

Upon being questioned by a neighbor regarding my activities, I explained my interest in collecting Coca-Cola cans. I sought help from my older sister, but her engagement was brief; she expressed disinterest and discarded the materials after an accidental injury. Undeterred, I requested assistance from my mother, who demonstrated considerable dexterity in handling the rope. Despite also attending to my younger sister, she facilitated the completion of my toy.

Testing the apparatus by turning its handle, I observed the mechanism function effectively, providing a sense of accomplishment. The experience underscored the practical value of perseverance and iterative creativity.

I became aware of some European wedding traditions involving the attachment of cans to vehicles—a custom that reminded me of the resilience inherent in diverse cultures and my own formative experiences.

My parents generally discouraged outdoor play, citing potential risks. Following a single attempt at soccer and subsequent parental admonishment, I refrained from the sport until adulthood. Throughout childhood, my self-made toys offered moments of enjoyment despite prevailing limitations.

# Part Four
# Becoming

# CLEANER, GAZA 2000S
## THE SON

At fifteen, I spent my summers on construction sites, my hands calloused and coated with dust from bricks and cement. From an early age, work defined my life. In our small shop, routines became a repetitive cycle of labor; it was all I knew, until August of 2000, when everything shifted dramatically.

My father was a pragmatic individual who valued hard work. "Find a job, even when you're young," he would advise, his tone reflecting his extensive experience. "It's your safety net for the future. You can begin at the bottom with modest pay and a basic role, then progress from there." He embodied his own beliefs; starting as a lowly clerk, he ascended to the position of general director of a government agency.

One afternoon in late August, my father informed me that I would be employed at the Municipality of Gaza. He stated that I would work as a cleaner but clarified that my responsibilities would not include collecting garbage from the streets; instead, I would remain at the office to maintain the surrounding gardens. At the time, I was still a teenager without an ID card, which would take over a month to acquire. My father viewed this position as a practical entry point into the workforce, offering an initial opportunity for independence and potential career development.

As Tuesday morning dawned, a gentle breeze wafted in from the west, bringing with it the scent of the sea. I awoke at seven, quickly dressed, and set out. My feet moved with unusual haste, driven by an insatiable curiosity. My mind raced with questions: *How can I be a cleaner? What if my classmates see me? Why not join the army?* Each query flowed into the next, unanswered, until I reached the beginning of the sloping road toward *Al-Zahra* School.

To my right loomed a remnant of the past—the Ottoman-era *Sabil*, a public water fountain that had remained dry and silent for almost a century. I'd always found it intriguing, a testament to a bygone era, but today I could only steal a brief look. My destination was beckoning. Turning left, I encountered a parking lot filled with yellow and orange cars poised to transport people to the southern cities of Gaza. I recalled my father's tales of this spot; it had once served as a police station, first under the British, then the Egyptians, and eventually during the Israeli occupation.

As I walked on, I recalled my father's story of a feared man from *Sheja'iyya* who terrorized a woman until she sought help from the Egyptian police in Gaza. They subdued him in public and cut off his mustache as a symbol of his downfall—a lasting reminder of justice served that I remembered each time I passed that spot.

At last, I arrived at the municipal office. There was Abu Raed, head of the environment department, surrounded by a group of cleaners—men we referred to as *Zabbal*, responsible for collecting the city's refuse. Approaching him, I felt small and out of place.

"I am Ayk," I introduced myself, my voice wavering between nerves and determination. "My father sent me to you." Without a word, he motioned me toward the office, and I stepped inside, bracing myself for what would occur next.

# GAZA 1994
## THE SON

On a humid Friday in Gaza, the city seemed to exhale its heat, prompting a mass exodus to the sea for relief. My brother-in-law arrived with a tent tied to the roof of his car and a cigarette perched between his fingers, his familiar grin lighting up his face.

"*Yalla*, let's go to the sea today," he exclaimed, his eyes sparkling with excitement.

He worked as a construction specialist in Israel. Once a brilliant student, circumstances forced him into labor due to the lack of universities nearby. After two years of diligent work in Israel, he married my sister, who had recently completed high school.

His daily life revolved around his job; he would wake up at three in the morning to take the bus, spend long hours on construction sites, and navigate through Israeli military checkpoints to return home around five. Israel's work schedule dictated his days off, giving him half of Friday and Saturday as his only breaks. This was a common fate among many in his generation, who were often relegated to being inexpensive labor for Israel. Yet, in the summer, these days off took on a special significance—a precious, fleeting escape to the sea.

At times, we travelled as a family, packing the car with watermelons and kebab skewers. Other times, my father would take us for a few hours in the afternoon. This Friday was different. For the first time, we were going to the beach without the sight of Israeli jeeps blocking the road or patrolling the coastal street. It felt like freedom, but in reality, it wasn't.

As the Peugeot cruised down *Al-Wehda* Street, we passed *Al-Shifa* Hospital, and I couldn't help but notice how strangely empty the streets were. A lone Palestinian army jeep was parked near the *Al-Yarmouk* football field. I leaned out the window, waving with a big smile as the wind whipped against my cheeks. My sister kept urging me to bring my head inside the car, but I enjoyed defying her, savoring the rush of air against my face.

We turned right onto *Omar Al-Mukhtar* Street, and as we neared the *Al-Kenz* crossing, the car started to slow down. Ahead of us, a crowd had formed, with people shouting and cars moving slowly. There was quite a scene.

In the midst of it, I spotted a young man, tall with striking red hair, running west toward the sea, brandishing a gun while others attempted to restrain him. He resembled a character straight out of an action movie, like "Rambo." I had never seen someone wielding a gun acting so casually, mingling with people as if it were perfectly normal.

"*Tousha! Tousha!*" people shouted—signifying a dispute. However, this was no ordinary disagreement. I had never seen a gun in the hands of someone from our side before.

As we followed the road, the car came to a stop, joining a line of over a dozen vehicles. "A checkpoint," my brother-in-law murmured.

I leaned in closer, trying to see. Men in civilian attire, armed with machine guns, stood in the middle of the road. They looked young— probably in their mid-twenties—and there was a woman among them, a cigarette casually held between her fingers and a rifle slung across her back. Their speech mirrored ours, yet their accents were softer and different.

"Who are they?" I whispered, feeling confused. "Why are they manning a checkpoint? Did the Israelis change into civilian clothing?"

When it was finally our turn, one of the men leaned into the car, laughed, and said, "*Emshi*"—Go.

"They're Palestinian," someone mentioned, almost like they were assuring themselves.

I later discovered that they were the sons and daughters of *Al-Sumoud*. These were children who had lost their parents in Beirut and Tunis during the 1980s and early 1990s. Many of them were brought to Gaza to live in hotels, afforded privileges, and given high-ranking positions. Their first action for a few of them was to establish checkpoints, imitating the Israeli soldiers they had grown up observing. My father once commented, "They think they're still in Jordan or Beirut," alluding to their behavior and display of power—a characteristic he believed had resulted in disastrous outcomes.

As we arrived at the beach and parked near the mosque, I dashed towards the water. I yearned to plunge in, experience the waves and salt, and allow the sea to cleanse the discomfort in my chest. However, my thoughts continually returned to those armed men. They belonged to our group, yet in that moment, they seemed like Israeli soldiers.

On that day, the sea failed to evoke its usual joy. It seemed heavy, weighed down by the awareness that our supposed freedom was merely an illusion. What began poorly was destined to conclude poorly. The Palestinian Liberation Organization had strayed from its path, transforming what once felt like a hopeful journey into one leading to despair.

# Yasser Arafat, Gaza 1994
## The Son

Yasser Arafat, the figure I admired, was a prominent presence in my childhood fantasies. Meeting him was more than just a dream; it became an obsession. I would spend countless hours writing letters that never reached him, expressing my feelings in words that floated like prayers in the breeze. I repeatedly painted his image on the walls of our home, capturing his iconic black-and-white *Kuffiya*. However, my parents were not as supportive of my artistic endeavors.

One day, after coming across yet another Arafat mural, my mother finally snapped. "*Inshallah*, Arafat, go to hell. Stop painting this Arafat nonsense!"

After Arafat returned to Gaza post-Oslo Accord, the city felt transformed and hopeful. I often told classmates that my father, who paid security forces as part of his financial job, worked with Arafat—even though this was only partly true. Clinging to the story, I insisted I would soon meet Abu Ammar himself, filled with childhood confidence.

In the summer of 1994, I accompanied my father to his office during my school vacation. This marked my initial visit following the departure of the Israeli forces, and I observed notable changes in the environment. The absence of Israeli soldiers and their previously prominent presence was evident. In their place, Palestinian soldiers were stationed, appearing at ease as they sat beneath trees and drank tea. This shift provided an early perspective on conditions associated with increased autonomy, though its full implications were not immediately apparent to me.

A towering tree stood outside my father's office, its branches reaching skyward like an ancient sentinel. I found solace beneath its canopy, playing with the leaves and earth. My affection for large trees was profound; they made me feel grounded and connected, as if they embodied my childhood essence. I had once heard that humans were formed from mud, a notion that intrigued me. I would spend hours manipulating mud and water in my hands, mesmerized by the act, although I never sought to sculpt a human figure. Even as a child, I recognized that creation was a power beyond my grasp.

As I paced between the tree and my father's office, I caught snippets of his phone conversation, but something felt off. His tone—his dialect—had shifted. No longer was he speaking in the rough, familiar cadence of Gaza. Instead, his words flowed softer and more refined, reminiscent of people I'd seen on television. I watched him, puzzled, questioning what had transformed him. Then I recognized it: he was conversing with Arafat's photographer, who had arranged for us to meet Abu Ammar the following day. My heart raced. Yet, amid my thrill, a lingering question haunted me: Why had my father altered the way he spoke?

Years later, he finally explained it to me. The individuals who returned with Arafat from Beirut and Tunis in 1994, known as the "*A'adeen*," occupied significant roles in the new Palestinian Authority. Their distinct dialect set them apart as both outsiders and influential figures. My father was able to fit in by imitating their speech, which helped him get his requests fulfilled more easily. This clever tactic was something I admired, and it showed me how language can be instrumental in navigating power dynamics.

The next day, my father smiled widely and said, "Today we will meet Abu Ammar."

I felt like I was floating home, my thoughts racing about the man I had admired for so long. I even sang a song I hardly understood—"PLO, Israel No"—as if the lyrics alone could bring me closer to him.

Once we arrived home, I rushed ahead, bursting through the door to shout, "We're going to see Abu Ammar today!" My sisters squealed in excitement, even though none really wanted to join.

My little brother, both cautious and curious, held onto my father's hand and said, "I want to come too."

That day felt ceremonial. I donned my best attire—a blue T-shirt I had yet to wear, paired with my new school jeans. My sunburned and worn face radiated excitement from playing outside. My father, ever practical, sported his old Soviet-style suit with square pockets, giving him an appearance as if he had emerged from a bygone era. He didn't begin wearing ties until much later, but it was inconsequential. To me, he looked like someone significant.

As we walked through Gaza, I rushed to keep pace with my father. After catching a taxi, we headed west; the distant sea sparkled and reminded me of Paris, which I had seen in magazines and newspapers. Excited, I shouted about the water, making my father smile and my brother grin quietly.

We reached *Al-Muntada*, Arafat's office, beautifully situated by the sea. I had often envisioned that Abu Ammar must cherish the sea; maybe that's why his office was so near it. The salty breeze filled my lungs upon exiting the car, and for a brief moment, I felt like I was on the brink of something extraordinary. We were mere meters away from the man I had longed to meet.

As we waited inside, the hours dragged on, and the excitement that had once kept me going started to fade. I gazed at the sea, yearning to run to the shore and feel the water with my hands. My father also grew increasingly frustrated as time passed. Eventually, after three hours, we decided to leave without meeting Abu Ammar.

However, we captured a few photos to remember a day that was filled with both hope and disappointment.

As we departed, my father gave an envelope to Arafat's photographer—it contained a promotion request. At that time, I didn't grasp its significance, but later I understood that Arafat's governance relied not on merit but on loyalty. He awarded promotions, jobs and money to cultivate allegiances and reinforce his power. While this system functioned for a period, it ultimately left me feeling disillusioned.

That day marked my initial heartbreak with Yasser Arafat, a leader I had elevated to such a height that even he couldn't attain it. It became a lesson I would carry forward: the beliefs we hold with unwavering certainty often led to disappointment. Years later, I would revisit *Al-Muntada* after Arafat's passing and again in 2022. Each visit stirred memories within me, reminding me not only of the hope and excitement but also of the disillusionment that arises when a child's dreams encounter the harsh realities of leadership.

# Contradictions and Brainwashing, Gaza 1995
## The Son

Shortly after Arafat's return to Gaza, everything appeared to shift, though not always in ways I comprehended. Some days, my father brought home newspapers with striking headlines like "Palestinian Police Raid Hamas Office" or "Preventive Security Arrests Suspected Militants." Other days, I encountered encouraging news such as "New Embassy Opens in Gaza" or "Plans for First International Airport Underway." A mix of hope and division surrounded me, leaving me bewildered and seeking clarity.

I would sit with those newspapers, attempting to unravel the contradictions. What did it signify to arrest and silence others who shared the same streets and prayed in the same mosques? My youthful mind struggled to grasp the fault lines emerging within the fabric of our society.

This changed during an orientation for *Fatah* youth activists, where I encountered words that would influence me for the next twenty years—words that sowed division within my spirit.

The speaker was a *Fatah* cadre, authoritative yet at ease, seated on one of those familiar white plastic chairs that came to symbolize 1993. He reclined with one arm over the backrest, a cigarette in his hand, its smoke drifting slowly toward the ceiling. Initially, his voice was steady, but it soon escalated, becoming sharp and commanding, his hand striking the desk for emphasis.

"They want to destroy Palestine and the future of our state," he asserted. By "they," he referred to *Hamas*, casting them as "the other"—an external enemy.

As a teenager, I wasn't scared; I was captivated, eager to absorb every word, and excited to be part of something bigger than myself. When I exited that room, I became more than just a teenager. I emerged as a Fatah member on a mission, ready to fight—even against my own people.

This new identity emerged at school, where I took charge of the *Fatah* Pioneers group. Across the courtyard, the Islamic Bloc represented Hamas's youth wing. During a tense exchange, I turned to Mohamed, my cousin and a compassionate classmate, and blurted out, "One day, I'll have you arrested." Those words hung heavily in the air between us. (He was killed by Israel in 2021)

Mohamed didn't retort. He uttered something faintly, a sound somehow stuck in his throat, before vanishing into the classroom, which felt suddenly like a dense jungle where I couldn't locate him.

Hours later, he spotted me and said just one line: "Righteous people always prevail." His words were soft yet piercing, akin to a light breaking through the darkness. They lingered in my mind, resonating long after the moment had passed.

Years later, I expressed my apologies to Mohamed, yet the guilt remained, a sharp edge in my consciousness. His words resembled water drenched over the toxic weeds within me. They compelled me to face an unpleasant reality: I had been indoctrinated. I wasn't advocating for inclusivity or democracy; I was merely a cog in the machinery of autocracy and division.

Reflecting on the past, I recognize how hate was planted in the receptive ground of my youth, nourished by fear-driven rhetoric and a false sense of purpose. I've learned that, in many respects, we are shaped by our childhood experiences—our beliefs formed by the surroundings we are part of. Nonetheless, we possess the ability to introspect, evolve, and remove the negativity.

The victim, I now understand, remains trapped in a moment frozen in time, completely overwhelmed by suffering. While the oppressors find peace, the victim endures a state of perpetual waiting—an experience that exacerbates anxiety, resurrects pain, and stirs a vivid fear of the worst outcomes. This was a cycle I once perpetuated, but now I am committed to breaking it.

# OUT OF THE PLACE, GAZA 1996
## THE SON

Gaza had transformed into a place that evoked mixed emotions in me, a blend of excitement and discomfort. What I had previously only viewed on TV was now materialising in my own neighborhood. The atmosphere felt different, imbued with both hope and unfamiliarity. One day, my oldest brother arrived home in a brand-new car, which shone brightly in the sunlight, contrasting sharply with the simplicity of our surroundings. He quickly showered and left again by late afternoon for his job at the newly created Ministry of Tourism and Antiquities.

For me, work was represented by what my father did—coming home by three, eating, and relaxing for the evening. But my brother's job was something entirely different—modern and thrilling. I recall gazing at the car, feeling proud that we finally had one, even though it did not belong to us. It displayed a red governmental plate, a symbol of authority that commanded respect. Only those who had accompanied Arafat back from Tunis and Beirut were allowed to drive such vehicles. These individuals held significant influence, nearly untouchable in society.

My brother wasn't a skilled driver. However, that didn't seem to be a concern for anyone. That evening, as he put on fresh clothes and spritzed a new perfume that he had purchased from a newly opened shop named *Al Andalus*, I stood at the door, watching him struggle to start the car. I felt my face flush with embarrassment every time the engine sputtered and stalled. People were observing, their looks sharp and critical. The contrast was glaring—this shiny new car in front of our unassuming home, which hadn't changed much over the years.

I believed my father could have provided us with a better house, but he opted to invest in our education instead. "Education will build you a life," he often insisted. I understood this principle, but couldn't help longing for a bit more at that moment.

The next day, my brother woke up late, took a shower, and got dressed slowly. While enjoying his tea, he told my mother, "We're going to the festivals tonight."

My mother, uninterested, replied, "I'm not into those things. Take your siblings instead."

Just as he was preparing to leave, my eldest sister and her husband entered. "Why are you late for work?" she reprimanded.

My brother dismissed her worry, clarifying, "Last night we kicked off the *Layali Gaza* festival, which lasts for a week. Dance groups from Egypt, Spain, Tunisia, and other nations are participating. You should come along—I can get you in for free."

The thought of the festival consumed me. I had seen it on television—colorful dances, lively music, performers in extravagant costumes. It was hard to believe that such a spectacle was taking place in Gaza, a place I had only known as simple and struggling. That night, I lay in bed, my imagination running wild. How would it feel to see them live? Would they dance in the same way as on television? Would the colors and sounds be as vibrant?

The next morning, I jumped out of bed before sunrise and walked into the kitchen where my mother was preparing tea. "What should I wear to the party?" I asked, my words spilling out before I was fully awake.

Without looking up, she replied, "Wash your face first," in a curt tone. I felt a sting from her words and a wave of defensiveness.

"If you don't want me to go, I'll just go alone!" I said impulsively.

She sighed, appearing half-amused. "Wear whatever you have," she replied, turning her focus back to the stove.

I washed my face at the outdoor tap near the main entrance, taking in the familiar morning sights and sounds of Gaza—a donkey cart passing, women with plastic nets heading to the market in the humid July air. Although routine, that day felt different as I briefly realized Gaza had used reusable bags well before environmental awareness became widespread.

As we prepared to leave, the differences between old and new Gaza became increasingly clear. The city was evolving and cautiously accepting modernity. Expensive cars, name-brand stores, and even bars were emerging, altering the social landscape. A new middle class was forming among individuals employed by the Palestinian Authority or international organizations, earning salaries in dollars. They were humorously called "the green group." This wealth was not distributed equally, revealing the fractures within society.

Finally, my brother called out, "Are you ready?" He, along with my mother, sisters, and brother-in-law, were getting into two cars.

My mother, laughing, refused to ride with my brother, saying, "He'll kill us before we even get there!"

As we headed to the *Rashad Al-Shawa* Cultural Center, the streets became increasingly chaotic. Traffic jams, honking horns, and military personnel attempting to manage the crowd overwhelmed me.

The frustration inside the car was palpable, prompting my brother-in-law to quip, "If they can't plan a street, how will they build a state?"

Upon arrival, the festival's magnificence took my breath away. Hundreds of people swarmed the entrance, the air alive with excitement and impatience. Cars were parked awkwardly, with drivers shouting, but all eyes were focused on the center.

My brother gestured towards a corner and said, "Wait here for me."

My heart raced as I stepped out, eager to witness the magic of *Layali Gaza*. It was more than just a concert; it was a glimpse of Gaza's potential—a vibrant place filled with color, music, and life. For one night, at least, Gaza transformed from a city weighed down by its history into a city that dared to dream.

As we waited for my brother to join us, the area surrounding the cultural center was alive with activity. Hundreds of people were entering the building, some ascending the wide stairs in groups while others made their way alone, their faces bright with infectious smiles. For the first time, I noticed many women without headscarves gathered in one spot. I had seen a few like that during the First *Intifada*, but now it felt more pronounced, almost as if the city had cast off some of its older restraints.

My brother took longer than anticipated to find a parking spot. When he finally showed up, looking a bit flustered and sweating from the July heat, he sighed, "There's no place to park!"

It was the first time I had heard a man discuss parking as if it were a puzzle to solve. For me, a car was simply a car, and any available area was a parking spot. That had always been my perspective. However, as I observed a policeman reprimanding another driver for trying to park in front of the center, a new realization struck me, and the rules surrounding cars and parking spaces took on a deeper significance. My mind was swirling with questions—some familiar, some fresh—and all buzzed louder than ever.

As we ascended the stairs together, we exchanged shy smiles, briefly scanning the faces of other attendees as if trying to decipher their thoughts. A strange tension gripped me, accompanied by an inner shame. I wondered, are festivals like this really meant for people like us? Coming from *Shuja'iyya*, a modest neighborhood, I couldn't shake the feeling that such gatherings were reserved for the "civilized," a term I didn't fully grasp but felt disconnected from. Even now, I'm uncertain of the origin of that belief, yet it loomed over me like a shadow back then.

In front of us, my brother, dressed in a beige suit, reached into his pocket to retrieve the tickets. He carefully counted them one by one as we stood in line. A man at the entrance noticed him.

"Come here," he called out with a friendly smile.

My brother stepped out of line, handed over the tickets, and shared a few words with the man. Moments later, he turned back to us, signalling for us to follow.

"It's alright, Engineer," the man assured my brother. "No need to count. Go ahead."

Inside the hall, I was amazed by the vast crowd. Thousands of individuals filled the space, their chatter forming a low, constant hum that mixed with the gentle breeze of the air conditioning. It was my first experience seeing so many people congregating in one location. The variety in their clothing, the spectrum of their expressions, and the diversity of their styles left me in awe. It felt like entering a scene from television, but this time, I was part of it.

As we searched for seats, it quickly became clear that there were none left. Chaos seemed to reign, yet no one voiced complaints. By seven o'clock, everyone was either seated or standing, eagerly waiting for the concert to commence. A half-hour passed, and still, nothing occurred. The air was thick with anticipation, but no one appeared discontented. Perhaps many were, like me, experiencing this for the first time. There were no expectations to be let down by.

At last, the hall erupted in cheers as the music began. A woman took the stage, adorned in dazzling dance attire, expertly balancing a straw bowl on her head. Her movements were fluid and graceful, accompanied by loud, rhythmic music. Soon, another dancer joined her, then another. It was mesmerizing, though not quite like what I had seen on television. I stood on my chair for a better view, but the woman behind me shushed me, her tone sharp yet gentle. I settled back into my seat, the excitement waning a bit.

Struggling to see the stage clearly, I started watching the audience instead. A woman joyfully clapped along to the music, her face glowing with excitement. A teenage girl giggled, covering her face with her hands as if to conceal her delight. The range of emotions surrounding me proved to be more intriguing than the performance itself. Eventually, I quietly shifted to the side of the hall for a better view of the dancers. While their movements were mesmerizing, I didn't experience the magic I had anticipated. Instead, I turned my attention back to those around me, their reactions enriching my perception of joy and celebration.

After about an hour, a singer took the stage. He was older and donned a traditional Egyptian *jalabiya*. While his voice was powerful, it didn't resonate with me. I couldn't grasp the lyrics and wasn't particularly fond of songs that lacked nationalistic themes or ties to the struggles with which I was familiar. Still, I listened, absorbing an experience far removed from my own world.

As the festival concluded, the crowd flowed from the hall, their faces illuminated with joy. The streets outside buzzed with energy. Police sirens echoed as they accompanied diplomats to Arafat's residence, their convoys speeding along *Omar Al-Mukhtar* Street. The city twinkled under the night sky, as if Gaza were putting on a dazzling display.

That night, while lying in bed, my thoughts raced. I understood that the world was far larger and more intricate than I had perceived in *Shuja'iyya*. Childhood, I mused, resembled a slow, gray canvas with sudden flashes of vivid color marking its most memorable moments. That festival was one of those memorable flashes—a new hue added to my understanding of life, a recognition that the world had far more to offer than I had ever envisioned.

# MASJID AL-HAQ, GAZA 1995
## THE SON

The mosque emerged gradually, brick by brick, like a soft prayer reaching for the heavens. I sat with my father outside our house when I overheard a discussion about it; "*Masjid al-Haq,*" they called it.

I often passed the construction site during errands with my father to buy supplies for our little shop or to pick up milk. The landowner kindly donated the land, and funds were largely gathered from Saudi Arabia to bring the mosque to fruition. At that time, it was a modest building, plain and barely resembling my vision of a mosque.

My family didn't follow Islam in a conventional way. Similar to my brothers, my father never had a beard, even though in the 1980s and 1990s, having one was considered a symbol of faith. Whenever my older brother would grow his facial hair, our father would disapprove and demand he remove it. However, during times of loss, such as when my grandmother passed away, my father would grow his beard in a sign of mourning for just forty days before shaving it off again.

Nevertheless, he was deeply committed to practicing his faith. He fasted during Ramadan, observed the months of *Shaban* and *Rajab*, said his prayers five times a day, and sought to perform numerous good deeds. His simple yet impactful guiding principle was: "Do good and throw it into the sea," conveying the idea of doing good without anticipating rewards in return.

Once *Masjid al-Haq* was completed, a group of young *Salafists*, recently returned from Saudi Arabia, took charge. The mosque, modest in size, was a simple white rectangular structure lacking a dome or minaret, yet equipped with loudspeakers projecting their voices throughout the town. As a child, I found these *Salafists* captivating. They were young men, likely in their twenties, dressed in short white *Jalabiyas* and wearing white scarves on their heads. They walked purposefully, their gazes unwavering, offering a brief yet genuine "*As-salaam alaykum*," as they went by.

One day, while playing outside, one of my neighbors—who was also a classmate—approached me. Sheikh Ahmed, a *Salafist*, called him over and reminded him that the *Dars*—the lesson—was scheduled after *Asr* prayers. My friend invited me to come along, and I was taken aback. I had never visited the mosque without my father before; it felt strange, like entering a world that wasn't mine. Yet, curiosity pulled at me. I rushed to my mother to ask for her permission.

"Why? You can pray at home," she replied. When I clarified that they would be teaching how to read the Quran, she agreed but warned, "Don't be late."

As I entered the mosque, an unfamiliar unease washed over me. My heart raced, sensing my lack of belonging. After the *Asr* prayer, the crowd dispersed, leaving just a small group with us. We formed a circle, and Sheikh Ahmed began by guiding us through Quranic verses. But soon, the focus shifted. He began discussing politics and society, listing items considered *haram*—prohibited. The atmosphere grew tense, and I felt a knot tighten in my chest as I listened. This wasn't why I was there. Nevertheless, I recited during my turn, surprising Sheikh Ahmed.

"You read well. Where did you learn?" he inquired.

"At home," I replied simply. "My father taught me."

After the lesson concluded, which lasted over an hour and a half, Sheikh Ahmed requested that we stay, clean the mosque, and wait for *Maghrib*. However, I had no inclination to stay. I informed him that my father was waiting, and I departed.

Upon returning home, my father looked at me with suspicion. "Where have you been?" he questioned.

"At the mosque," I answered.

His expression turned serious. "Which mosque?"

After a moment of hesitation, I replied honestly, "*Masjid al-Haq*."

His response was immediate and resolute. "You will not go there again," he stated firmly. "This is the first and last time."

Even with Sheikh Ahmed trying to pull me back to learning, I never went back.

Years later, my father clarified his choice; "Religion," he said, "should not be exploited. Those individuals are hazardous. They distort children's thinking with notions that mislead them. If you were older, around 20, I would have allowed you to decide for yourself. But you were merely a child."

Reflecting on the past, I recognize that my father viewed my life not merely in the moment but as part of a larger journey where he aimed to guide and safeguard me. His insight protected me from journeys I wasn't prepared to take. With his calm and consistent approach, he meticulously crafted my life, piece by piece, as though he had orchestrated it for my improvement all along.

# The Policeman, Gaza 1995
## The Son

I sat on the steps, observing the policeman. He had dragged a chair from one of the classrooms and sat there in the stifling heat of late June. A few months had gone by since the Palestinian police and military returned with Arafat, and the Israeli soldiers had withdrawn from Gaza City. The police now donned dark blue uniforms featuring the Palestinian flag. I wasn't fond of the dark blue; I favoured the olive-green military uniforms typically seen in newspapers and magazines worn by Palestinian fighters. That felt more like home to me, more like a symbol of resistance.

"Why do you have this? Is it to fight Israel?" I asked him, embodying a child's innocence as my small fingers reached for the gun next to him. It was long, black, and unfamiliar—nothing like the iconic *Kalashnikov* I had often seen in photos.

Before he could respond, I scrunched my nose and remarked, "This gun is ugly. It looks like the military's gun," referring to the Israeli army.

He smiled, set his tea on the ground, and rested the gun on his lap. "This is an American M16," he explained patiently.

A nearby boy proudly remarked, "My father has one like this."

The policeman barely acknowledged this comment, simply asking if the boy's father worked for the police. The boy nodded in response.

The officer reclined in his chair. "We're supposed to be civil police, not soldiers," he stated, his voice calm yet firm. "But we still need these guns because we're still fighting Israel."

For me, Palestine represented more than just a place; it embodied everything—a goal, a home, a heartbeat. I frequently thought about Haifa and Yaffa—ancient cities that attracted me with an inexplicable gravity, even more so than Jerusalem or Gaza. The stories I had heard, and the narratives of historic Palestine, left me longing for both the past and the future.

The officer completed his shift and left quietly, while I remained on the steps, eagerly looking forward to the next day. Tomorrow would mark the start of the summer camp organized by the Palestinian army. I was going to become a soldier. At 11, I felt prepared.

That night, I went to bed early, eager to sleep in, but woke at six despite it being summer vacation. With no school and no responsibilities, we typically spent our three months of break wandering aimlessly or sometimes accompanying our fathers to work. Our mothers grew irritated with us, their tempers short, and longed for the return of school.

I didn't even wash my face; I rushed outside to see if the street was alive yet. Poking my head out the door, my heart raced at the sight of jeeps and military vehicles parked near the school. Adrenaline surged through me, excitement thrumming in my veins. I dashed back inside, splashing water on my face and frantically searching for my shoes.

In the meantime, my father was getting dressed while my mother worked in the kitchen. "Get my shoes, Ayk!" called my father.

I noticed his brown shoes close by, covered in dust and scratches. I picked them up, splashed some water on them, and settled down with my legs apart, using a rag to scrub the shoes clean.

My father's voice became louder and more impatient as he

fastened his belt. He stepped outside, noticed me diligently polishing his shoes, and smiled. "Good boy, *Wallah*," he remarked, his previous irritation fading away.

Once he was prepared to depart, my mother presented him with a steaming cup of tea. The moment he left, I dashed to the school. I needed to arrive first to sign up for the camp.

At the school, dozens of children, mostly teenagers, lined up obediently, waiting. A tall officer, with a sharp face and dressed in a strict military uniform, barked commands. His authoritative voice resonated through the warm morning air, firm and commanding. I found it appealing.

The twenty minutes I waited felt like an eternity. I overheard the boys in front of me discussing the weapons training. One of them said to his friend, "You're too young. You're ten. You need to be thirteen or older to train with the *Kalashnikov*."

At that moment, I understood that I wouldn't be permitted to learn to use a real weapon. I considered lying about my age, pretending to be thirteen, but I hesitated; I thought that if I died as a *shaheed*, I wouldn't go to heaven if I lied. So, when my turn came, I stood tall and truthfully told the officer, "I'm 11."

He then directed me to a classroom, and as I entered, I saw children from my neighborhood sitting quietly at their desks. Two large soldiers stood at the front, their uniforms pressed and faces stern, although they offered smiles now and then, providing a small sense of reassurance in the tense silence.

More kids flowed in, some donned t-shirts featuring the Palestinian flag, others were barefoot, and a few arrived with their parents. It felt like a festival, akin to a national celebration. One man came with his two sons: one about my age and the other just a year old, cradled in his arms. The baby sported a tiny military uniform and held a toy soldier.

After a short while, a higher-ranking officer entered the room, handed the soldiers a list, and announced, "This company is complete." He then faced us, his voice resonating with pride. "You are Palestine's cubs. The future lions of Palestine."

The soldiers opened large boxes and started giving out yellow caps featuring the Palestinian logo and flag. They also distributed white T-shirts adorned with the same emblems. Excited by the symbolism, I quickly put on the new shirt over the one I was already wearing. In that moment, something changed within me. I was no longer just a kid; I was part of something larger, something significant. My aspiration to become a freedom fighter, like those I had seen on TV from Beirut and beyond, was gradually turning into reality.

# The Speaker, Gaza 1996
## The Son

"You will be the keynote speaker at the graduation parade." —I was just 12 when the camp leader, a major in the national security forces, told me this.

He likely recognized my reading skills, yet I never considered myself a strong speaker. Nonetheless, by reading the news daily and mimicking speeches I'd seen on TV, I had been unknowingly preparing myself for this moment.

We referred to it as a camp, although it wasn't a typical one. We would come in the morning and return home by evening. During my final camp, I spent a significant amount of time in the kitchen, which turned out to be surprisingly enjoyable. I learned from the chef, and as a bonus, I was allowed to take home extra food—bread, fruits, and vegetables. My mother appreciated it. It was during this experience that I first encountered the responsibility of leadership and the burden that accompanied it.

One day, we found ourselves with over twelve bags of pita bread, each bag containing about fifty pieces, along with several boxes of produce. The chef wasn't able to take anything home; while he was compensated, we had never been instructed on how to handle the leftover food. I could have easily taken half or even all of it without anyone noticing. Instead, I enlisted the help of the school guards and cleaners, distributing everything except for two bags of bread and some vegetables, which I had already been taking home regularly. From that moment on, the way people regarded me changed significantly.

When the established figures began showing me more respect than I had extended to him, I experienced the true weight of power for the first time. This was my initial lesson in politics—that respect is purchasable, and leadership can lead to corruption. If something as basic as a loaf of bread could influence people, how much more would money and jobs affect them? That day, I experienced the sorrow of witnessing how effortlessly dignity can be exchanged.

On graduation day, I chose not to join the parade. Instead, I stood by the podium. My father had assisted me in crafting my speech, and while I felt nervous, I was not afraid. As guests arrived—generals, community leaders, and the public—I paced back and forth. They took their seats, waiting for the ceremony to start. The sun was low in the sky, casting light on some faces as it moved eastward. Even though it was July, the weather remained delightful.

The ceremony began with the Quran recitation, followed by the national anthem and the march. Sitting near the podium, separate from the other children, I experienced a strange blend of pride and detachment. Due to my kitchen duties, I had missed the training sessions with the others, which, ironically, granted me certain privileges. Living across from the school allowed me to assist with morning deliveries at six o'clock. Sometimes, life is about circumstance—a combination of luck and timing that positions you where you might not actually fit.

At last, my moment came. "Now, let's hear from the participants —the Cubs of Palestine," announced the speaker. My legs trembled slightly as I approached the podium, clutching the paper tightly. This was no longer just a school radio program; this was the real deal.

I started, "The Palestinian revolution was born to thrive and to triumph." The applause erupted, growing louder with each sentence I delivered. Though I was only twelve, I felt a rush of energy and confidence. I set the paper aside, adrenaline coursing through me as I spoke from my heart: "We are the warriors of dignity and freedom. When Israeli army minister Moshe Dayan declared he would crush the Palestinian revolution like an egg in his hand, he encountered the fighters of *Karama*. Thirty years later, here we stand—the new generation of *Karama*."

I glanced around; my cheeks flushed with enthusiasm. The general looked on, both amused and approving. Then came my blunder. I started expressing gratitude to the various security forces, but mistakenly thanked general intelligence instead of military intelligence. A major general corrected me, a moment I will never forget. It was my inaugural impromptu speech—my first experience speaking in front of an audience.

From that point forward, I developed a passion for speaking and lecturing. That experience taught me a vital lesson: any effort to restore a person's inner strength must first illustrate a future goal, even from a young age. Life's signals may arrive slowly, but they do arrive. That speech marked the first indication for me.

# Study or Politics, Gaza 1996
## The Son

During my university years, I stood apart. I never engaged in political activism within *Fatah's* youth faction, as it didn't resonate with me. The organization's corrupt, unethical, and tribal customs felt stifling, with power solely in the hands of politically active extended families. Campuses transformed into spectacles, showcasing a select few who manipulated and displayed their power. Throughout my four years there, I refrained from voting but chose to identify as *Fatah* instead of joining *Al-Shabiba*, its youth branch.

My father frequently reminded me, "We're here to study, not waste time on fruitless politics and competitions." Over time, I've come to fully appreciate the depth of his words.

It became clear that those fixated on temporary political status ultimately held little worth, while individuals dedicated to their education made significant progress. Contributing to society is not merely about grasping transient power or titles; it's about being knowledgeable, earning respect, and honoring every opportunity and role with its rightful significance. Unfortunately, universities in

Palestine have turned into battlegrounds of division, corruption, and favoritism.

One day, a lecture was interrupted by chaos outside as shouts drew our gaze to the windows. We leaned forward, wanting to understand the scene unfolding in the main square. There, the university rector was being pulled along by members of a prominent family. He had declined to meet some of their requests, probably concerning scholarships or job placements for their relatives. Following that incident, the university was closed for weeks. On another occasion, gunfire resonated throughout the campus.

I detested my experience there. I worked after university hours but longed to finish and depart. The feelings I had since childhood were validated: I didn't fit into that society. In 2004, a campus explosion claimed the life of a lecturer when a bomb was hidden beneath his seat. This event marked a turning point, unravelling the sense of security and ultimately leading to Hamas assuming control of Gaza. Rumors swirled about some members of *Fatah's* leadership being involved, casting a dark cloud over everything.

Politics in Palestine feels like navigating a path lined with fragile eggshells and sharp spikes. If you walk it for too long, you'll inevitably get hurt. Even worse is when ordinary citizens become the very fuel for the fire that harms them. By 2004, I had made my choice. I had to leave, as that society would have engulfed me if I had remained.

# Khamra, Gaza 1997
## The Son

My father often remarked, "Every era has its own men and its own state." This was one of his favorite sayings, a piece of wisdom that matured alongside him, shaped by the harsh realities of his life. He also had another, more pragmatic phrase: "In the time of rulers' change, one must save his head." This emphasized that during political turmoil, it's crucial to steer clear of the conflict to ensure one's survival.

As a teenager, my curiosity was relentless. One day, I noticed a black nylon bag on the second floor and wondered what was inside. When the house was quiet, I quietly crept to the room, heart pounding with anticipation as I approached the mysterious bag.

The nylon bags crackled as I opened them, signaling my intrusion. Startled, I paused, taking a few steps back and scanning the area, half expecting someone to appear and catch me in the act. However, the second floor remained eerily silent. Gathering my courage, I moved forward once more and uncovered the contents—two large, dark bottles with unreadable English labels. They were completely foreign to me, heavy and peculiar, undeniably not juice or milk. They exuded an air of mystery—something illicit, something adult.

Carefully, I returned them to their place and discreetly exited the room, descending the stairs under the burden of the secret weighing on me. But halfway down, I halted abruptly, my hand flying to my head in panic—I had forgotten to reseal the bags.

My mother was making her way upstairs to tidy the room. "Go buy coffee and sugar," she instructed, handing me ten orange shekels, unaware of my inner distress.

I rushed to the shop, gripping the coins as if they were a lifeline. On my return, with my hands full of sugar and coffee, I mentally prepared for the unavoidable confrontation. What would I say? Would she find out? The house was silent when I got back, and I heard her faint voice from her room asking me to put the groceries in the kitchen. My heart relaxed; she hadn't discovered anything—yet.

That evening, my father came home to a simple meal of *Molokhia*, chili peppers, onions, and bread. After eating and preparing for prayer, he noticed my mother's tense demeanor. When he asked what was wrong, she glanced at me and told me to go to the garden behind the house.

A sense of anxiety coiled in my stomach. Why was I feeling guilty? I hadn't purchased the bottles, nor had I opened them properly. Still, the burden of the secret weighed on me as though it were solely my responsibility.

The confrontation unfolded when my brother came home from work. He ate quietly, oblivious to the tension that was escalating. Once he finished, my father gestured for me.

"Go to the *Hakoura* and water the roses," he instructed. His voice was steady yet authoritative, ensuring that compliance was the only choice.

As I stood outside, I heard the faint murmur of voices. Then, sharp and distinct, my father's voice pierced through: "*Khamra. Haram.*" Wine. Forbidden. The words resonated in my mind like a verdict. Soon after, my name echoed, pulling me back into the room where the two men sat like judges. My brother's face flushed with embarrassment, concealing simmering anger, while my father gazed at me with intense eyes, calm yet resolute.

"Did you open the bottles in your brother's room?" my father inquired, his voice slicing through the quiet.

My brother repeated the question, his tone harsher and more accusatory. That moment felt like it stretched into eternity. My mouth moved, but the words that emerged were a jumble of incoherence.

"So, you did." My father's voice resonated like a quiet thunder as he pointed a finger at me, his words precise and piercing: "Never touch someone else's bags or belongings. Never. Go."

Shame flushed my cheeks as I walked out of the room. Later, I uncovered the truth about those bottles. They were a gift intended for a Palestinian political leader who asked to bring them from the West Bank, meant to build connections and facilitate promotions, or better access to decision-makers. My brother may have never known what the bottles were. My father explained it plainly, as he always did: "Every state has its own representatives, and your own knows how to engage with them. One cannot treat everyone equally based on a single religion or culture."

On that day, my father imparted the importance of privacy. The lesson remained with me, underpinning my respect for boundaries and instilling the value of leaving others' property undisturbed. Though my curiosity may have lessened in some respects, the wisdom I acquired proved invaluable.

---

A few weeks later, we chose to visit the beach on a scorching summer day. This trip was unusual, taking place not in the tranquil morning hours but during the golden afternoon, following Friday prayers and lunch. For some reason, my brother-in-law thought starting late was a good idea. Unlike our usual trips, we didn't bring a tent this time. Instead, we opted for plastic chairs, which were becoming a common sight in Gaza after 1994. Previously, wooden or bamboo chairs were typical, more beautiful, and enduring. Though we had two low wooden chairs at home, we purchased six plastic ones in 1996, which squeaked a bit when you sat on them.

As the vehicles left the driveway, Gaza's streets were mostly empty under the August sun. A small number of police vehicles remained at intersections or roundabouts, with officers resting in shaded areas. Many of these officers were young locals employed by the police or security forces. In contrast, senior officers had returned with Arafat, indicating a change in the city's power structure.

When the sea came into view, my excitement surged. Gaza's sea has a unique scent—salty, raw, and vibrant. As the car slowed near *Sheikh Ejlin*, I was already clutching the door handle, eager to jump out. The moment the vehicle stopped, I threw open the door, jumped out, and stretched my arms wide like a kite catching the wind. I sprinted toward the water, kicking up sand beneath my feet.

My oldest sister's voice pierced through the air, filled with fear: "Don't go in until we're there!" she yelled, terrified I would drown before they could catch up with me.

Understanding my curiosity, my mother was hesitant about my joining this outing. Despite my sister's objections, I allowed the waves to wash over my legs, the cool water brushing against my feet before pulling away. While the others got ready to swim, I settled where the sand met the sea, captivated by a singular question: What lies beyond that vast, unending water?

Engrossed in this thought, I started digging a hole, creating channels to direct the water from the waves into my small kingdom of sand. Suddenly, something caught my attention—a bottle, partially buried in the damp sand. Intrigued, I picked it up. It was brown and glassy, its surface dulled by the ocean air. I held it up to my nose and took a sniff, instantly recoiling from the odd scent. My nose crinkled in distaste, but I chose not to discard it. Instead, I filled it with water, believing it could be useful for my sand creations.

When my brother-in-law spotted the bottle, he chuckled and shook his head. "Throw that away," he said. "It's *khamra*—alcohol." The term was new to me, but the way he pronounced it made it sound almost forbidden, like a secret. This was my first brush with beer, and that brown bottle became forever etched in my mind. Each time I see a brown beer bottle, I am transported back to that beach moment, asking myself the same question I pondered then: What's hidden beyond this sea? Although I now know the answer, I still wonder what remains of the place where I once sat, wide-eyed and curious.

As we headed home, my brother-in-law brought up the bottle to my sister. "He found a bottle of *khamra*," he said with a grin.

My sister let out a heavy sigh, clearly disapproving. "Where did you find it? Did you wash your hands?" she questioned, her tone suggesting I might have been tainted by it.

The conversation shifted when my brother-in-law mentioned a new open bar in Gaza selling alcohol. He drove toward *Ansar* Square, then down *Jamal Abdelnasser* Street, stopping near the French Cultural Center. There, he pointed out a small kiosk under Arcadia trees, with a man arranging chairs and bottles visible on a shelf.

"Look," he said. "That's it."

We all gazed in astonishment. My sister gasped, her hand covering her mouth. "*Khamra* in Gaza!" she exclaimed, her voice filled with shock and disbelief.

The image lingered in my mind, a striking view of a changing Gaza—a place situated between its age-old customs and the encroaching modernity of a new and intriguing world.

In that very location—or perhaps nearby—over 1,500 years ago, the world's finest wine was produced. Gaza's white wine was renowned far and wide, its fame stretching across the Mediterranean to cities in both Europe and Africa. From the bustling ports of Gaza and Ashkelon, this esteemed wine travelled to distant shores, achieving such lasting recognition that its containers were named after it—"Gaza jars." Crafted from the rich mud of Palestine's fertile land, these jars became as emblematic as the wine they held.

As a child and teenager, I frequently envisioned myself on a beach, so often refilling a glass that I would lose count, the numbers whirling like clock hands. I had seen such scenes on television—a sun-soaked shoreline, a wine glass in hand—and I yearned to step into that reality. Later, in Beirut, those images returned whenever I spotted older men lounging by the *Corniche of Ein El Mraisseh*, with the gleaming waves and the poignant music of Umm Kulthum wafting through the air. They would relax in wooden chairs, an *argileh* beside them. I often pondered if, tucked away among their possessions, there was also a bottle of wine—perhaps not from Gaza, but one that possessed a similar essence.

Cities, much like individuals, are molded by their past—a past intricately tied to their identity. While Gaza may not be famous for its wine today, it still holds a memory of its jars. One day, its vineyards and winemaking may make a comeback, restoring their former significance. Nevertheless, even without current acknowledgement, Gaza's heritage as a maker of exceptional wine remains firmly embedded in history.

Cities inherit passions from their forebears. Grapes, jars, wisdom, and architecture are not temporary fads but lasting legacies. Much like humans, cities possess a DNA that time cannot change. Gaza's DNA speaks of vineyards, lively ports, and artisans shaping clay. It narrates the tale of a place that once captivated the world's palate, its wine flowing across the Mediterranean like a liquid thread that links civilizations. This is the reality that Gaza endures.

# Deliberations and hope, Gaza 1998
## The Son

In 1998, my older brother took me to a political debate show hosted by Marwan Kanafani, an advisor to Yasser Arafat and a member of parliament. Marwan wasn't just a close family friend to us; he was also the brother of revolutionary thinker Ghassan Kanafani, who was killed by Israel in Beirut during the 1970s. Marwan's commanding personality shone through on his show, modeled after Western programs that featured aggressive questioning and confrontations with officials. With his position and strong connections to Arafat, he boldly confronted policymakers.

I can still picture myself in front of our new color TV, watching the show with my brother and father. When I saw Marwan on screen and then got to meet him that same week, it filled me with happiness. I was truly impressed by someone who appeared on television.

As I matured into my teenage years, the show grew in importance within our community. It relocated to Gaza's primary cultural hub—the *Rashad Al-Shawwa* Cultural Center (bombed and destroyed in the Gaza genocide). It was my first time visiting a venue like this. I took a service taxi, paid one shekel and asked the driver if he was heading to *Al Majlis Al Tashri'i*, the legislative council, located across from the center.

Upon my arrival, I was welcomed by a grand staircase that ascended to a massive gray building topped with a vibrant dome. Towering trees surrounded the structure on the southern and eastern sides, creating the illusion of a forest embracing the edifice. Inside, I noticed my older brother, who was assisting in coordinating the program and its broadcast. A diverse crowd had gathered—Mukhtars (head of extended families), young people, politicians, police officers, and security personnel. I was curious about the presence of the Mukhtars and family heads, as they were typically esteemed figures who refrained from political matters. Later, I realized they attended in hopes that Marwan could facilitate a connection with President Arafat, often to seek favors or assistance. Arafat leveraged jobs and financial support to gain the backing of extended families.

That day, I listened attentively, becoming increasingly fascinated by how Marwan questioned policymakers regarding public concerns. Fearless and straightforward, he pressed them, which only heightened my respect for him and drew me closer to the political sphere.

It was also my first visit to the *Rashad Al-Shawwa* Cultural Center—a tidy, enclosed hall with rows of seating. The building enchanted me; I felt an inexplicable connection to it. The ambience, the design, the temperature, even the scent—it all resonated with me. While some people bond with objects, I found that place to be my own.

After the program concluded, I allowed my feet to lead me, feeling a soft breeze from the western gates. Just before leaving, I spotted a doorway to the left that opened to a space with chairs and tables. I crept inside quietly, like a thief, discovering new moments I hadn't known existed. *Is this really in Gaza?* I wondered. The area was partially open, featuring a man behind a bar stove, and tables a few meters above ground, with trees providing cover from the street. It was sunset, and the distant sound of car horns punctuated the evening air.

A man came up to me and inquired about my order. For a brief moment, I was unsure. Then, the scent of Nescafé wafted towards me.

"Nescafé. How much is it?" I asked, anxious that my ten shekels might fall short.

"Two shekels," he answered.

Feeling relieved, I nodded in agreement. I took a seat at a table facing south, alone in my corner, while another man and a couple sat nearby. In the distance, I noticed new buildings being constructed along with police convoys, their sirens blaring as they escorted Western officials to Arafat's nearby office.

I took a sip of my Nescafé, reflecting on the future of this place and pondering if other cities worldwide had similar structures. Gaza served as a testing ground for the state of Palestine's development and planning. I often heard that they aimed to transform Gaza into a version of Singapore. I was unaware of where Singapore was or the reasons behind wanting Gaza to resemble it. My only lingering thought was why Gaza shouldn't become the next Beirut, a city that has long been etched in my mind and spirit, as the center of resistance and struggle.

The man who helped me came back and inquired if I was from *Sheja'iyya*. He was tall, had sharp eyes, a kind face, and spoke in a calm voice. Within minutes, I discovered that he was employed by the Gaza municipality and managed the café. He was familiar with my family. Upon realizing this, he returned my two shekels.

"You're my guest; I can't take your money," he said.

He informed me that the building contained a library that I could visit for free. From that moment on, I became a regular at both the library and the café. It transformed into my beloved sanctuary, where I discovered myself as a teenager and a young man. A year later, the man who first introduced me to the library and treated me to Nescafé was killed by Israeli soldiers during the Second *Intifada*.

Cities are filled with treasures, and Gaza's cultural center was one of its jewels. The libraries in these centers captivated me and fostered my love for reading, pulling me toward peaceful moments in that secluded café. Each time I remember those days, I perceive cities as reflections of the spirits of their inhabitants. Their unique characteristics distinguish individuals, much like a library bursting with various books.

# SECOND INTIFADA, GAZA 2000
## THE SON

In July 2000, the *Fatah* leadership encouraged large-scale demonstrations to support Yasser Arafat. Despite extreme summer heat that made outdoor gatherings challenging, these calls were taken seriously by many. Discussions within households reflected uncertainty and apprehension regarding future developments.

My father, experienced and wise, frequently remarked, "If this fails, we will go to war."

These circumstances prompted contemplation about personal roles and responsibilities during times of political tension, fostering a sense of anticipation about future participation.

By the end of July, the peace negotiations at Camp David crumbled, like fragile sandcastles disappearing beneath a rising tide. Evenings had us huddled around the TV, engrossed in *Al Jazeera* or the Israeli Arabic channel, our eyes tracking the tense faces of Arafat, Ehud Barak, and Clinton as they manoeuvred through the carefully maintained gardens. For a fleeting moment, a small glimmer of hope surfaced—fragile and tender, akin to the first green shoot in an empty field. Yet, as I concentrated and absorbed the newscasters' words, that hope faded, engulfed by a daunting sense of dread. It was as if a flickering candle had been snuffed out, plunging us into darkness as we faced a terrifying unknown.

I was eager to participate in the protests against the Israeli occupation, to be part of the crowd and represent our voice. However, my father prohibited me.

"Not yet," he said, his eyes reflecting a sadness I couldn't fully grasp at the time.

Being young and still bound by the rules of summer break, I found it difficult to defy his wishes and set out alone into the heat. The day felt unusual, as if the world was holding its breath—humid, oppressive, and eerily still. There was no breeze or relief from the heaviness in the air, as though the sky was indicating something profoundly wrong.

On that day, the streets were filled with public employees and *Fatah* members assembled to welcome Arafat. Although they demonstrated resolve, a sense of uncertainty was evident in their demeanor. My family and the media repeatedly raised the same question: "What is next?"

I observed Arafat as he exited his vehicle on TV; his expression was notably more reserved, and his remarks conveyed a heightened gravity. He proceeded directly toward *Al Montada*, his office in Gaza, moving with purpose and urgency, suggesting a profound sense of responsibility for the future of our people.

As Thursday dawned in the final week of September, the long-awaited rains finally arrived. This downpour brought with it a much-needed reprieve from the oppressive heat. In Palestine, the first rain represents more than just a shift in climate—it heralds the onset of the olive harvest. We refer to it as *Saliba*, the rains that signal when the olives are ripe for picking, a cherished annual tradition for families throughout the region.

My father, with a rare smile, declared that we would come together next weekend to harvest olives from our trees. My spirits lifted at the thought. Since childhood, I have cherished the olive harvest—the thrill of climbing trees, the simple yet profound joy of collecting each olive, the laughter, the conversations, and the bond of family as we worked side by side, cousins, nephews, and nieces sharing in the work and the joy.

That Thursday was different. As I made my way home, an unmistakable shift lingered in the air—something heavy and foreboding. My mother stood in front of the television, her face grave, her gaze fixed on the screen, while the room filled with the haunting sound of a song that carried an unsettling weight. The melody sent chills down my spine, reflecting a collective despair, a prelude to the storm that was about to engulf us.

The lyrics floated through the air, and while I couldn't grasp every word, I sensed that something monumental had occurred. The olive harvest, the gathering, even the rain—all seemed to pale in comparison to the burden of the world we inhabited, a world precariously poised on the brink of something far greater and more perilous than we had ever known.

*"Where have the millions vanished, lost in the folds of betrayal? / Where does the spirit of Arab youth wander, adrift in the currents of despair? / Where lies the ember of Arab rage, smoldering beneath the weight of silence? / Where hides the dignity of Arab souls, obscured by shadows of indifference? / Where are the millions? / We stand as the truth, the flame of revolution burning bright, / While they, the oppressors of Al-Fil, fade into obscurity. / We are the generation of truth, the heirs of revolution."*

Once I heard it, I realized we were entering uncharted territory. The TV was set to the official Palestinian channel, playing nationalistic songs and reminders of the revolutionary days in Beirut, their anthems awakening something deep within me. The screen displayed images of individuals shot at *Al-Aqsa* Mosque, students fleeing in terror, their voices strained with cries that filled the air like smoke. Ambulances darted back and forth, red lights flashing amid the chaos, their sirens merging with the cries of the injured. And then, to intensify the pain, there were images of Ariel Sharon storming the sacred grounds of *Al-Aqsa* Mosque, heavily guarded by Israeli soldiers.

The following day, after Friday prayers, the news arrived: many dead in *Al-Aqsa*. I hadn't attended the mosque that day. There was something inside me that held back. It wasn't merely fear—it was deeper, more troubling. A slow-growing skepticism, a diminishing trust in the sacredness of everything, in God, in the convictions I had held until that point. My heart grappled with questions that seemed too vast for me. *What was happening to us? What was happening to me?*

As the day wore on, I found myself glued to the television, mesmerized by the endless stream of death, destruction, and despair. More images of bodies being carried away, mothers wailing, the streets drenched in blood and grief. By the end of that day, it felt as if all the hopes and dreams I had carried, like a bag over my shoulder, had been ripped away. Once so bright, the future I had envisioned vanished into the smoke of gunfire and shattered glass.

After two months of oppressive silence in the political arena, everything changed abruptly. The atmosphere, once heavy and stifling—almost as if we could sense the very heartbeat of the land—was shattered. A button had been pressed, unleashing a cacophony of gunfire—sudden, forceful, and relentless. The violence that had long simmered beneath the surface now broke free, and once it erupted, there was no let-up.

In that instant, the future became irrelevant, eclipsed by the present, dominated by a storm of anger and grief. As for the past? It seemed to reveal one harsh reality: the peace process we had cherished was a grave error, with hope proving to be a cruel fantasy. Our yearning for peace had led to our own betrayal, buried deep with the deceased.

That day signified the conclusion of an era—the era of hope. It was interred with the bodies and the aspirations of a generation. In its place, something new emerged. The child within me, who had clung to a naive belief that the world could improve and that change was possible, matured instantly. There was no space for innocence any longer. I stood there, gazing at the TV, feeling the burden of a world collapsing around me, and I realized I had entered adulthood into a realm darker, harsher, and far more unforgiving than I had ever envisioned.

# An Appointment with Death, Gaza 2000
## The Son

Caught in a dance with destiny, I found myself on the brink of mortality on that fateful Sunday, October 8, 2000. I gazed into the abyss of two daunting possibilities—either the oblivion of death or a life overshadowed by monocular vision. Fighting fiercely against fate, I triumphed over both fears. That day, the gap between discussing an event and experiencing it was laid bare before me. Each year, as October 8 approaches, the memories that have long been imprisoned in the depths of my past break free. Like will-o'-the-wisps, they obscure my vision, creating an annual eclipse that blurs the line between past and present.

That Sunday marked the start of the second week of the second *Intifada*, with a storm looming ahead. My school stood strong, located 1.5 kilometers from the route regularly taken by Israeli tanks and armored vehicles heading from Israel into the heart of the Gaza Strip, specifically the Israeli settlement of Netzarim. As the clock hit 11 a.m., we left the school. Heavily laden with backpacks filled with books, I felt a new determination arise within me—an unprecedented decision to partake in the act of throwing stones at the Israeli tanks. In groups, we walked along the paved road, our steps alternating between urgency and sprinting, as if we were in a high-stakes race.

During this march, a classmate and I paused to buy sunflower seeds—a little treat to enjoy as we set out on our journey. He leaned in and said, "Let us revel and find solace in these sunflower seeds on our journey."

Now, as I look back, I can't help but think of the many young and old souls who walked that same path but never came back to the embrace of their families.

Gradually, we approached the epicenter of the unrest—a battleground where clashes erupted before us. The acrid odor of burnt rubber filled the air, creating a dismal barrier between us and the Israeli soldiers. Ambulances, a massive tank, a crowd of men and children, and a distressed mother searching for her lost son all came into view.

I was only 300 meters away when suddenly, a searing projectile struck my forehead just above my right eye. It felt as if my breath was expelled through my eyes. I desperately attempted to open my eyelids, but they wouldn't budge. In that instant, the toxic smoke from the smoldering rubber seemed to infiltrate my being, its sharpness embedding itself in my mind whenever I saw it on television. The previously dark rubber clouds morphed into a blinding white void, intensified by the burning in my eyes. Everything around me became white. Instinctively, I reached for my eyes, my hands rubbing them desperately. The pain grew sharper, the world started to spin, and an overwhelming urge to relieve myself surged within me.

"Rubber bullet, rubber bullet!" my classmate shouted, his voice laced with alarm.

I searched for clarity in the turmoil. Once more, I tried to open my eyes, but they stubbornly stayed closed. A severe pain pulsed through me, reminiscent of a scorpion's deadly claws scraping my eye. The paramedics who arrived at the scene incorrectly assumed I had been affected by tear gas. They immediately washed my face and instructed me to go home.

At that moment, the reality of my situation hit me hard. How could I tell my father that I had participated in the protests against Israeli soldiers that he had passionately warned me against? His wise words had always reinforced the belief that knowledge and writing were the true tools to fight challenges. I spun a web of lies at home, creating a story that hid the truth.

My mother, her eyes filled with worry, noticed blood trickling from under my eyelid, while my eye was obscured by a gruesome, bloody mess. She quickly called my father at work to inform him. Within 10 minutes, a relative arrived in a car, rushing me to the ophthalmology hospital, where my father awaited.

After examining me, the doctors discreetly called my father aside to share the dreadful news: my injury wasn't from just a hand but from a rubber bullet. They spoke softly, informing him that I might never regain sight in my right eye.

The internal damage was severe, and the bleeding persisted relentlessly for an agonizing 24 hours. For six interminable weeks, darkness shrouded my sight, robbing me of the visual tapestry that once adorned my existence. Though the blood eventually dried and my vision slowly returned, the scars of that ordeal persisted. Scars that refuse to heal remain silent wounds long after the pain has subsided.

My father never mentioned it again, as he realized I had learned the hardest lesson possible. Even prior to my physical recovery, he quickly removed me from that school, making sure my daily travels led me far from the center of turmoil—West Gaza became my new destination.

# "SEE ME, MY AUNT," GAZA 2000
## THE SON

At noon, a call for food resonated. A man in a tattered beige Soviet suit perched like a hawk on a backless chair beneath a towering electricity pylon. He held stacks of cash: dollars, Jordanian dinars, and Israeli shekels. His workplace, simmering under June's intense sun, transformed into a fierce opponent, driving him to adjust his chair slightly every ten minutes, seeking shelter in the broad shadow cast by the metal giant.

Close by, another man nonchalantly leaned against the red and white striped barriers that divided pedestrians from the chaotic flow of traffic. Both men would spring into action like coiled snakes whenever a car came to a halt nearby. Their business involved trading cash, earning small amounts of money from every hundred dollars. They were the underground experts in currency exchange, the pulse of the black market.

During my teenage years, their presence was integral to my life, becoming familiar faces as I worked as a park guard at seventeen. Balancing a full-time job from the afternoon until the evening with school, I patrolled the vast park. It transformed into my outdoor classroom, where I would recite and memorize lessons. Math posed a challenge, requiring my focus to decode its problems. In contrast, Islamic studies were a more welcoming companion, as I could learn by memorizing Quran verses while on duty. Chemistry and English, on the other hand, were my beloved subjects.

As I walked from west to east, a multitude of life unfolded around me. Some rushed towards shared taxis, shouting their destinations into the swirling chaos. Others vanished into the winding alleys of *Omar al-Mukhtar* Street, seemingly consumed by the city itself. There were instances when I paused, book or notebook in hand, resembling a statue caught in motion. At other times, I would lean on a plastic chair behind the park fence, watching the stream of humanity as if overseeing a complex nuclear plant console.

On that peculiar day, I noticed a figure rushing across the street —a young man in his early twenties. He wore sunglasses, jeans, and a T-shirt, with a plastic bag swinging from one hand and a Steyer TMP machine gun casually hanging in the other. It was both unsettling and captivating to see a civilian wielding such a weapon. I couldn't shake the persistent question that entered my mind: *Why was this man displaying a gun?*

This question lingered stubbornly, remaining unanswered. It was the first year of the second *Intifada*, a time when there were no Israeli soldiers in our city. The man seemed to be an inexperienced civilian, unfamiliar with combat.

A voice echoed from afar, *Shufeni Ya Khalti*, "See me, my aunt," —a local saying that ridicules those who act without substance, merely putting on a show of bravado. That day ignited numerous questions within me about the Palestinian struggle for freedom.

The image of that seemingly innocent civilian wielding a weapon in a time with no immediate threat creates a poignant illustration of how neglecting the small details of that era contributed to the militarization of our society. The fallout shattered Palestinian unity, leading to devastating consequences. Small, overlooked fragments, like shards of a broken mirror, reflect a distorted reality.

# Joining a Militia, Gaza 2001
## The Son

I t was 2001 when the Israeli invasions became brutal, suffocating every aspect of our lives. My head and soul were in constant turmoil, wrestling with the reality surrounding me. Questions echoed inside, endlessly swirling—*Is this what you wanted? Isn't this the fight you longed for? To be a freedom fighter?* But reality was cruel, and death was creeping closer each day, shadowing everything.

Mohamed, a 12-year-old relative and neighbor, was shot in the head by an Israeli soldier. He was funny, mischievous, and constantly stirring up trouble. I remember his laughter, and I remember how quickly it was silenced.

With the invasions, new committees were formed by Arafat called the "Popular Resistance Committees." Many of our friends in *Fatah* became members, enthusiastic and ready to sacrifice themselves. Then, in 2002, Israel assassinated their leader in Gaza, Jihad Al-Amarin, a *Fatah* commander close to Yasser Arafat.

"Do you want to join?" a friend and neighbor asked one evening, inviting me to join the resistance.

I hesitated, reflecting on everything—my family, my future, and my anger. "We're all part of the resistance," I eventually responded. "I contribute, and when the time comes for me, it will happen."

It wasn't bravery, nor was it fear; it was something different—a profound frustration. I didn't want to fight for a cause that felt inherently corrupted while others benefited. My choice wasn't logical; it stemmed from my anger.

The previous night, I listened to my father and brother discussing Arafat's approval of financial aid for one of his advisors. This assistance was intended so that his children, aged nine and 13, could avoid the traumas of conflict by traveling to the U.S. and Europe, costing €9,000. In my mind, I thought, *What about me? Why must I bear the burden while they enjoy comfort?*

That same day, the Israeli army invaded the eastern part of our neighborhood in *Sheja'iyya*. Dozens were killed, and several people were arrested. From that night on, I slept in my jeans for weeks, ready to run west towards safer areas of Gaza at a moment's notice. The fear of arrest outweighed the fear of death. We stayed awake until three or four in the morning, waiting because most invasions occurred around that time.

After a week of sleeping in the same clothes, I felt exhausted. I wore my jeans to university, work, and bed. My mind started racing: *What is the point of life if our only activity is running, only to ultimately end up dead?*

I questioned whether it was time for me to join the militias. If death is unavoidable, perhaps it would be better to die as a fighter instead of someone who is always fleeing.

That week brought tragic news. Two men from our community were killed by the Israeli military. Both were members of *Fatah*, and their funerals would be organized by *Fatah*—an elaborate event featuring their photos and extensive propaganda. *Fatah* and Hamas, together with other factions, vied to honor the deceased. Martyrdom had become a core element of Palestinian identity, serving as a measure of value.

This situation reminded me of Naji Al-Ali, the Palestinian artist and cartoonist who once illustrated a profound reality: "Anyone who writes or paints for Palestine must know that they are already dead."

He suggested that every activist in Palestine effectively signs their death certificate as soon as they raise their voice. He was correct. Naji Al-Ali was assassinated in London. Those who give their lives become the prophets of truth.

That evening, I went to the funeral and stayed late to discuss new initiatives and possible actions with others. Upon returning home, I found my mother, father, and eldest brother waiting outside. They were not just angry; they were frightened. My father conveyed his thoughts with his usual clarity: "The biggest fight, the best battle, is education. We must fight with knowledge, not weapons."

With that, I buried the thought of joining a militia or ever owning a gun. From that moment, I realized my fight wasn't on the streets; it was in classrooms, books, and the minds of future generations.

# Part Five
# The Exodus

# Desires to Escape, Gaza 2006
## The Son

As my final year at university came to a close, the already difficult conditions in the Gaza Strip seemed to deteriorate even more rapidly. The once-vibrant life slowly faded, transforming into a desaturated, sepia-toned version of its past self. In this unpredictable environment, my position as a software engineer managing the efforts of garbage collectors felt like a surreal and dissonant tune that did little to soothe my restless spirit. The societal structures that had once guided and grounded me now felt like a tightening grip around my soul.

My psyche, akin to an ethereal echo, had already surpassed Gaza; I felt ready to physically follow. This sense of imminent departure, this desire for escape, had been embedded in me since my youth. The foundations of exile, immigration, and displacement are often sown long before the actual journey begins, subtly thriving in the fertile ground of the mind long before they become evident externally.

For me, exile and immigration encompass more than just physical relocation; they embody significant mental states and cognitive transformations that take place prior to any geographical shift. The decision to leave is merely the concluding step in an extended psychological journey, a concrete manifestation of an internal migration that has already occurred.

One afternoon, my mother found me captivated by glossy magazines, my eyes hungrily scanning images of lush trees, pristine beaches, and busy streets crowded with cars. I believed these ideal scenes were glimpses of a European paradise. Curiously, she inquired about my fascination, and I shared a wistful dream of buying a house in those verdant surroundings.

Her laughter echoed in the room, infusing a hint of humor that brightened her words. With a twinkle in her eyes, she suggested that I should learn to clean up after myself before considering homeownership. A warm, playful smile played on her lips, recognizing the irritation her words would provoke in me.

There was a period when my days were governed by a nocturnal pace, with my work starting only as the sun set. I often found myself at the heart of the evening, anticipating the familiar rumble of the garbage collection truck as it wound its way from Gaza's central square to the end of the street. The driver and I would spend those hours in our moving vehicle, exchanging stories and sharing wisps of smoke that floated lazily into the night. The truck was more than just a vehicle; it was a meeting place where routine intertwined with defiance.

Each shift commenced with a ceremony: I distributed cigarettes, my small gift to the tired workers. As the cigarettes sparked to life, so did our expressions, reflecting the glowing tips. Our conversations flowed freely, often returning to the pressing issue on everyone's minds—the erratic payment of salaries. From 2004 until I left, wages were elusive, arriving either halved or only every three months, as unpredictable as a capricious lover.

Among the workers was Adel, a man in his mid-thirties, shouldering the burdens of two marriages. If he arrived late, he would ask me to excuse the delay, explaining that it was due to the challenges of keeping peace between his two wives. I never penalized anyone's pay; these men meant more to me than mere workers. They were comrades, real people who provided relief from the suffocating expectations of civilized society that I was supposed to uphold.

As time passed, my eyes began to scan the horizon, yearning for a life beyond Gaza. My opportunities felt limited by my circumstances: my command of English was shaky at best, and my university grades remained average, too far from excellence to qualify for a prestigious scholarship. A "good" grade seemed like a distant dream, while the keys to potential scholarships remained elusive. My father, either unwilling or unable to support my education in Europe, provided no comfort.

In this context, I broadened my search by looking into scholarships available in nearby countries such as Jordan and Egypt. One day, I came across an online portal aimed at young people from Europe and the Mediterranean. Their mission focused on non-violence and peace, which strongly resonated with my aspirations. With enthusiasm, I drafted an email outlining my interests and asking about possible opportunities.

A few days later, my eagerness paid off when I received a response full of interest. The allure of someone from Gaza wanting to engage piqued their curiosity; it added a distinctive element that might enhance their donor funding. As our communication progressed, it led to an invitation to join their programs in France. I instantly dove into the complicated process of visa applications, collecting all the necessary documents.

On a pivotal day, while visiting the French Cultural Center to submit my application, the clerk issued a blunt warning: "Only students get visas to France, but you can try."

Despite the harsh reality of his words, my determination remained unshaken. Though my hope endured some bruising, it continued to burn brightly.

Even after six months of studying French and positioning myself as someone who would never even think of illegal immigration or seeking asylum, my visa application was rejected without any explanation. It felt like attempting to dance in quicksand—the harder I tried to demonstrate my worthiness, the more I appeared to be bogged down.

Years later, having received European citizenship, I discovered from the same clerk who had given me the ominous warning that my application had never even left the room in the Gaza Strip. It turned out that the French consul—a native Gazan himself—was a sort of gatekeeper, rejecting all visa applications from Gaza unless they had the backing of the French government.

"He was more royal than the king," the clerk remarked. Indeed, after this consul stepped down from his iron throne, many Palestinians were able to successfully secure French visas as self-supporting students, conference participants, or volunteers.

Months after my initial rejection, a new opportunity emerged. I received an invitation to join the European Voluntary Service Program, which attracted thousands from the region. With approval from the organization and proof of funding for a year, covering my housing and living expenses, along with a document from the European Commission validating the project funding, I submitted my reapplication.

Despite this, I kept visiting the center to study French, like a moth drawn to the faint light of a flickering bulb. Each day, I hoped they would announce my long-awaited visa approval. However, that announcement never came, remaining an elusive specter even after ten years. Perhaps my application had been condemned to serve as fuel for the consul's fireplace.

In Gaza, a city skilled at making its residents wait, my existence revolved around an unending dance of expectation. Always on standby for something to happen, to alter, to transition. I often reflect on how people born just two kilometers from me—at that very moment, beneath the same stars—can navigate the world swiftly, free from the burden of bureaucratic complexities or even the necessity of knowing a consular's name. That consul's name lingers in my mind, a painful reminder of a story that could have taken a different turn.

One day, while I was caught up in Microsoft Messenger(an early 2000s chat messenger on the computer), the notification of a message broke the quiet—a chat from a classmate who had faded into memory over the last six months. I was absorbed in translating my certificates and official papers into English, envisioning a future beyond Gaza's restrictive borders, even though the chance of obtaining a visa felt as distant as a mirage.

The message from my friend was akin to an unexpected gust of wind, steering my small boat of aspirations toward uncharted shores. His announcement of being in Malaysia for nearly seven months struck me like a comet darting across my static sky, evoking surprise and curiosity. Malaysia, an emerging destination for Gazan scholars seeking master's and Ph.D. programs, was largely unfamiliar to me, apart from the fact that it is a Muslim country.

"Doing my master's degree, then I will pursue a PhD," he wrote, which stirred a pang of jealousy within me. Here I was, trapped in Gaza, my aspirations suppressed like a songbird confined in a cage, while he was out there, exploring new horizons, his life unfolding like an endless scroll.

I asked him about his financial situation and what brought him to Malaysia. His straightforward answer, "A bird in the hand is worth ten in the bush," captured the reality that clung to us like a second skin. He meant, a real chance to study in Malaysia was better than trying and keep dreaming of an opportunity in Europe.

His message became a powerful catalyst. My mind raced as I considered the possibility of life and study in Malaysia. Having abandoned my aspirations of obtaining a prestigious scholarship and a European visa, I found myself on a ship adjusting its sails to uncertain winds. I asked my friend if he could help me with admission and a visa to Malaysia. He quickly agreed and asked for a few essential documents.

As a chronicler of my own life, I had digitized every piece of paperwork I had accumulated since I first started using a computer and scanner. The fear of losing everything to Israeli invasions or airstrikes motivated me to store my life's records in the virtual space. Everything from birth certificates to university transcripts was sent to my friend within minutes.

With the few hundred USD fees securely transferred and the visa application underway, a wave of relief enveloped me like comforting balm. I was no longer a castaway lost in a sea of uncertainty. I was moving forward; however, the way ahead remained unclear. This choice to venture into the unknown marked my personal Exodus.

That morning, I confronted my mother with my decision. She was apprehensive, her perspective shaped by the names of prestigious European universities that frequently echoed over the airwaves. Although she had never attended university and did not speak English, her inherent wisdom often outshone that of many graduates. Despite her hesitations, I successfully transferred the application fees.

The ensuing weeks were filled with daily dialogues about life in Malaysia. Then, one ordinary morning, my routine was interrupted by a brief but powerful email from my friend—an admission letter for the master's program. I rushed to tell my mother, excitement pouring out of me.

Her reaction was subdued, laced with a mother's concern, emblematic of the paradox I faced. "*Mabrouk*, when is the travel?" she asked, a silent prayer evident in her tone.

# TO ITALY, FAREWELLING GAZA, GAZA 2007

## THE SON

My life flowed on, shrouded in anticipation for an uncertain day. I was uncertain about the reason for my waiting. Was it the upcoming arrival of my Malaysia visa that kept me on edge, or was it a lingering hesitation—a dissatisfaction with the notion of Malaysia itself—that consistently postponed my decision to start my journey? Days slipped by, each one stripped of purpose and meaning.

Each morning began in the same dull routine. I woke up, navigated through a flood of emails, and immersed myself in the constant stream of messages. The online world became my solitary refuge, with the internet serving as a lifeline—a hint of connection in a world growing distant. Every moment I shared my life with others via the screen offered a brief, sweet glimpse of our shared journey.

Two weeks faded into nothingness before an email appeared in my inbox in the form of an email. It carried news from a friend, simply asking me to book my ticket by the end of the month to join the upcoming semester. A harsh truth enveloped me: my departure wasn't a light decision. The two gates offering an exit from the Gaza

Strip remained firmly shut. Leaving Gaza was not merely about travel plans; it represented a grand journey, a daunting and formidable challenge.

Borders, those artificial divisions in the sand, have acted as cruel puppeteers, extinguishing the futures of numerous individuals. The lives of Palestinians in Gaza have become distorted into a grotesque game, manipulated by the fickle whims of a senior Egyptian army officer or an Israeli committee that played with the Gazan spirit, as if trying to erase their humanity, leaving them in a state that lingers between that of animals and shadows.

When my eldest brother returned from the United States, adorned with academic honors, he proposed an alternative path that I clung to like a lifebuoy in a storm. He indicated that the new MA program in Italy represented more than just a change in location; it was a paradigm shift, guiding me away from my past and toward a fresh horizon, which I have always liked. I agreed without hesitation, motivated by a silent awareness that at times we need to let go of our past to embrace our future. I trusted my eldest brother in everything; he would guide me, exactly like a father. As I age, I sometimes regret not listening to much of his advice.

For me, departure represented not a conclusion but a new beginning. Every new beginning is like dawn, filled with promise and accompanied by challenges, resembling a beautiful puzzle that is fulfilling yet filled with obstacles and anxieties.

That week, my older brother—a man who wore his youth like armor, despite our 16-year age difference—entered our home, his steps echoing the vigor of his spirit.

"Today, we submitted Ayk's application for the scholarship in Italy," he said, his words spilling out over a sip of tea.

"Ahh, Italy! It's so different from Malaysia," my mother replied, her lips curling into a knowing smile.

"But it's not a full scholarship. He'll need to pay for the flight and some fees," he added.

"We can handle that. He's working; he can contribute from his savings," she suggested.

My father's voice, resonating with the melodic hum of Quranic verses recited in the *Mujjawad* style—a nostalgic melody that has filled my dawn and dusk since my earliest memories—signaled his approval. As his prayer concluded, he turned and blessed us simply with, "*Aa'ala Barakat Allah* (God bless)."

My mother, her laughter echoing like a cheerful anthem, joked, "Yes, he'll leave to come back with an Italian wife, just like the ones we see in glossy magazines and on television!"

Parents frequently view the eldest son as the family's guiding compass, whose insights are rich in experience and authority. This view was familiar in my family, particularly given my eldest brother's impressive education and clear understanding of his choices. What appeared to be a simple decision actually carried the urgency of a rescue mission, aimed at swiftly freeing me from the suffocating confines of Gaza.

He eventually admitted that he would have taken on the financial burden himself to rescue me from the impending storm of political oppression caused by my ties to *Fatah* and my position towards political Islam. He wanted to protect me from the harmful effects of danger, and his efforts gradually bore fruit.

That evening, I slipped into sleep, embraced by newfound joy, although laced with the troubling anxiety of possible admission rejection. My hopes were delicately poised between an exhilarating academic opportunity and the risk of remaining trapped within the walls of Gaza. Remembering that after almost twenty years, I admit that my life unfolded like a colorful Persian carpet, filled with new experiences, cultural exposures, ideologies, and a priceless education. This journey provided me with a spectrum of perspectives, enabling me to examine life from various angles. I felt liberated from the boxes of rigid political beliefs, and a wave of relief swept over me, as if I had shed an unseen burden.

After a grueling three weeks, an email from the Italian university landed in my inbox, announcing my admission to the cultural studies program with a partial scholarship. A wave of joy surged through me, prompting an unexpected victory dance. I dashed to share the news with my mother, but her reaction was lukewarm, a smile tinted with a mother's instinctive concern. I couldn't help but wonder if she anticipated the prolonged separation this opportunity might entail.

"Tell your brother the news," she advised, her hands caught up in the rhythm of making lunch.

After a quick phone call, my brother shared my excitement, proposing we go over the details when he got back. As the exhilarating thrill of my success faded, the reality of the conditions outlined in the rest of the email set in. They requested a fee of 5,000 Euros but hinted at the possibility of relief through a UNESCO scholarship.

With a heightened sense of urgency, I reached out to the embassy in Jerusalem regarding the translations needed. To my relief, the Palestinian representative assured me that the fees for translation and visa would be waived for Palestinian students from Gaza. This unexpected advantage ignited a glimmer of hope in me, prompting me to collect the required documents.

That evening, my brother suggested reducing the fee to a more manageable amount of 1,000 Euros. Within the same week, we received a response agreeing to this sum as both a seat reservation and a starting point for the visa application process.

Bank transfers presented another challenge. The Bank of Jordan appeared to be the only one able to facilitate the transfer. My father reached out to an old friend, the bank manager, requesting assistance in our time of need. This served as a poignant reminder that human connections can provide hope even amid the most formal and impersonal transactions.

The next morning, sunlight brightened my room like an eager intruder, stirring me from slumber. The oppressive heat felt like a tyrant, and the stifling humidity of Gaza made the air feel dense. My mother gave me 1,000 Euros, wisely advising me to divide the cash into different pockets as protection against theft. This hard-earned lesson came from painful memories reflected in my father's eyes.

His story often surfaced during our talks—a time when he was given his manager's salary alongside his own and my sister's. A bustling market, a fleeting distraction, and a nimble thief forever altered our approach to handling money. Now, we carefully distribute cash among various hiding places, a routine ingrained in our lives. Some lessons arise from personal challenges, while others are imparted through shared experiences and inherited wisdom.

As I left the house, I turned left and paused at the large cemetery, which is an informal shared taxi service stop, waiting for a taxi to take me to *Al-Sahha*, the vibrant central square of Gaza. It is also named "Palestine Square." This well-worn path was etched in my mind; I could navigate it without thinking. In Gaza, taxi routes are not dictated by official guidelines but crafted through shared social awareness—a map living in the hearts of its inhabitants.

After 15 minutes, a taxi arrived, a shared ride with three other passengers. In Gaza, public transportation has been supplanted by "service" cars, driven by money, their routes dictated by the flow of income. A driver once candidly told me, "We don't see people; we see Shekels."

Once settled next to the driver, I faced a familiar question: "*Ya Mussahel?*" (Where are you going, by the guidance of God?)

I held back a retort, finding the intrusion annoying. In Gaza, though, taxi drivers were kings of the road, embodying a unique mix of awareness and ignorance. Despite the occasional overstepping, I valued the camaraderie and humor that characterized these exchanges. In contrast, European taxis provided anonymity, with drivers serving merely as a backdrop to the ride.

In his relentless pursuit of conversation, the driver asked again, this time inquiring if I was going to the European Hospital. I responded tersely, denying his assumption. Positioned around 30 kilometers from the city center, the European Hospital represents a hub of modern healthcare in Gaza, drawing patients from the city square.

Intrigued by the unusual question, I inquired about the hospital, only to hear from a backseat passenger about an upcoming Turkish delegation visiting to handle complex cases. This surprising information reinforced my faith in the streetwise intelligence of taxi drivers.

The taxi slowly made its way along *Baghdad* Street, mired in the relentless traffic at *Sheja'iyya* crossing. As we moved up *Al-Wihda* Street, one of the vibrant Gaza's busiest areas enveloped us. It means Unity Street. A road that connects *Al-Wihda* and the other busy street that hosts the Palestine square is named for the revolutionary Palestinian Fahmi Beyk, linking *Omar Al-Mukhtar* Street with Unity Street.

When the taxi finally reached the inevitable congestion, I opted to complete my journey on foot. After settling the fare, I narrowly escaped another round of the driver's musing about the European Hospital.

As I strolled, the air became rich with the intoxicating mix of freshly made *Shawarma*, morning coffee, and the tempting scent of Arabic desserts. The aroma of *Knafe* acted as a beacon, leading me toward the vegetable market street and to the second floor of the corner building. The Bank of Jordan has been a reliable fixture there since the 1980s.

The manager warmly welcomed me and designated an employee to assist me in opening an account. After thirty minutes, my account was set up with a deposit of 1,000 Euros. However, an unforeseen complication occurred because of a missing Swift Code, which made the money transfer process more difficult.

I had just 20 Shekels on my prepaid mobile. The oppressive limitations of Gaza's telecommunications weighing down on me. The paper from the Italian admission office was in my hand, a gateway to a completely different world. With a deep sigh, I dialed their number, hoping my limited funds would be enough. The ticking clock echoing with my call seemed to mock the imminent end of my balance.

The soothing voice of the woman in charge of fees came through the line, but just as we were about to engage in a meaningful conversation, my 20 Shekels disappeared, and my call was suddenly cut off. I muttered curses at the expensive nature of Gaza's telecommunications, doubting the viability of my quest. Would I be able to finish the task today and make it back home? The bank closed at noon, adding another hurdle to my already challenging situation.

Defeated, I started my journey home, weaving through the bustling *Omar Al-Mukhtar* Street towards the east. Upon reaching the main crossing in *Sheja'iyya*, I hopped into a shared taxi and within ten fleeting minutes, my home's familiar silhouette came into view.

My mother greeted me with a hopeful, "Did you transfer the money?"

Sighing, I explained the obstacle of the missing Swift code and my unsuccessful attempt to obtain it that same day. My words lingered, casting a shadow of doubt, but her eyes remained bright with hope.

That evening, my friend from Malaysia ignited my thoughts by asking about my plans. His words resonated with me, forming a mix of joy tinged with a bit of regret. I shared news of the partial scholarship from Italy, and a soft sigh on the other end revealed his understanding—I would not be going to Malaysia. I had to decline his request for help, as my journey was now taking me in a different direction. Our conversation concluded with a sincere wish for good luck, a testament to a friendship that had endured many challenges.

Situated in front of my desk, I reached out to the Italian admissions office to request the elusive Swift code. As dusk softly settled over Gaza, I remained still, my gaze fixed on the screen, anticipating a reply. After what felt like forever, an email notification appeared, presenting the sought-after Swift code.

A victorious smile spread across my face as I mused, "It is going to work."

The next morning, dawn welcomed me with its radiant fingers slipping through my window, dispelling the shadows of doubt. Sunlight began its daily dance, twirling around the room and enveloping everything in its golden glow. The warmth was like a quiet wake-up call, gently prompting me to rise from my sleep. I curled my legs to my chest and tossed aside the light blanket. As I cautiously opened my eyes, the room embraced me with a comforting familiarity. The calming presence of my mother at the end of the house brought a wave of reassurance over me.

She expressed her surprise at my early wakefulness with a raised eyebrow. As I made my way through the expansive hall, the familiar scent of a Gaza summer blended with the less pleasant odor of burning garbage. My mother's concerns about the practice filled the air, her anxiety for our health echoing alongside the rising smoke. I retorted with a sarcastic remark about our situation, pointing out the municipality's financial limitations that resulted in this issue.

The second day at the bank was just like my earlier experience. After waiting for an hour, I stood once again in front of the bank manager, who seemed absorbed in his paperwork and distracted by a phone call. He gestured for me to take a seat, his silent command evident in his manner.

Ahmad, who works at the bank, was my savior. Following the manager's guidance, he collected my account documents and began the fund transfer process.

The manager's tales of my father served as a comforting relief for my anxieties, his cherished recollections of their shared experiences flowing over me like a gentle breeze. It was akin to embarking on a journey into my father's history, uncovering a hero who donned his humility like armor. His accolades were given with a warmth that deeply moved me, reflecting my father's legacy. The manager's concluding remark regarding my father's commitment to our independence instilled in me both pride and a revived determination.

I was taken aback when the manager tried to invite me for coffee; his hospitality was a clear sign of his profound respect for my father. I politely turned him down, using the urgent nature of my tasks as an excuse, yet his friendly attitude had already made a lasting impression on me. As I left the bank holding the transaction confirmation papers, the manager's narratives about my father continued to resonate in my thoughts.

# Holding on, letting go, Gaza 2007
## The Mother

When you talked about leaving, it unsettled me deeply. Every mention of travel brought a rush of fear and anger, as if I were losing you even before you left. I told myself you'd return quickly, that it would only be a matter of weeks. But your love for exploring was part of who you were—a part I always admired and worried about. I still remember the softness of your first word: "Bye," spoken as you said farewell whenever a family member stepped out the front door.

Your grandfather often said that a child senses their path from the moment they see the world. For me, travel stirred a deep anxiety I couldn't easily explain, places one might go, *Hajj* to Mecca, or medical trips to Jaffa. It was a fear born not just of distance but of what could be lost along the way.

I have known loss firsthand. My two sisters were taken into exile, disappearing without a trace. I missed out on the childhood of my youngest brother when he left early and returned only to bring his own family. Their absence leaves a silence that feels endless.

That same fear fills me when I think of losing my sons to the unknown. When my eldest brother first spoke of leaving, it cut deeply, but I held onto the hope he would stay with us, that he would come back.

When my sister married and moved to Saudi Arabia, it felt like she carried a part of me away with her. Nights passed restlessly, her name echoing in my mind, a constant reminder of what was lost.

Even your short ten-day trip to Egypt made my heart race. Your father, calm and steady, reminded me to let you grow; to let you face life on your own terms. Yet my connection to you, as your mother, stayed strong, holding tight to love amid uncertainty.

When you graduated high school with top marks, pride filled me like the morning sun breaking through darkness. I dreamed of what your success would bring. But behind that joy was the memory of your long, hard days—seven hours of work after school. I believed in you then, as I do now. You have always been bright and inspiring.

As a child, you didn't often pick up books unless exams approached, yet your teachers always recognized your sharp mind, calling you one of the brightest in the school.

We gathered in our living room, simple chairs around us, and plates of baklava—sweet like a reward for your hard work. Then your father asked the big question: "Do you want to study Engineering or Medicine?"

At that moment, my heart stopped. I watched you carefully, afraid you might choose Medicine, which would take you far away. Since there were no medical colleges in Gaza at that time, you would have to travel. When you said Engineering, relief washed over me. The thought of you leaving for a distant land was the storm I hoped to avoid.

Frequently, I felt stranded in a sea of emptiness, merely sitting in my chair while my mind drifted into daydreams of Italy. To me, dreams acted as the blueprints of the future.

As time moved forward, you found yourself returning to familiar patterns, now tempered by experience and carrying your hopes clearly in your heart. You wanted to leave, to step into the unknown. But beneath that desire, I sensed you were seeking more than just travel—you were ready for freedom.

Over many years, I watched you slowly pull away from the stories and life of Gaza. As a child, you dreamt of the excitement of Beirut or the quiet of snowy landscapes. I still smile remembering how you used to pretend to be the president, wearing your father's *Kuffiya*, playfully imitating Abu Ammar.

Your university graduation marked a turning point; you had grown into a resolute young man ready to stand on your own. One day, you told me you wanted to continue to a Master's degree. Hearing this, alongside your brother's long absence and your developing strength, made your choice easier to accept. The ongoing political unrest and your activism, shared by your younger brother, intensified my feelings about your leaving. Yet your maturity and achievements gave me hope. Even though you were far away, knowing you were alive was more bearable than the unbearable pain so many mothers face in losing their sons to conflict.

When you asked for money to travel to Malaysia, I worried it might not be the best path for your dreams. You seemed to be chasing hopes tied to others rather than your own strength. Still, I encouraged you to explore all options. A mother rarely refuses her child but tries to teach lessons of resilience and independence. The day I gave you the 70 USD, your brother and I quietly worked to find you a scholarship in Europe.

I watched you closely when you returned from work or downtown, trying to see your inner struggles through your eyes. It was hard to watch you navigate life's challenges. When the scholarship from Italy came through, my heart lifted even more than yours did. Though my formal education was limited, I had learned extensively through the news and radio. Italy represented safety, opportunity, and most importantly, being closer to home.

Your father and I made the biggest sacrifice by accepting your distance, all to protect you and nurture your dreams. We saw you start as a hopeful youth, and now the years have passed, your youthful hair giving way to silver, carrying wisdom earned along the way.

# Between Choices, Gaza 2006
## The Son

I woke up feeling ready to submit my application for a European visa. I knew the chances of approval were slim, but hope was still alive. The thought of the visa lasting only a year made me uneasy—I wished I could stay longer. Still, my father's wise words echoed in my mind: "A bird in the hand is worth ten in the bush." His advice reminded me to appreciate the opportunities I had, even if they were temporary. Parents might come from different times, but their wisdom remains timeless, passed down like priceless lessons from one generation to another.

While waiting for my official admission letter, I kept to a daily routine. I'd wake at ten, make strong coffee, check emails, eat, nap, go to work at dusk, come home, and check emails again. Nights ended with chats on MSN Messenger before I drifted off around midnight. After a week of this, I arrived home one evening tired, secretly carrying two packs of Lucky Strike cigarettes — a small rebellion hidden from my parents.

As I turned on my computer, there it was—an email shining in the dim light: my admission letter. It felt like hope breaking through the darkness, though reality remained harsh with the *Rafah* crossing closed. Still, having the visa was like holding a small light that could guide me forward. I printed the letter, packed it with my documents and passport, and went to sleep with anticipation in my heart.

The next morning felt different. I woke early, and my mother noticed, joking with an old saying, "*Sarih Sraha*," about waking early for work. It reminded me of past generations, Palestinian workers rising before dawn to start their day.

I had to send my passport to the embassy. When I returned from the bathroom, I found my mother had made me coffee. It was funny but touching—she often said I drank too much coffee, but always made me a cup each morning. While I prepared to leave, my brother-in-law stopped by, and over coffee, we talked about the conflict between *Fatah* and *Hamas*.

Soon, I headed to the post office near the municipal park. My brother-in-law laughed, teasing me for being restless, reminding me that the plane wouldn't leave from there. He warned me, "In Europe, you must be careful. Israelis operate openly, looking for collaborators."

At the post office, a relative greeted me warmly. I handed over my envelope with all my important documents for the Italian embassy in Jerusalem, including a fee of about 50 USD. Others arrived too, carrying visa applications for embassies in Spain and Germany.

The manager joked, "Most people apply to study and never come back."

In Gaza and the West Bank, the postal system is unreliable. There are no postcodes in Palestine because Israel refuses to allow them, so mail must go through Israeli control. An Italian friend sent me a postcard and a book in 2005; they didn't arrive until 2008 to Gaza, while I was already in Europe.

In 2009, I sent a book to a friend in Gaza, but it only reached him in 2014 after being held by Israeli authorities. The book was damaged beyond recognition—its spirit lost. It made me question reason in such struggles. But then I wondered: is there any reason for the colonization of Palestine?

Before the room cooled, I thanked my hosts and asked if I could confirm my application's delivery with the embassy the next day. Outside, a cold breeze hit my face, bringing the comforting smell of nearby coffee.

Heading home, my thoughts raced. *What will I do until one o'clock?* I wondered. My watch said it was nearly 11:30.

As I walked, my mind leaped forward to Italy, then snapped back. How would I manage the travel? Classes start in a month. Would I make it? Overwhelmed by doubts, I felt trapped between my dreams and reality—ambitions that felt both distant and urgent.

---

As time moved on relentlessly, I found myself stuck in a place of uncertainty. Waiting was all I could do, and anxiety filled my mind with endless scenarios that vanished as quickly as they came. I feared losing myself as my carefully made plans seemed to dissolve into indecision. I longed for something solid to hold on to amid this storm of waiting.

The period before receiving a decision was both difficult and strangely familiar. It amazed me how the people of Gaza live with this constant uncertainty, never knowing what fate will bring next. Life here is marked by endless waiting—a kind of emptiness that leaves many feelings invisible. Often, I joked with friends that a verse from the Quran (*Al-Ahzab*) described Gazans perfectly: some have fulfilled their vows and others still wait, never losing their resolve. My atheist friend would reply that not all Gazans are truly believers; there are many pretenders among us.

The media was full of news about Hamas's control over Gaza, and I felt powerless as my world seemed to crumble like fragile building blocks. Just as I was preparing for news about my visa, an unexpected call changed everything. The Human Resources team at the Gaza municipality unexpectedly transferred me from the Environment and Public Health Department to the computer and IT unit.

This sudden shift left me confused. My engineering studies felt irrelevant, and I longed for simpler clerical work. My heart was already drawn away from IT toward culture, history, and social sciences. Life had taught me that the brightest people create their own paths and seek places where they can truly excel.

Adjusting to my new role was uncomfortable. I had to start my day very early, facing rows of computers and a few coworkers. Over time, it became clear I didn't quite fit in. My coworkers saw me differently, and my routines changed. Without a personal computer at work, I couldn't check emails during the day. Weeks of dull, repetitive tasks made me feel isolated, but I learned that intolerance of difference is all too common.

Often, I found myself lost in thought, dreaming of Italy. For me, dreams are plans for the future, and I knew that giving up on them would mean losing hope for a better path ahead.

After two weeks, I took a day off—the only leisure day I had among twenty workdays that year—and called the embassy in Jerusalem to check on my visa.

When the consular officer answered, I barely had time to introduce myself before the line cut out, then she said, "We recognize you. You're the only applicant we have from Gaza. Your certificates are ready; we're just waiting to issue your visa."

I asked about the costs for document translation.

"No fees for Palestinians from Gaza with scholarships," she replied.

Relief washed over me. I saved some money.

When my father heard about my trip, he said, "Italians are good people. They remind us of Palestinians—we must be distant relatives from Roman times." He said that with a laugh.

His laughter reminded me of the 1998 World Cup, when Gaza was mesmerized by Italy's team. Our connection wasn't just about appearances but shared solidarity. Italians even dedicated their 1982

World Cup win to the Palestinian cause during the Beirut siege. To me, Italy was a place of hope, creativity, and new beginnings.

That day, traveling to Jordan felt far away, like a faint crescent moon in the morning sky. But getting a Jordanian visa was necessary on my way to Italy. I gathered the required papers and visited the embassy in Ramallah, then headed to the DHL office to submit the visa application to Jordan. At that moment, my future depended on two visas. On the way home, I thought of all possible outcomes—what if Jordan accepted me but Italy didn't? Or vice versa? Life is full of uncertain chances.

Weeks passed in the dull routine of a job that didn't feel meaningful compared to my previous work. I decided to apply for vacation days and resolved that once I had the Italian visa, I would ask for a year-long unpaid leave.

Then, one day while working quietly, my phone rang.

"Hello, is this Ayk?"

"Yes, speaking," I said, heart pounding.

"This is the Italian embassy. You can collect your passport."

I paused, questioning, "Does it have the visa?"

"Yes, and the certified documents," she confirmed.

A smile spread across my face, bridging the distance from Calabria to Gaza, and the sea between them. I felt joy and excitement for the future. I planned to pick it up the next day and checked with EMZ post—luckily, the courier was already in Jerusalem.

Two days later, I could hardly believe it—my passport showed the Italian student visa. Dreams I had imagined had become real. Taking another day off, I collected my documents. Suddenly, Gaza felt temporary, and I was already preparing for a new journey. Holding the passport, I traced the visa with a proud smile.

"*Mabrouk*," said the office manager.

"Thank you. May your children achieve this too," I replied warmly.

"When do you travel?"

"As soon as the Rafah border opens," I said.

He laughed. "*Filmishmish, Inshallah.*"

*Filmishmish* is an Arabic phrase meaning "when pigs fly," expressing how unlikely the border opening seemed.

After leaving the post office, I decided to call the Jordanian embassy. On my way to *Al-Remal*, a lively neighborhood, I looked again at my passport and smiled, holding it close like a treasure.

When I spoke with the Jordanian official, he told me, "Your visa was issued and sent to Gaza two days ago."

I was shocked, asking him to check again. After confirmation, I rushed to the DHL office. That day, it felt like a heavy weight had been lifted and the chains of uncertainty broken.

# Rafah Crossing, Gaza 2007
## The Son

The Rafah crossing had been closed for over nine months, turning Gaza—under strict Hamas control—into one of the world's largest prisons. I held visas for Europe and Jordan, but the chance to cross borders felt distant and unreal. Rumors of Palestinian reconciliation floated around our home, but my father viewed them with skepticism born of experience.

"Every era has its leaders and nations," he often said. "*Hamas* thrives on this situation. They drive expensive cars and hold power tightly, so why would they want to reconcile with *Fatah* and share their gains?"

As months passed and the start of the Italian academic year neared, my anxiety grew, swallowing me in deep darkness. I often woke up late, sometimes only rising when the sun was already high. Still, I stayed wrapped in my sheets until my mother's voice broke through, urging me awake with a mix of humor and firmness. Some days she joked the clock was "eighty," other times "a hundred," trying to shake me from my sluggishness.

One afternoon, I watched the news on *Al Jazeera*. The report said nearly 100,000 Palestinians in Gaza were trapped, unable to continue their studies, jobs, or lives. Thousands more suffered on the Egyptian side, blocked by the Rafah closure and the blockade. On screen, women cried, men shouted in frustration, and the collective despair was palpable, dreams disappearing with no clear end in sight.

Then, the *Hamas* government announced that anyone wishing to leave Gaza could register at the Rafah crossing. That evening, as the sun set, I told my father and brother-in-law that I wanted to sign up.

"My friend, don't provoke them," my brother-in-law warned carefully. "They suspect former *Fatah* activists. You'll draw unwanted attention."

My parents and older brother agreed. "Wait for the crossing to open and leave quietly with the crowd," my father advised.

In the days after, I balanced preparing for my university journey in Italy with constant internet searches, mindful of rising phone bills. One warm evening, a radio announcement sparked hope: the British embassy was helping scholarship holders travel via the Erez crossing to Amman, then on to the UK. I thought about contacting UNESCO and the Italian embassy for help.

The next day, my eldest brother suggested, "Why don't you write to UNESCO?"

I hesitated, "Will it even help? Do they care?"

"Even if it feels like sending a message in a bottle, write honestly about your situation. You have nothing to lose," he encouraged.

The following morning, despite a restless night, I woke early and kept to my routine, anxiously waiting for 10 o'clock—the moment I planned to call UNESCO and the Italian consulate.

When the hour came, I dialed the Italian consulate, nerves tightening.

"I have a visa, but I need assistance. I'm from Gaza," I said.

"Okay, from Gaza! Let me check with the consular secretary. Please hold," came the reply.

While waiting, my mind spun through worst-case scenarios. The rest of the day was spent trying to reach UNESCO—no one answered. Their silence reminded me of a classmate's harsh words, calling UN agencies in Palestine ineffective while earning high salaries.

Later, I contacted the UNESCO representative's office. To my surprise, the representative was Italian. This small fact lifted my spirits, and I found myself imagining her and the Italian consul discussing my case over dinner. Sometimes, a bit of humor helps lighten the heaviest moments.

---

I can't remember the exact day, but I will never forget when my younger brother came to my room with important news, as if returning something I'd lost.

"The Rafah crossing will open for three days, starting the day after tomorrow," he said. Those words sparked a flicker of hope in the darkness and gave me the strength to get up and confirm the news.

The news was true. Energized, I went home and told my family I planned to try to cross.

My mother teased my younger brother, saying, "Ah, you want to send him to Europe so you can have the place to yourself. You're excited to get married."

That evening, my eldest sister—someone I call "my second mother"—came to help me pack. She was surprised I wasn't taking my laptop. I explained it was too heavy and that I planned to buy a new one once I got to Italy.

After a final check of my passport and money, we arranged a taxi to Khan Younes. *Hamas* had organized buses from there to take travelers to the Rafah border. Saying goodbye to my siblings was hard. I struggle with showing emotion, but parting from the faces I had known all my life was deeply moving.

As we passed familiar landmarks on the way to Khan Younes, memories flashed through my mind. When we reached the stadium, the crowd waiting there felt overwhelming. The streets were packed with people, faces full of desperation and worry, as if facing a harsh judgment.

My brother and I could only go so far before the crowd blocked the path. He left to check on the registration while I sat next to my suitcase, watching the chaotic scene unfold. When he returned, he was exhausted; no progress had been made.

Despite the difficulties, a stranger offered a special coordination to get through the Egyptian border—but it came at a high price. My brother didn't trust it and suspected a scam.

As dawn turned to morning, the exhaustion of the crowd was palpable. The waiting felt endless—like a festival without joy, everyone hoping for a miracle that didn't come. Eventually, I gave in to fatigue and despair, accepting that my attempt to leave had failed.

Returning home, my mother greeted me with a warm laugh, "*Ahlan Wa Sahlan*—you traveled and came back."

I was overwhelmed with tiredness and soon fell into a deep sleep, seeking comfort in rest. Later, I learned that only 300 out of 70,000 people waiting actually crossed the border. My brother was blunt: "They were the ones who paid. The ones with money."

Refusing to lose hope, I resolved to keep trying. As my father reminded me, "The best is what God has chosen."

The strongest weapon anyone has is their determination to keep fighting, and when that is lost, dreams begin to fade.

# Doubt and Hope, Gaza 2007
## The Son

As the sun set and darkness crept in, the warmth that once touched my forehead vanished. I was tired and craved sleep, the kind of rest I hadn't had since morning.

Growing up, I often heard warnings like, "Wake up before the sun goes down; it's not safe. Devils come at sunset; you'll get sick." Folklore surrounded me: sleeping at sunset lets evil loose, leaving shoes upside down brings bad luck, and eating watermelon at night might summon danger. After leaving Gaza, I realized these stories came from communities trying to explain life and fill gaps in belief.

Still half-asleep, I moved through the house like a man battling a hangover.

My mother smiled and teased, "Don't think you're in Italy. You're here—sleepwalking."

After a quick wash, I made a simple sandwich with cheese, Gazan *Dogga*, and tomato. Back in my room, I turned on the computer and found a welcome email for the new semester, with a list of classmates. I hoped to find someone who would help gather study materials if my trip to Italy was delayed. The memory of forced online classes during the SARS pandemic was chilling—two kinds of confinement:

one from a virus with a vaccine, the other from occupation without any remedy.

Hours passed before I fully felt awake, like I was coming out of a vivid dream. The suitcase in my room reminded me of what lay ahead. I studied the syllabus and downloaded the course materials. Changing my major from engineering and leaving Gaza felt overwhelming. The first modules were "Cultural Economy," "Post-conflict and Culture," and "Tangible and Intangible Heritage." I felt lost and unsure where to start, but I reminded myself to be patient: *You had a rough night; tomorrow will be better.*

Through Facebook, I connected with classmates and received a message from Lolua, a cultural activist in Tajikistan. She understood my experience and offered to share her lecture notes daily. I thanked her and told the program coordinator about it.

While writing my first paper, one idea caught me: changes in political and historical contexts can reduce the significance of cultural heritage. It made me wonder, *could change also diminish humanity?* I realized change doesn't happen on its own; it requires action. No force outside can transform us—we must be the change we wish to see.

A heavy feeling settled in me. Familiar things in the room, full of memories, seemed larger, almost overwhelming. Fear pushed me to turn off the computer and head to the bathroom for *ablution*, a cleansing ritual before prayer. Back in my room, my brother offered tea, but I declined. I said I would pray and sleep instead, unrolling my prayer mat gently.

I began my *Ishaa* prayer. After the required units, I prayed two extras, seeking guidance. During the second unit, in *Sujood*, despair flooded me. Tears fell as I whispered, "Why me, God? Why must I suffer? Please help me."

In that moment, my vulnerability opened, and I sought comfort and strength from the presence I have always trusted.

---

Outside my room, the heavy heat and bright images of another scorching day surrounded me. This day felt different—something was off. My mother, who usually wakes me like a reliable alarm clock, didn't call me.

Slowly, my tired body moved as my mind nudged it awake, my feet sliding over the worn tiles that had been in our home since the 1970s. My hand rubbed my eyes awake, and I felt the salty trace of a tear on my cheek. Had I cried in my sleep, or was this the quiet residue of last night's grief?

As I left the room, I leaned on the doorframe, tired. My mother saw me sitting by the tree she had lovingly nurtured for seven years. She admitted she let me sleep, joking that my long travel day deserved a break.

Then, teasingly, I said to her with mock annoyance, "It's because of you. You don't want me to travel."

Seeing my discomfort, she playfully added, "*Roh Tnnayl*" (Go to hell), but her smile made it clear it was a joke.

Looking back, I understand why she wished I wouldn't leave Gaza and why her teasing hid relief whenever I was home. Years ago, a relative who sees the future through reading hands and a cup of coffee, the traditional way of seeing the future, predicted, "You will travel far and long."

When I asked if that was all, she said, "That's what I see now."

Those words stayed with us, filling the days with quiet waiting, sleep broken by worry, and too much time spent staring at my computer screen. The online world became my main connection with classmates, while my phone's constant buzzing threatened bad news. Despite it all, I treasured the moments spent with my aging parents.

My father, who had retired by then after decades of work, refused to stop his morning routines. "A man dies when he stops working," he would say.

Even after retirement, he rose early, walking to his beloved mosque, *Ibn Othman*, and returning by sunrise. His determination to avoid rest echoed in my mind, blending with his words: "It is better to travel with dignity and comfort than to just arrive."

When news came that Rafah crossing would open on Wednesday, I felt a strange mix of hope and dread. The weight of despair can cloud good news. Still, the announcement spread on every media platform and pushed me to prepare. I planned to be at the stadium early, ahead of the crowds, knowing well the gatekeepers' tactics. An officer once confided to me that some guards accepted bribes and used crossings as opportunities to make extra money. That made me feel like a helpless dog, trapped and ignored.

When registration started, uncertainty gripped me. Friends couldn't help with the complicated coordination; the 1,500 USD fee was impossible, and signing my name in front of Hamas militants felt like walking into a fire. As an opposition activist, I knew this was risky.

On a cool Monday morning, I walked along Gaza's sandy beach, feeling small amid the crowd of footprints. The calm waves and fresh breeze offered peace, but that peace was shattered when I returned home to foul sewage smells from a nearby broken system.

"My God, enough!" my father exploded, cursing the municipal neglect. "When they built this in 1986, only a few hundred lived here. Now, 10,000 depend on this broken system."

Years later, whenever I saw broken sewage pipes in Beirut, I was instantly transported back to Gaza.

Yet life went on. I saw a woman lifting her long *Abbaya* to keep it clean, children making sleds from plastic to slide over sewage pools, and the mosque's *Imam* adjusting his *Jallabiya* as he headed to pray. Despite protests, the children laughed and played, their resilience shining through the stench. We often joked that any new virus coming to Gaza would turn back, defeated by the strength and immunity built from years of hardship.

At home, our neighbor sent a plate of food. The house buzzed with food smells; my mother had prepared a lunch fest on the floor—

okra, rice, green chili, raw onions, bread, and an unfamiliar dish called *Rummaniyya*.

My mother said, "Your mother-in-law loves you," a common phrase when guests arrive as meals are started to be served.

My father joked, "He should find a wife before the mother-in-law."

I asked about the unknown dish and learned it was made from eggplant and pomegranates, called "poor man's meat" because the eggplant chunks look like meat. I had never tried it before, but found it surprisingly tasty. That day was my last encounter with *Rummaniyya*; I've never seen it since. This made me realize how our tastes are tied to familiar foods from home. Food, like people, carries stories that fade when we leave.

After the meal, my father lay back and quickly fell asleep for an afternoon nap. I wanted to ask if he remembered *Al-Zeer Salem*, a story he told in my childhood, but the moment passed. His quiet rest filled the house, while I faced a stack of unread emails. I hoped for news from UNESCO or the Italian embassy, but the silence deepened my despair. My sigh echoed through the quiet rooms, a reminder of disappointment.

Later, dark clouds gathered overhead, signaling the first rain of the season. At seven, on an impulse, I decided to travel to Khan Younis.

My brother Mohammed offered to accompany me, saying, "I'll stay with you until you leave."

Our mother worried and insisted Mohammed return after dropping me off. My parents were sadly used to seeing my travel bag by the door promise of departure that often didn't come true.

Stepping outside, my father called after us, "If they start shooting, just come back!"

*Salah Eddin* Street, the main road from north to east Gaza, was alive with taxis and travelers carrying bags. This was the road where I first traveled as a child to visit the home of martyred fighter Osama Najjar, a place heavy with memories.

Near Khan Younis, we faced many Hamas checkpoints. Thousands waited for Rafah to open in two days, the crowd overwhelming. It felt impossible to outpace them and secure a spot. Later that evening, we found brief comfort over hot tea at Shareef's house.

But stepping outside again, police laughter at the struggles of travelers cut deeply. Their vague remarks suggested corruption was widespread.

# Despair, Gaza 2007
## The Son

Under the night sky, my brother and I lay on rough cardboard, surrounded by many others doing the same. The possibility of rain looming, threatening to turn our gatherings into a muddy mess. In the quiet, a baby's cry pierced the stillness, jolting me from my restless sleep.

An elderly woman nearby whispered sadly, "What wrongs has this innocent child done to suffer like this?"

Her words cut deep, filling me with a quiet self-reflection. I wondered why I had come to witness such pain in this broken place. All wanted to travel and leave Gaza.

Around me, everyone carried their own heavy story. A mother searching for a quiet spot to nurse her young baby, an old woman shivering in a thin shawl, an 18-year-old clutching a worn backpack and dreaming of university in Cairo, a middle-aged engineer fearing job loss in Doha. Their hardships filled the air, mingling with the scent of sorrow and hopelessness, like being trapped in quicksand with no rescue.

At dawn, a *Hamas* police officer's voice echoed from his car, ordering everyone to move to the stadium where buses would take us to Rafah. We exchanged bitter smiles but pulled our bags and joined the rush.

The orange taxi back to Gaza City felt burdened with my sadness. Despair etched my face, and the phrase "Gaza, the land of death" haunted my thoughts. I felt trapped in a bubble of hopelessness as the taxi sped on.

The driver, marked by harsh lines from a hard life and a cigarette always between his fingers, broke through my gloom by mentioning a relative who might help with 'coordination.' I asked if this relative was with Hamas or the Egyptians. His hearty laughs briefly lifted the heavy air.

The hope faded with the phone call—spots were taken by 1,500 people, each paying a bribe of 700 USD. Hearing passengers called "heads" stunned me—freedom had become a commodity. Discouraged, I returned home, the driver's bitter jokes echoing inside me.

At home, relief and disappointment tangled. My father's calm words on patience and faith offered some comfort, though I didn't know then that a call from the Italian embassy that night would change everything.

During the ride, the driver's voice shifted from excitement to grave acceptance. My brother and I listened closely as he explained that all spots were booked for the next three days, with 1,500 reserved travelers. His frustrated curses hung in the air.

I asked about the cost—it was 700 USD per person. The dehumanizing term "head" replayed in my mind, picturing travelers as livestock to be sold. Some years, the price soared as high as 3,500 USD. With a heavy heart, I went home.

The driver's cynical remarks about Hamas and the struggles of the people stayed with me as we traveled familiar roads.

Returning home felt full of contradictions. My mother spoke words of hope and faith, my father rested, confident in divine timing. But in my room, I felt broken. I collapsed on my bed, fully dressed, overwhelmed by emotion. Eventually, sleep came and gave me a temporary escape.

At three in the morning, my phone rang insistently. I barely noticed at first—it was the Italian embassy. I hesitated before answering, weighed down by hopelessness. Hearing the voice from Italy sparked a flicker of hope, though the thought of a meeting in Israel filled me with fear.

I thought through the possibilities, wondering if it was a trap. I decided to go and reassess afterwards.

When I told my parents, my father's words comforted me: "I told you, Allah is preparing something better." He reassured me that my political activism wouldn't pose a problem.

That night, my brother-in-law, a former *Fatah* security officer, gave me valuable advice about the meeting.

So, with a nervous heart, I waited for the dawn of a new day—one that could change my life forever.

# Erez, Gaza 2007
## The Son

Under a calm blue sky, the rooster's morning call woke me at five. The creak of the front door announced my father's return. His soft prayer floated through the quiet morning, a familiar comfort woven with faith.

Rushing through the morning routine, I resisted my mother's insistence on a shower, worried about being late. Stepping out, the rich aroma of coffee wrapped around me, both comforting and nerve-wracking. Despite her objections, my father eagerly poured himself a cup—his traditional remedy for nerves.

Breakfast with my parents felt almost dreamlike in its quiet intimacy. As I sipped coffee, I studied my father's weathered face, a map of time and hardship. His advice about my upcoming interview with the Israelis carried a serious weight amid the peaceful morning.

Humor lightened the mood with my mother's playful reference to the second *Intifada*: "Meeting Sharon"—her euphemism for a long bathroom break—lifted our spirits before I faced the day's uncertainties.

The taxi ride toward the Erez crossing took me past the raw beauty of dawn in Gaza. The landscape's simplicity stirred deep reflection, while fears of manipulation and collaboration hovered like dark clouds above an uncharted sea.

At the deserted Hamas checkpoint, a sharp reminder of our precarious reality, anxiety grew as the Palestinian Authority officials recognized me and the others and asked for our IDs.

Our movement felt like a solemn procession under constant surveillance—an eerie dance in front of ever-watchful Israeli cameras. Walking the long corridor in silence, each of us wrestled with our own worries.

A seasoned businessman, familiar with this routine, broke the silence with bold advice and carefree humor, contrasting with the fearful tension of another traveler. I found myself torn between quiet defiance and cautious fear.

Crossing the "red line," we entered the narrow, fence-lined passage—the maze leading to Erez. Six cameras and a loudspeaker watched silently overhead. The fear thickened as we moved down this sealed corridor.

The businessman, our unwelcome guide in the darkness, grew quiet, increasing our collective unease as we neared the final gate. We slowed, instinctively holding our breath in the stillness.

A sudden voice crackled through the speakers—a distorted female voice. The businessman stepped forward, lifted his shirt for inspection, then disappeared as the gate closed behind him.

When my turn came, I duplicated the ritual, the weight of fear and hope mixing in my mind. Inside, the sterile scene was one of heightened security—empty except for steel fences and the faint scent of soldiers.

Separated by fences, solitary confinement felt real. I recalled stories of Israeli intelligence attempts to recruit Palestinians and vowed silently that I would refuse even at great cost.

As the next gate approached, paranoia crept in again: Did they have something compromising about me? I stole myself with a sharp mental reply, determined not to give in.

Inside the heavily guarded area, time slowed. The X-ray machines scanned us, and finally, we faced the young soldier demanding our IDs. Her youth contrasted sharply with the power she held over us. Being herded into a corner to wait, the harsh reality of occupation settled heavily around me.

Sweat formed on my brow as I stood, my mind swirling with questions: Why was I here? How had I ended up like this? It felt like a nightmare, and part of me wished I could fly away back to the chaotic familiarity of Gaza. No soldiers brandished weapons, only a few scattered guards, yet the atmosphere was heavy with confinement and humiliation.

A stern officer in civilian clothes appeared. His sharp features were hidden behind dark sunglasses. He commanded us with a curt "*Taal*" in broken Arabic, collected our IDs, lined us up against the wall, and searched us carefully with a handheld scanner—as if the previous X-ray wasn't invasive enough.

He disappeared for a moment and returned with black plastic bags and long black flex cuffs. A chill ran down my spine. I feared arrest—because of my *Fatah* affiliation, or simply my family ties. Sweat poured down my face.

Inside a room, I saw my three companions, stripped to their underwear and handcuffed, standing in a human chain. Their left hands rested on the shoulder of the man in front, while their right hands held bags containing their clothes.

The officer ordered me to undress. My movements were mechanical, fueled by fear and obedience. He inspected my naked body with heavy, invasive hands. When he touched my private parts, I swatted his hand away despite his command to remain silent. He handed me a plastic bag to hold my clothes, but abruptly snatched my belt, declaring it dangerous.

Fully undressed, I joined the human chain, placing my hand on the shoulder of the young man ahead of me. The officer blindfolded me with a tightly secured plastic bag and bound my legs with flex cuffs. We were told to move slowly, following the lead of the first man.

We descended stairs and twisted through corridors for fifteen minutes, an ordeal that felt like a descent into hell. Blind, restrained, and at the mercy of our captors, we were mere pawns in their cruel game. Whenever the line faltered, the officer rejoined us, like misplaced links in a chain.

The cycle of isolation and forced reconnection cast a dark shadow over us, a psychological torment designed to break spirits. It was a humiliating procession, echoing the suffering of countless men before—and those yet to come.

After the march stopped, we were guided into an elevator whose mechanical hum filled the confined space like frantic wings. Two floors later, we moved through a maze of hallways and climbed about fifty stairs.

A heavy silence settled over us. With every minute, frustration grew as we faced the painful reality of our dehumanization.

I wondered who was watching us—male or female soldiers—staring at our naked vulnerability. This exposure was unlike anything I'd experienced before. When the monotone beep of an unlocked door sounded, a sudden cool breeze hit our blindfolded faces and bare chests.

Inside the room, the officer began removing our blindfolds. We were told to sit on small chairs, our nakedness painfully exposed. I wondered how long this would last, but the officer, accustomed to this torture, quickly cut our leg restraints one by one.

With a harsh "*Elbis*," put your clothes on, he ordered us to dress and left, leaving us in silence.

Looking around, the small white room felt stark and cold. A window showed a calm sea, contrasting the tension inside. A large mirror likely served as a one-way observation point. Fear hung thick, silencing all conversation.

After 30 minutes, the door opened again. Every 15 minutes, an officer returned to escort someone out. One by one, companions were taken until I was the last left standing. Rather than fear, solitude strengthened me. My heartbeat steadily, and my eyes reflected the fierce determination of a lion ready to face whatever came next.

For a moment, a wild thought crossed my mind: what if I laughed loudly and unexpectedly, making them think I had lost my mind? Instead of letting them control my emotions, I wanted to be the one to unsettle them with my laughter. There I was, trapped alone in a small room, enduring a grueling two-hour wait that gnawed at my sanity.

I wondered about their intentions—whether they wanted something from me or were simply playing a cruel psychological game. Through the haze of uncertainty, only one urgent need stood out clearly: the need to use the bathroom. I wasn't concerned with their plans, only fearful of their hinted threats of imprisonment.

After what felt like an eternity—two and a half hours—the door finally creaked open. An officer led me into an office lined with trophies, scattered files, and the Israeli flag hanging silently. A man in his mid-40s, calm and composed, sat behind the desk like a spider in its web. He stood and shook my hand politely, a hollow gesture before the ordeal ahead.

He began with a twisted apology for the body search, calling it a defense against "harmful demons." I didn't respond, wearing my discomfort quietly. Then, opening his laptop, he started demanding details about my life.

The interrogation had a strange rhythm. He offered me a cigarette, which I declined. Then coffee—also refused.

"*Badri o Haniya* Coffee is the best, isn't it?" he said, naming Gaza's popular coffee brand.

His offers weren't kindness, but tactics in this uncomfortable game. His flawless Gaza Arabic surprised me. My brother-in-law, who was an officer in the Palestinian Intelligence Anti-collaboration unit, later explained these interrogators had served in Gaza since the first *Intifada*, still hunting collaborators.

After an hour of relentless questioning, he summoned a soldier via a button. I was escorted back to the first room, sharing space with a tall man whose face looked like a ripe apple, his eyes weary from many battles. Silence hung heavily between us, broken only by small gestures. We were puppets, controlled from another room.

Half an hour later, a distressed businessman arrived, sweating and gasping. I pressed the red button to call for water. It took another 30 minutes before any came.

The tall man remarked bitterly, "Lucky you got water. I asked, but they never brought me any."

Just then, the door slammed open. Fear gripped me, expecting punishment for our conversation. Instead, they called me back for harsher questioning about people from my neighborhood, including a childhood classmate.

"My life is about studies, work, and home," I said firmly, meeting the interrogator's gaze.

He shouted, "You're lying! You know them!"

Calmly, I replied, "You understand them better than they understand themselves. Why are you asking me?"

I marveled at my own boldness—it surged within me like a storm. They pressed me about phones and jobs of my family members, as if they had all the information. It felt like they were weaving an intricate web, building a detailed dossier on every Palestinian.

Our day began at an ungodly hour outside an empty shipping container and ended near sunset. Before leaving, the officers ordered us to cover our heads with plastic bags again. The tall man then asked if we could leave Gaza.

The officer's cold reply haunted me: "We will see."

The arrogance in that simple phrase revealed the power imbalance of colonization—the dominant "We" towering over the controlled "us."

# Borrowed Time, Gaza 2007
## The Son

Friday morning, I woke up overwhelmed by fatigue and despair. Two weeks had passed since my interview, lengthening into a heavy shadow. My movements felt slow and forced as I sat on the edge of the bed, trying to convince my eyes to accept the new day.

"Wake up, the clock's struck eight," my mother called softly.

"I'm awake," I replied, stretching as I pressed my eyes, trying to shake off the exhaustion. Checking my phone, I saw no missed calls. Standing by the door, I looked out into the backyard where sunlight gently touched the rose bush my mother had planted ten years ago. Our family's connection to nature ran deep, intertwined with generations of memory.

Fridays usually meant family gatherings. The kitchen would buzz with the aroma of *Maqlouba*, *Maftoul*, or sometimes *Geddra*, filling the house as we anticipated the post-prayer meal that stretched into the evening. This Friday, though, felt different—quieter, smaller, missing the usual warmth.

"I won't cook today," my mother's voice came from the entrance, tired but firm.

"Why not?" I asked.

"I'm exhausted. No one is visiting, and you're not helping. Take some money and get kebab for everyone," she replied, shaded by sunlight.

"But you should cook *Geddra*. I want to eat it before Ramadan, and I might leave soon," I urged.

Her face softened. After a deep breath, she moved toward the kitchen. "I'll do anything for you, *Habibi*," she said kindly.

Grinning, I went to freshen up. In the bathroom, my breath fogged the mirror. I wiped it like a windshield and caught sight of myself. My eyes were red, and exhaustion clear on my face.

"Why do I look this tired?" I asked my reflection, anger bubbling beneath the surface. Determined to push away anxiety, I decided to shower before prayers.

"Is there enough water for a shower, Mom?" I called out.

"I don't know. Check yourself," she said. No matter what age, a mother's voice comforts. Feeling the warm water on my face, her reassurance mattered.

"It's warm enough," I said. In Gaza, power outages meant boiling water or letting the sun warm it.

"Don't use too much; we might not get more for three days," she warned.

I simply said, "Okay."

After the shower, the air felt thick and humid. Sweat trickled down my face, sunlight sparkling in my eyes. I longed to escape the house's tightness. As I walked through the corridor, a breeze from the backyard brushed my skin, tempting me with a glimpse of freedom.

In a simple blue t-shirt, faded jeans, and worn sandals, I stepped outside toward the mosque. But which mosque? Every Friday, I found myself walking to a different place of worship. The promise of air conditioning called me on this hot day. I headed for the *Al-Hikma* Mosque.

Once vibrant, the mosque—over three centuries old—now stands with only a weathered minaret remaining after the Israeli attack in 2014 destroyed the rest. I had walked this path many times; every stone held memories, casting a ghostly veil over the renewed sanctuary. When asked what remains of Gaza, I think of its scars. Physical structures crumble, but the impressions etched in my soul endure.

After a brisk twenty-minute walk, I left my sandals at the entrance and stepped onto the worn carpets. The Imam's sermon filled the old walls, bringing peace to my body, but my mind drifted to the winding streets of Milan and Rome—imagining freedom. With closed eyes, I sensed the sweet taste of liberty along distant canals.

That daydream shattered as the Imam's voice rose to close the prayer. My peaceful smile turned to frustration. Like sprinters, the worshippers rushed for the exit puzzling scene I always struggled to understand. Among the crowd, I felt caught in a slow-motion sci-fi escape.

I rose from the carpet, resting my hand on my heart to finish the last two *Rakats Sunnah* quietly. The mosque, once full of life, now felt hollow, allowing me to leave unnoticed. At the door, shoes were piled chaotically. I found mine and stepped out, my phone buzzing with a call from an unfamiliar Jerusalem number.

The voice belonged to Chiara, UNESCO's manager in East Jerusalem. She spoke gently about my request to leave Gaza. Time stretched as she gave the bitter news: "Permission was not granted. The Israeli security wants to meet you again."

Anger and despair rose fiercely inside me. My voice cracked as I responded, "No, I will not meet them again. They asked everything last time—they knew everything. Is this the peace they want? Preventing students from learning and traveling? Helping the UN achieve peace?"

Her silence was understandable. I was sure she understood the hopelessness this causes. Denying young people's education and opportunity fuels extremism. When hope dies, radical ideas grow, and death feels inevitable.

Looking back, I know I was right. Wars, internal strife, despair, and a lost faith in the future could have ended me. I tell friends and colleagues that since 2007, my life has been borrowed time. I could have become one of many casualties.

After my father passed, I took on a stoic mask, hiding tears in public, adhering to an outdated idea of masculinity. I reserved my grief for solitude, trying to protect a fragile pride.

Now, I see these norms for what they are: chains that trap men in unhealthy expectations. Grieving and showing emotion aren't only for women. Men can cry and still command respect and dignity.

---

In the soft morning light, I held a cup of coffee, my eyes heavy with fatigue and my body tired. That day, I left my usual routine and sat under the tall tree in front of the house, greeting neighbors as they passed by. My thoughts were restless, struggling against the limits I faced. I wanted a cigarette sharply, but I didn't smoke out of respect for my father sitting beside me. In our conservative Gazan family, a son never smokes in front of his father.

As time passed, my brother-in-law arrived from the nearby streets, breaking the quiet morning. We spent an hour talking about the difficult political tensions between Hamas and *Fatah* until he asked, twice, "When are you traveling?"

His question finally reached me. Others laughed and teased, "His mind isn't here—it's in Italy."

I gave a vague reply and went back to check my email. There, an email from UNESCO awaited me, promising faster permission to leave Gaza through their link with the Italian embassy. My studies were to start in two days, but I was stuck, relying on the internet to learn.

Days went by slowly as I waited for approval. The Italian

consulate called to say they had appealed to the Israeli Defense Minister for an emergency permit. After the call, I thought about how fragile power is—how my future depended on the decisions of an Israeli officer or a young soldier watching drones.

The reality hit me hard. I kept my pain inside, even around my older brother. This silent suffering was difficult, but I held on to hope and strength.

As Ramadan began and classes started, my hope faded. Supportive messages from colleagues and classmates were my only comfort through the heavy workload. I felt trapped physically but mentally free, studying economics, culture, tourism, and politics—subjects new and interesting to me.

One afternoon, while buying hummus, carob juice, and pickles for Ramadan, my old Nokia suddenly rang loudly, cutting through the market noise. Seeing an unknown number, fear washed over me—was it another attempt to recruit young Gazans? I quickly hid the phone and kept walking, bumping into my younger brother.

The phone rang again, this time from Jerusalem. Summoning courage, I answered and heard a voice with a gentle Italian accent. The news was difficult: approval was coming, but the timing was uncertain. The farewell I wanted to give my family felt sudden and incomplete.

This uncertainty was hard to accept—a pause between staying and leaving. It reminded me of nights spent afraid of invasion. Now, I was waiting again—not for danger, but to leave. My bag had been packed for months, but leaving now felt different—more serious, filled with both excitement and fear. I felt this deeply in my heart.

# The Last Ramadan and the Unspoken Fears, Gaza 2007

## The Son

On the last Thursday of Ramadan, as the clock struck six, I navigated my way home from downtown, trapped in a reality that felt as desolate as an abandoned city. The oppressive heat, the sandpaper-like roughness of my dry throat, and the heaviness of fatigue pulling at my eyelids were my only companions until my phone buzzed. An unfamiliar number from Jerusalem appeared on the screen. A wave of dread settled in my stomach, and my hands shook like leaves caught in a storm before I could finally answer.

"*Buongiorno*, I am Francesco from the Italian embassy in Jerusalem. Is this Ayk?" he inquired, his accent wrapping Italian silk around his words.

"This is me, Ayk," my voice wavered, my heartbeat pounding at an anxious tempo as I braced myself for the coming words.

"Tomorrow, you are traveling, leaving Gaza," he said.

I cut him short, my words slicing through the thick tension. "You mean the Israelis have granted me the pass to travel?" I clarified, my voice measured and slow, echoing the beat of the question that throbbed in my veins.

"Yes, your journey starts tomorrow. Arrive at Erez Crossing by seven in the morning. An Italian diplomat will be there to meet you. Don't be late," his words concluded our conversation before he ended the call.

Standing frozen like a statue, I gripped my phone as if it were a lifeline. Then, the weight of his words washed over me like a wave: I was leaving the neighborhood that had nurtured me since birth. As I scanned the familiar faces and shopfronts that had become fixtures in my life, an exceptional sense of finality took hold. It was as though an inner compass signaled that many of these faces would soon dissolve into the fabric of my memory, never to reappear. Turning toward home, my feet instinctively followed the well-known path, drawn by the comfort of familiarity.

As I entered, the rich aroma of Ramadan delicacies enveloped me like a tempting promise. Plates of vivid colours lay scattered across the floor, waiting for the fasting day to end. In an unusual scene, the only guests at our table were my immediate family—a contrast to the usual flow of relatives who filled our home during Ramadan.

Spotting me, my mother asked, "What do you want to eat tomorrow? *Maftoul* or *Maqlouba*?" Her question lingered, heavy with the anticipation of our last Friday of Ramadan.

"I won't be here to break the fast tomorrow," my response landed heavily in the conversation.

"Allah, are you invited elsewhere?" her question bloomed with a smile.

"No. I'm leaving tomorrow. The embassy just let me know," I shared, a smile tugging at the corner of my mouth.

Time seemed to freeze around us. My little sister halted mid-step, a dish clasped in her hands. My mother rose, an uncertain smile playing on her lips.

"*Yalla! Inchallah Khair*, let's hope this time it works out," she voiced her prayer.

My father, who was the last to know, nodded and said, "Good. Go, pursue your studies, and return when you have finished. Avoid politics and forbidden practices." His tone was firm and resolute, emphasised by the closing of the holy Quran.

As the *Maghreb* call rang out, marking the end of the day's fast, my father did something unusual: he chose to pray before we broke our fast. The room was heavy with silence, enveloped in a dense fog of melancholy. I felt adrift in a sea of conflicting emotions, with the sadness reflected in my parents' eyes clashing against my unrestrained excitement and desire to discover what lay beyond.

After breaking our fast, I withdrew to my room. My suitcase and backpack, silent witnesses to my failed attempts to escape Gaza, patiently awaited their final packing. After seventeen years, I decided to send the suitcase back to Gaza after the genocide, as a hint that whoever leaves, shall go back, one day.

As I packed, my mother entered the room and sat on the bed, tears glistening in her eyes, reflecting her sorrow. She gave me a stash of money, her words revealing the fears of a mother sending her child out into the world. When she left, her silence conveyed so much.

"You're going to study, not for tourism, not to pursue politics. Study and return," my father's words, filled with his hopes and anxieties, served as my only farewell. He handed me an envelope, a safety net for the uncertain future ahead.

Upon opening it, I discovered a pile of 100-dollar bills. His generosity served as a touching reminder of his love and care, acting as my direct connection to home. His sadness reflected the grief of losing another son, highlighting the emptiness their absence left in his life. Nevertheless, life presented itself as a blank canvas for us sons, and we were the artists meant to infuse it with our unique narratives.

That night is a significant entry in my memories. Shortly after midnight, my mother appeared at my doorway, her silhouette framed by the light. I pretended to be asleep, keeping my eyes tightly shut. Despite my many unsuccessful attempts to cross the Rafah border, I always returned home, greeted by her laughter and the words, "You traveled and returned—thank God! *Hamdella A'asalamah.*"

However, that night, the atmosphere was laden with a sense of finality, like a closing note to a long melody. With international guarantees and support from the Italian embassy and UNESCO, I was ready to leave the large prison we called home. Life in Gaza, which felt almost familiar then, was about to become a mere footnote in my history.

I sensed my mother's approach through the whisper of her footsteps, or perhaps it was my imagination painting a picture of her silent tears cascading like dewdrops. As the weight shifted on the edge of my bed, I could feel her presence. I continued to pretend to sleep, aware of her gaze exploring my face as if trying to engrave it into her memory. I could feel her silent tears tracing the contours of her cheeks.

Mothers possess a sixth sense; they always know. My plans had been mapped out just one year abroad, but did she realize I might not come back? I lay there, pretending to sleep, aligning my breath with hers. I yearned to shatter the pretence, to face her, to ask why she lingered. Yet, I allowed her to watch me, to absorb the sight of me. The clock indicated 12 in besieged Gaza, and I was meant to rise at four to journey toward the Erez crossing, the northern gate of our collective prison.

My determination to keep up the facade of sleep stemmed from an intense fear of goodbyes. Goodbyes embodied a terrible contradiction – the hope of seeing each other again, contrasted with the haunting possibility that it might be our final moment together. I feared the farewell deeply. Eventually, I would understand the reason behind this dread, as my father would die before I had the opportunity to greet him once more. I opted to leave in an ordinary manner, mirroring my earlier failed attempts to escape in an effort to outsmart fate.

My mother understood I would set off on this journey of life, knowing I might never return. Years later, I still struggle with this question: Did she truly know? Why did she allow me to go? How could she choose to endure the constant pain of longing amidst countless possible outcomes? The options were numerous: a joyous reunion, the heartbreaking chance of never seeing me again, or the unimaginable horror of my return in a coffin. How did she come to terms with these thoughts? How did she find solace in the face of such significant loss while already living amid the consequences of multiple wars, stringent sieges, rampant unemployment, and the grim reality of an unlivable Gaza?

My heart aches with these inquiries: How did my mother's grief evolve, contradicting the saying "sadness is born big and then shrinks"? How did she survive the years and months, consumed by an overwhelming tide of sorrow?

# The Last Goodbye, Gaza 2007
## The Son

At four in the morning, I woke and looked out my window, confirming the sky was still dark before dawn. The first light was beginning to appear on the horizon.

I quickly got out of bed; my mind was still foggy but calm. I went to the bathroom, splashed cold water on my face, and brushed my teeth with a practiced routine. Walking back, I noticed my mother praying quietly in the corridor, her whispers filling the empty space.

In my room, I carefully packed my toothbrush and toothpaste into my travel bag. This ritual, repeated on many trips, had become a steady routine, the last to pack and the first to unpack. The familiar path from my room to the bathroom was a reminder of the many mornings I had spent in Gaza; comforts I would later miss.

In my new life, I appreciate having a place for these simple items by a clean sink. I often think about how others care for their oral hygiene. Do children in remote places brush their teeth in front of mirrors? How do they access water to do so? The genocide of Gaza has shown me that in the most horrific ways.

I picture myself in a small village far away, walking a long way to find water. I imagine holding my toothbrush and toothpaste as I hurry to the communal water source. I imagine feeling the cool dew on my bare feet and the sun's first rays as I brush there.

This image shows the daily struggles that many face to meet basic needs. These thoughts remind me that there is a bigger world beyond my own experiences.

I looked at the bag holding the clothes and memories of my life. I left behind some clothing, knowing they would never be worn again and would soon be forgotten, like parts of a past life.

When I grabbed my bag and pulled it along the floor, my heart skipped a beat. Was I really leaving? A wave of emotion washed over me as I stood caught between staying and going. I had reached my goals and was ready to leave the walls that confined me, but something still held in my heart. It was a turning point major change in my life.

"Your brother Mohamed will accompany you to Erez," my mother's voice wafted over to me as she concluded her prayers.

"No, I don't want him to. The Hamas checkpoint might give him trouble," I replied instantly, my words interlaced with concern.

Out of the corner of my eye, I noticed my younger sister standing at her door. A complex mixture of emotions played across her face—a bright smile contrasting with the tears welling in her eyes. This was her first goodbye to a brother, with an uncertain amount of time stretching out until we might reunite. Sisters are much like fortune-tellers or second mothers, able to sense the shifts of change before they unfold. Maybe she already understood that our time apart would be lengthy.

When the taxi arrived, my younger brother leapt into action, helping me with the bag. I suggested he join me at the mosque so I could say goodbye to our father before heading home with him. His nod confirmed our plan.

My mother stood by, her eyes filled with quiet strength and unfallen tears. I felt a familiar warmth as I grasped her hand. The embrace offered a fleeting refuge, her kiss on my forehead serving as a final blessing.

"Take care of yourself," she murmured, her words fluttering like a fragile bird.

"*Inshallah*," I echoed, my assurance in the tense air.

Next came my sister, her eyes brimming with a constellation of teardrops ready to overflow at the faintest tremor. "Don't cry. I'm not disappearing into oblivion. Take care of our parents," I encouraged her as I wrapped her in a reassuring hug. My last footsteps resonate through the hallways of our shared childhood.

As I stepped out of the house, I locked eyes with my mother one last time, her expression a blend of silent sobs and flowing tears.

"Mom, this is unbearable. If my departure hurts you so much, I'd rather stay. But please, don't cry. I promise I'll come back," I reassured her. Yet, I understood that the stirrings of *Ghourba* had already taken hold of her heart, a flame that would linger on. *Ghourba* is an Arabic word that describes many emotions in one word: exile, homesickness, estrangement, and alienation.

As the taxi's engine hummed and we began our journey to the west, my eyes remained fixed on my mother and sister, who stood like sentinels at the door. Their figures slowly faded from view, shrinking until they were just tiny dots in my rear-view mirror.

The road ahead stretched out, a dull strip of asphalt bordered by winter-bare landscapes on both sides. A chill enveloped us. My brother and I were uncertain about our father's whereabouts, hoping for a glimpse of him coming back from the mosque. As we approached the cemetery, we spotted a solitary figure coming from the east, who paused as our car drew near, recognition lighting up his face.

A wave of fatigue hit me as I stepped out of the taxi, the weight of finality leaving me in a state of emptiness. I took a few slow breaths to steady myself, struggling to keep my emotions in check.

Once I neared him, he nodded, "Ah, you're leaving."

"Yes, I am ready, with good intentions, *Inshallah*," I replied.

"Make me proud, do you hear that?" His voice wavered as he dabbed his tear-streaked face with a tissue.

"I will make you proud, rest assured," I replied, adding, "You've raised me to be independent and filled me with wisdom and knowledge. I won't just fly; I will soar, carrying on your legacy."

After sharing a final embrace, I let my younger brother take him home. I later discovered he cried for the rest of the day. At that moment, I wasn't aware it was the last time I would see him, the final face-to-face conversation between us.

As the taxi drove me towards Erez, I struggled with my overwhelming feelings, holding back tears that still managed to flow silently. I shifted my gaze back and forth, committing to memory the sights and sounds of Gaza—its trees, homes, the distinct scent of its air, and its landscapes.

Years later, I remembered a conversation with a college friend who once asked, "Where do you think you'll be in ten years?"

That question, my departure from home, and the image of my parents' tears provided a fresh perspective on life. The broader concept of life's meaning became less significant; what truly mattered was the specific meaning of one's life at a certain moment and in a unique context.

# Freedom, Unfreedom, Gaza 2007
## The Son

A desolate world stretched before me, holding me down like a specimen in a biological study, caught in the scene of Gaza. As I handed my ID to the soldiers from *Hamas* at the first checkpoint, I sensed I had relinquished a portion of my independence. A young man in his twenties approached our vehicle, his anger emanating like a raging wildfire. Dressed in loose, dark blue trousers and holding an AK-47 machine gun as if it were a prized possession, he looked inside the car.

His face, framed by a thin beard, showed clear signs of hardship. I couldn't help but notice his sandals—a simple pair that revealed him to be a dedicated *Hamas* supporter. In Gaza, everyone recognized these "Napoli Sandals" as an unspoken symbol of affiliation. Years later, when I arrived in Napoli, a sign welcoming us sparked ironic laughter from me, as memories of those notorious sandals starkly contrasted with the city's real elegance.

I said, "I am traveling to Italy to study, courtesy of the embassy."

He demanded my ID and ordered the driver to open the car's boot. An uncomfortable silence enveloped us, interrupted only by the anxious hum of the engine and the soft rustling of the papers inside. Suddenly, a call from a private number broke the quiet, sending my heart crashing into a void of fear. A myriad of possibilities played out in my mind, like a thrilling movie unfolding in mere seconds. The thought of my permission being revoked chilled me to the bone, yet a part of me felt an odd sense of relief at the looming disappointment.

"Ciao, Ayk. I am Francesco from the embassy. Where are you?" The voice carried a clear Italian lilt, sounding both slow and disgruntled. As a result, my first encounter with the informal Italian greeting "Ciao" was far from delightful.

"I am at the *Hamas* checkpoint, waiting," I replied, an anxious knot forming in my stomach.

"We've been waiting for an hour now. We said seven, and now it is eight," came his pointed reply.

"I'm sorry. I'm on my way," I assured him, ending the call just as the soldier handed back my ID and signaled for me to leave. It was the day to turn to wintertime. I got confused.

The Hamas checkpoint was only 500 meters from the Palestinian Authority checkpoint. The road, narrow and riddled with potholes, had a damaged asphalt surface. A layer of sand blanketed much of the road, swirling in a dance stirred by the wind, forming a symphony reminiscent of a farewell serenade from Gaza's sands.

As I opened the taxi door, a man in a bright white shirt, holding a walkie-talkie, stepped out from a makeshift container room.

"Are you Ayk?" he inquired. After I confirmed, he continued, "They've been expecting you." He then spoke quickly in Hebrew while signaling for my ID. Later, I discovered that the Israeli army required the white shirts.

"We don't have any small cars or carts. You'll need to carry your luggage to that entrance and walk there. Here's your ID," he remarked, emphasizing his words with a long drag of his dwindling cigarette.

Before I could move, he requested that I open my bags for a routine search for weapons or explosives. Taking advantage of the moment, I removed my jacket and tucked it into my bag. The morning air nipped at my skin, but the excitement of the journey ahead provided a sense of warmth.

As I trudged down the bumpy path, a familiar scent caught me, evoking memories that surged back like an unyielding tide: the distinct, stark smell of the army. This aroma, unique to them, was a mixture of fear, authority, and something indescribable that had been ingrained in my memory since childhood.

With each step towards the north, I lugged my heavy black bag, marked with orange stripes – a subtle nod to Jaffa's renowned orange groves—in addition to a backpack. The rhythm of my footsteps seemed to mimic my racing heart, creating a jarring beat that resonated in the quiet surroundings.

A sudden wave of dread washed over me, immobilizing me instantly. I recalled the small collection of medals featuring the Palestinian flag hidden deep within my bag. It felt like I was swimming against a current; the thought that finding these items could result in imprisonment engulfed me like quicksand. My fear twisted inside me, transforming my confident steps into cautious shuffles, while my hands busied themselves, frantically searching through the bag for the incriminating items.

Once my left hand grasped the cool metal of the medals, relief fluttered in my heart—a small triumph over the tidal wave of anxiety. I quickly transferred them to my right hand, acutely aware of the risk of being observed. I had heard whispers about their far-reaching surveillance cameras; was I now a target of their keen watch?

With a firm grip on the bag's handle, my right hand discreetly released the medals. Like silent confessions, they cascaded over the back of the bag, their fall slowed by the rough fabric before landing on the sandy ground below. One by one, they disappeared completely.

A wave of relief washed over me, but it was tinged with a sorrow that lodged in my throat like a lump of unshed tears. The medals I had discarded were intended as gifts for friends in Italy, but the harsh reality of my situation overshadowed those intentions. I stood on the brink of the unknown, stepping onto a long and winding path leading to a future that felt both inviting and ominous. My entry into this new chapter depended on the mercy of the Israeli forces, the occupiers of my land. The fear was no longer just a distant murmur; it had transformed into a deafening roar. The possibility of being turned back loomed large, casting a long shadow over my unwavering resolve.

Reaching the entrance brought a sense of relief, as I knew my burden could now be dragged along the smooth cement that stretched for another kilometer and a half. Moving through the long alley, completely sheltered and lined with countless watchful cameras, I felt acutely aware of every action, careful not to raise any suspicion. The last time I traversed this path, I was with three others, but today, the echoing solitude was my only companion. With each step, my imagination spun tales of soldiers hiding behind these daunting walls. This was a borderland, a no man's land, a threshold experienced by only a few hundred souls.

When I reached the first gate, a disembodied voice came through the microphone, commanding, "Stop." Swift orders followed: "Put your backpack on the floor. Raise your shirt. Move around."

The left side of the corridor slid open, allowing my oversized luggage to pass through the turnstile, an electronic gateway designed for both security and size limitations.

As I moved forward, I approached a second gate, the main building towering ahead. The gate creaked open, and sweat started to trickle down my face. Soon, I was faced with another gate, its enigmatic exterior concealing whatever lay beyond. After a tense pause, a small electronic portal activated. Eager to proceed, I pushed my bag through the opening toward an X-ray machine for larger luggage, with an entrance for individuals stationed on the right.

In that moment, a deep realization struck me. Histories are chronicled in books, retold countless times, but there are also the histories we embody, etched into our very DNA. The oppression, anxiety, and confinement were part of my narrative, ingrained within me. The history we learned, even from Palestinian literature, was often reduced to terms like "occupation" or "apartheid." Yet even those terms seemed insufficient, failing to convey the depth of my history, the history of Gaza, which was woven into our essence.

Stepping inside, I found myself surrounded by metal and stainless-steel walls. A woman's voice floated towards me, her words a mix of English and hesitant Arabic. I couldn't make sense of it and began scanning for the camera, encountering only unfamiliar signs.

Realizing my confusion, she switched to simpler instructions; "Bag in," she said, and activated the X-ray machine. I watched as my luggage disappeared into the machine's cavernous mouth.

Upon stepping through the individual gate, I found myself before the place where I had once interviewed. My body instinctively moved, hands raised, steps precise. Thoughts of arrest surrounded me like phantoms, casting a shadow over my mind. But as I emerged on the other side, my gaze met the sight of the Italian consul waving at me from a distance, behind a glass wall. His familiar figure seemed to form a protective barrier around me, calming my racing heart to a steady rhythm. I was no longer alone in this sterile, metallic environment.

In one corner, a heavily armed sentinel stood guard, accompanied by a female soldier in an olive-green uniform. I realized that it was her voice that had been guiding me through the microphone. She gestured for me to open my bags, scrutinizing the contents before giving me the signal to close them and approach the counter.

At the counter, I handed my ID to a soldier who was focused on his computer screen, a piece of paper clutched in his hand. This piece of paper, my permit, held the power to grant me passage or confine me, turning me into a ghost in my own land.

Within a minute, fortune smiled upon me. My ID and the permit were returned, an innocuous slip of paper representing the line between life and death. To this day, I keep that paper as a vivid reminder of my escape from the world's largest open-air prison, a liberating symbol ironically given by the very oppressor who aimed to dehumanize me.

As I emerged, the Italian consul greeted me with a firm handshake and offered assistance with my luggage. While we walked outside, he called for the diplomatic car, noting that lingering near the building was not allowed, so the vehicle was waiting a few hundred meters away. Our destination was now Jericho, marking the start of my journey to Amman, Jordan.

# Leaving 2007
## The Son

Francesco, the Italian consul—a bald man with authority—and the driver, a gray-haired Jerusalemite, accompanied me on this journey. I looked around, taking in the changed surroundings. The green fields, smooth traffic, and clean environment sharply contrast with the hardships on the other side of the border. It was clear how much privilege meant when measured against the suffering of others.

"What will you study in Italy?" Francesco asked, breaking my thoughts.

"Cultural studies," I replied with a small smile. Before we could continue, the driver pointed out entrances to destroyed Palestinian villages. He knew the area well, and it was clear I didn't.

"How do you know them all?" I asked.

"I drove taxis and buses here for 25 years," he said, looking at me through the rearview mirror with a depth of stories behind his eyes.

I watched the scenery outside—cars, trees, and landscape—while the driver occasionally commented, "You Gazans love Palestine and its old villages."

"Absolutely," I agreed. Francesco then joked, "Will you marry an Italian?"

"Maybe," I said, laughing.

After 40 minutes, we saw the Dome of the Rock. I had expected to go straight to Jericho, but they planned a stop in Jerusalem to get a visa stamp on my passport.

In Jerusalem, the architecture looked familiar from pictures and TV, but seeing the Israeli flag flying above was hard to accept. Leaving Jerusalem, we passed settlements with signs pointing to Ramallah and Bethlehem. Francesco listed their names as we drove.

We began descending toward Jericho through roads known by harsh nicknames: "Death Road" and "The Snake's Road." Memorials stood quietly along the way, honoring those who had died on this dangerous path. The driver told us to speed up—Friday crossing hours were shorter.

A sign pointed to the Allenby Crossing, but there was no clear sign for Jericho.

At a checkpoint, a soldier checked documents. After five minutes, he said, "No," then spoke to the driver in Hebrew. Their expressions told me something was wrong, and worry filled me.

Still, a strange relief appeared.

The driver explained, "Because you're from Gaza, we have to go to Jericho first, then get a permit at the Israeli checkpoint."

Frustrated, Francesco failed to persuade the soldier to allow a shortcut.

At the Israeli checkpoint near Jericho, we waited behind a car carrying Tayeb Abdelrahim, a senior Palestinian official. He was ordered to step out briefly to show his papers—an obvious display of control.

When it was our turn, Francesco gave the soldier our documents. After a quick check, she said simply, "Ok!"

"Are we going?" Francesco asked, surprised.

A sharp reply in Italian followed. We were sent back to the first checkpoint, where the same soldier checked us again and then let us pass. My heart raced—finally, I was leaving.

Francesco complained about the soldiers' rudeness, interrupting my moment of relief.

We traveled in a diplomatic car to the VIP hall. A female soldier with determined eyes took my documents and motioned me to follow.

"Now you have to go. We can't cross after this. Good luck with your studies," Francesco said, shaking my hand.

From nearby, the soldier called out sharply, "*Yalla!*"

As I approached, the heat in Jericho made sweat form on my forehead. I smiled gratefully at the driver, whose worn face reflected my own feelings.

The soldier led me into a room with high-backed chairs and portraits, including Isaac Rabin and King Hussein of Jordan, with inscriptions in Arabic, English, and Hebrew reading, "Peace of the Brave." I smiled quietly at the irony—Rabin's history did not fully match the image of peace.

Looking out the window, I saw Palestinians controlled by soldiers watching them closely. I thought of the crossing's original name, "*Ma'abar Al Karama*," meaning "Dignity Crossing." After what I saw, it felt more like a place of humiliation.

A woman entered, her red diplomatic passport drawing attention. She asked if I had a Jordanian visa, then said I couldn't travel without it.

Showing my visa, the relief on her face was clear. No buses were available, so a taxi would take me to Jordan.

A white taxi labeled "VIP Allenby Bridge" arrived. While crossing rocky terrain, I admired the hills and city views, dotted by Israeli settlements interrupting the landscape. The scene stirred strong feelings—I wanted to remember it, knowing it might be the last time I saw it clearly.

At the Jordanian crossing, I felt calm. The driver asked for 80 USD for the fees and the taxi ride.

Though the amount seemed high for a short trip, I reminded myself of the 2,000 USD bribe I once considered paying for a harder route through Egypt. Money can sometimes make borders easier to cross.

After an hour and a half, we reached the old city of Amman and the *Alquds* Hotel—known among Gazans for its affordability.

The hotel's aged doors, like the city itself, marked the end of my long dream, and the start of it, full of hardship and hope. The squeaky doors of the shower and bathroom echoed quietly, welcoming a traveler from a land he was now leaving behind.

# Lingering, Gaza 2007-forever
## The Mother

That night, it was my last chance to look at my son.
My sadness for your *Ghourba* is born small and grows and keeps growing.
Your clothes are still in the cupboard. For many years.
I went back to your room, crying.

Abdalhadi Alijla
Stockholm
31 December 2024.

# About the Author

*Abdalhadi Alijla* is a Palestinian-Swedish political scientist, author, and advocate for social justice. He is the author of *Trust in Divided Societies*, co-editor of *Rebel Governance in the Middle East*, and a senior fellow at the Arab Reform Initiative. A scholar of governance and democracy, he has worked across Europe and the Middle East. In 2025, Alijla lost his mother and over fifty relatives during the genocide in Gaza. *Fearful in Gaza* is his reckoning, his tribute, and his call to remember.

# A Word from the Publisher

Thank you for reading *Fearful in Gaza!*
We hope this book offered a deeply personal glimpse into Abdalhadi Alijla's life and the lives of those around him—people navigating fear, faith, and resilience amid the relentless realities of war.

If this story moved you, through its honesty, its quiet strength, or its reminder of the humanity that persists even in devastation, we'd be truly grateful if you shared your reflections. Your review, whether on Amazon, Barnes & Noble, Kobo, Apple Books, Goodreads, or wherever you discover powerful works, helps other readers find *Fearful in Gaza* and hear its vital voice for themselves.

Thank you for helping to keep these lived histories alive, and for supporting the work of *Vita*, where we honor lives worth telling.

www.ingramcontent.com/pod-product-compliance
Lightning Source LLC
Chambersburg PA
CBHW060513080526
44586CB00012B/465